D0076037

Second Edition

Corporate Financial Analysis

Diana R. Harrington

Brent D. Wilson

BPI

Corporate Financial Analysis

Corporate Financial Analysis

DIANA R. HARRINGTON
University of Virginia

BRENT D. WILSON
Brigham Young University

1986

Second Edition

BUSINESS PUBLICATIONS, INC.
Plano, Texas 75075

ISBN 256-03413-3

Library of Congress Catalog Card No. 85-62775

Printed in the United States of America

4 5 6 7 8 9 0 ML 3 2 1 0 9 8

For Will and Renee

PREFACE

This book was written with the objective of discussing financial analysis as it relates to decision making. We believe that analysis is useful only as it assists the manager in making better decisions and that the goal of the decision-making process is to enhance the value of the firm. We believe that it is possible for managers to create value through the financial decisions they make, and we have used the concept of value creation as the basic framework of the book, relating techniques of financial analysis to this objective.

As a result of our practical orientation toward value, we have chosen not to present abstract financial theory. Rather than deriving rigorous mathematical proofs, we have explained how the tools, concepts, and theories of finance can be used to improve financial decision making. We have followed this practical approach throughout the book by using examples of actual business situations to illustrate the application of modern financial theories and techniques.

The book was written for three different groups of readers. First, the book has been and will be useful for students studying finance. While we first wrote the book as a companion reference for students taking a finance case course, the book also will be, and has been, useful for students who want a simple supplement to a more advanced textbook or for instructors who may wish to discuss the applicatons of concepts derived in more theoretical finance courses.

Second, we have found that the book has been useful for executive management education in courses where basic techniques of financial analysis are needed or used. Our experience in teaching corporate executives suggests that a straightforward, pragmatic approach is required in such courses, and we wrote and revised the book with this in mind.

Third, the book can serve as a useful reference for the practicing manager who wants a review of current concepts and techniques in finance. Thus, we have found that the book can be effectively used as a stand-alone reference.

Since we believe that managers and students of management can best develop the ability to apply techniques and concepts to financial decisions through practice, we have included problems at the end of each chapter. These problems are meant to provide an opportunity to practice the material contained in the chapter. We encourage the reader to work through the problems and refer to the solutions in Appendix C at the end of the book.

We believe the use of computer-based financial modeling systems greatly enhances the ability of the manager to analyze financial problems and decisions, and we have included explanations as to how this can be done. Recognizing the advances in financial planning and analysis that have come with the microcomputer, we have included a primer on financial modeling as Appendix A and a primer on one of the most popular of the electronic spreadsheet programs, Lotus 1-2-3 (a product of Lotus Development Corporation), as Appendix B. The manager or student wanting to enhance their skill in modeling can do so by executing the problems at the end of each chapter and comparing their solutions in Lotus 1-2-3 with the Lotus 1-2-3 solutions contained in Appendix C. [Note: for those of you who are using the IFPS, Interactive Financial Planning Service, modeling system, the solutions to the chapter problems using this language are also contained in Appendix C.]

The book is a compilation of ideas and materials developed during the past few years at the Colgate Darden Graduate School of Business Administration at the University of Virginia and at Brigham Young University. The material has benefited from the response of students in the MBA classes and has been refined through the comments of executives attending executive management courses.

We wish to express our thanks to our colleagues at the Darden School and Brigham Young. We are appreciative of the support provided by numerous students and executives who not only encouraged us to write the book, but provided suggestions for improving the presentation of ideas and concepts. We want to thank the following reviewers for their helpful suggestions: Joseph Finnerty, University of Illinois; Kendall Hill, University of Alabama–Birmingham; Robert Klemkosky, Indiana University; John U. Miller, San Jose State University; Robert A. Olsen, California State University–Chico, and Henry Oppenheimer, SUNY–Binghamton. The mistakes are my coauthor's.

Diana R. Harrington
Darden School—University of Virginia
Brent D. Wilson
Brigham Young University

CONTENTS

CHAPTER 1

Corporate Financial Analysis

The financial performance of a corporation is of great interest to many different groups and individuals. Lenders are concerned with the corporation's ability to repay loans as well as its adherence to applicable loan covenants. Purchasing agents are concerned with the viability of a company as a supplier of goods or services to ensure that it is a qualified vendor and will be able to fulfill any contractual obligations. Potential investors are interested in determining the financial strength of a company as an element of assessing the value of the company's securities.

In addition to these external analysts, managers within the corporation are also concerned with analyzing the financial performance. Comparison of actual performance with budgets or objectives and evaluation of different divisions of a company are only two examples of the type of analysis that internal analysts are likely to perform.

The primary sources of information that these analysts use to evaluate a firm's performance are its financial statements. These statements are always historical in that they record past performance. Many groups are, however, more interested in future performance. The past performance, as shown in the financial statements, is typically used to predict future performance. The methods used to project future performance will be discussed in Chapter 3.

I. FINANCIAL STATEMENTS

The kinds of financial information included in published financial statements vary. Each country has different regulations regarding the publication of financial information. The regulations of the United States and the United Kingdom require the most disclosure; however, most industrialized countries require disclosure of sufficient information to allow a meaningful analysis. In all countries, the public disclosure requirements apply only to publicly owned companies. Privately owned corporations may not be required to publicly disclose financial information; however, certain groups, such as banks, may have access to financial statements from a privately owned company.

In the United States, publicly owned companies are required to prepare four statements: the statement of earnings, the statement of financial position, the statement of changes in the financial position, and the statement of changes in share owners' equity. Collectively, these statements are referred to as the financial statements. Typically, they are prepared quarterly; however, annual statements satisfy the minimum legal requirement.

1. Statement of Earnings

The statement of earnings is also known as the *income statement* or the *profit and loss statement*. Its purpose is to show the total revenues earned by a company during a specific period of time as well as the total expenses incurred during the same period. The difference between the revenues and expenses is called the *net income* (also known as *earnings* or *profits*) or *net loss* for the period.

This statement reports all of the revenue or expense transactions during a specific period of time, the reporting period. A quarterly report would include only the transactions made during the three-month reporting period. An annual report includes all income and expense items for the year. An example of an annual statement of earnings is shown on Exhibit 1–1. This is the 1984 statement for the Whirlpool Corporation, a major manufacturer of household appliances such as washing machines, clothes dryers, and refrigerators.

2. Statement of Financial Position

The statement of financial position is also referred to as the *balance sheet*. The statement reports the corporation's assets, liabilities, and owners' equity at the end of the reporting period. The corporation's assets must balance with the sum of the liabilities and owners' equity, hence the term *balance sheet*.

The balance sheet differs from the statement of earnings in that it reports the firm's status as of a point in time, the end of a reporting period. While the earnings statement reports on a flow of transactions or funds, the statement of financial position reports on the resulting status of funds. Thus, a quarterly report would specify the status of the assets, liabilities, and owners' equity at the end of the quarter; an annual report would indicate their position at the conclusion of the reporting year. The Whirlpool Corporation's annual statement of financial position for 1984 is included on Exhibit 1–2.

3. Statement of Changes in Financial Position

Also known as a *funds flow statement* or *sources and uses of funds*, this statement reports the amount of funds generated and used by the company during the period as well as their source and disposition. The difference be-

EXHIBIT 1–1

WHIRLPOOL CORPORATION
Statement of Earnings
(in thousands except per share data)

	Year Ended December 31 1984	1983	1982
Income:			
Net sales	$3,137,482	$2,667,682	$2,271,305
Equity in net earnings of affiliated companies	27,411	17,495	25,652
Other	42,919	49,113	43,274
	3,207,812	2,734,290	2,340,231
Deductions from income:			
Cost of goods sold	2,476,235	2,102,740	1,827,326
Selling and administrative expenses	388,591	309,384	271,749
Interest on long-term debt	4,892	5,287	5,497
Other interest expense	1,665	885	634
Provision for plant closings	4,564	23,156	—
Income taxes	142,300	129,800	98,800
	3,018,247	2,571,252	2,204,006
Earnings from continuing operations	189,565	163,038	136,225
Gain from discontinued operations	—	4,000	2,790
Net earnings	$ 189,565	$ 167,038	$ 139,015
Per share of common stock:			
Earnings from continuing operations	$5.18	$4.47	$3.75
Gain from discontinued operations	—	0.11	0.08
Net earnings	$5.18	$4.58	$3.83
Average number of common shares outstanding	36,585,557	36,495,995	36,315,108

tween the sum of the sources of funds and their uses is typically reported as a change in cash or in net working capital. The sources and uses are determined by comparing the current statement of financial position with that of the previous reporting period. This comparison highlights the significant changes that have occurred in the corporation's financial position during the period.

A corporation generates financial resources through several methods. These include borrowing additional funds; increasing the owners' equity; retaining the period's earnings; or decreasing assets by selling any excess equipment. The resources thus generated can be used to increase assets, through the purchase of new equipment; to decrease liabilities, by paying off loans; or to decrease owners' equity, by paying a dividend from earnings.

The statement of changes in financial position from the 1984 annual report of the Whirlpool Corporation is shown on Exhibit 1–3.

EXHIBIT 1-2

WHIRLPOOL CORPORATION
Statement of Financial Position
For the Years Ended December 31, 1983 and 1984
(in thousands)

Assets	*1984*	*1983*
Current assets:		
Cash	$ 22,535	$ 32,673
Short-term investments	288,086	385,737
Receivables, less allowances for doubtful accounts (1984—$1,480,000; 1983—$1,760,000)	199,476	182,777
Inventories	359,726	264,480
Prepaid expenses	34,719	9,481
Deferred income taxes	7,890	29,901
Total current assets	912,432	905,049
Investments and other assets:		
Whirlpool Acceptance Corporation	137,517	125,949
Affiliated foreign companies	118,060	104,252
Other assets	10,095	8,172
	265,672	238,373
Property, plant, and equipment:		
Land	9,834	9,055
Buildings	212,072	187,155
Machinery, equipment, and tools	391,980	336,161
	613,886	532,371
Less: Allowances for depreciation and amortization	226,975	209,290
	386,911	323,081
	$1,565,015	$1,466,503
Liabilities and Stockholders' Equity		
Current liabilities:		
Accounts payable	$ 195,613	$ 185,236
Payrolls and other compensation	84,899	83,811
Taxes and other accrued expenses	71,341	82,227
Income taxes	3,922	26,200
Product warranty	19,979	18,280
Total current liabilities	375,754	395,754
Other liabilities:		
Long-term debt	52,751	56,648
Product warranty	14,432	14,748
Deferred income taxes	25,796	21,705
	92,979	93,101
Stockholders' equity:		
Capital stock	36,617	36,535
Additional paid-in capital	32,620	30,450
Retained earnings	1,027,045	910,663
	1,096,282	977,648
	$1,565,015	$1,466,503

EXHIBIT 1-3

WHIRLPOOL CORPORATION
Statement of Changes in Financial Positions
(in thousands)

	Years Ended December 31		
	1984	*1983*	*1982*
Operating activities:			
Earnings from continuing operations	$189,565	$163,038	$136,225
Noncash charges (credits):			
Depreciation of plant and equipment	33,444	33,064	32,286
Amortization of tooling	36,726	28,218	21,639
Increase in noncurrent deferred income taxes	4,091	3,376	2,014
Equity in net earnings of affiliated companies:			
Whirlpool Acceptance Corporation	(11,568)	(8,014)	(7,027)
Affiliated foreign companies	(15,843)	(9,481)	(18,625)
Decrease in long-term product warranty	(316)	(1,655)	(906)
Dividends received from affiliated foreign companies	4,255	4,352	4,815
Changes in components of operating working capital other than cash and short-term investments	(135,172)	33,299	59,311
Cash provided by continuing operations	105,182	246,197	229,732
Cash dividends paid	(73,183)	(67,530)	(59,940)
Cash provided by continuing operations retained in the business	31,999	178,667	169,792
Gain from discontinued operations net of noncash items	—	4,000	2,790
Cash provided by operations retained in the business	31,999	182,667	172,582
Investing activities:			
Additions to properties	(86,947)	(38,182)	(39,646)
Additions to tooling	(50,147)	(45,310)	(41,582)
Disposals of properties	3,094	3,031	1,522
Increase in investment in and loans to affiliated foreign companies and unconsolidated subsidiary	(2,620)	(52,945)	(5,800)
Repayment of loans by affiliated foreign company	400	1,200	800
Decrease (increase) in other assets	(1,923)	(465)	172
Cash used for investing activities	(138,143)	(132,671)	(84,534)
Financing activities:			
Repayment of long-term debt	(3,897)	(4,200)	—
Stock option transactions	2,252	3,066	4,170
Cash provided by (used for) financing activities	(1,645)	(1,134)	4,170
Increase (decrease) in cash and short-term investments	(107,789)	48,862	92,218
Cash and short-term investments at beginning of year	418,410	369,548	277,330
Cash and short-term investments at end of year	$ 310,621	$ 418,410	$ 369,548

EXHIBIT 1–3 *(concluded)*

WHIRLPOOL CORPORATION
Statement of Changes in Financial Positions
(in thousands)

	Years Ended December 31		
	1984	*1983*	*1982*
Changes in components of operating working capital other than cash and short-term investments:			
Receivables	$ (16,699)	$ (16,492)	$ (10,116)
Inventories	(95,246)	(36,210)	28,276
Prepaid expenses	(25,238)	(1,815)	(1,923)
Deferred income taxes	22,011	(16,950)	(243)
Accounts payable	10,377	76,261	34,151
Accrued liabilities	(8,099)	53,229	(5,157)
Income taxes	(22,278)	(24,724)	14,323
	$(135,172)	$ 33,299	$ 59,311

4. Statement of Changes in Share Owners' Equity

This report also may be called the *statement of retained earnings*. This statement provides additional detail on the composition of the owners' equity accounts of the corporation. Its purpose is to highlight changes in the owners' equity or retained earnings that have occurred during the reporting period.

This statement is similar to the statement of changes in financial position for the corporation; however, it focuses specifically on the changes within the owners' equity segment of the balance sheet. The statement of changes in owners' equity is frequently combined with the statement of earnings since the earnings disposition has a major impact on the owners' equity account.

Exhibit 1–4 shows the statement of changes in share owners' equity for the Whirlpool Corporation from the 1984 Annual Report.

In addition to the data contained in these statements, corporations also include significant financial information in notes to their financial statements. These notes provide additional detail on many items included in the financial statements. Typically, one can find additional information about taxes; the composition of debt; contingent liabilities; depreciation of property, plant, and equipment; and nonconsolidated subsidiaries.

Since specific accounting conventions and policies can have a significant impact on the financial statements, companies usually include an explanation within the notes of the significant accounting policies used in preparing the statements. In the United States, companies with operations in different industries or different countries are required to provide a segmentation of income and assets by industry and by country.

Recent changes to accounting policies require that U.S. companies report inflation-adjusted earnings data. This information is included in the notes to the financial statements.

EXHIBIT 1-4

WHIRLPOOL CORPORATION
Statement of Changes in Share Owners' Equity
(in thousands)

	Years Ended December 31		
	1984	*1983*	*1982*
Common stock:			
Balance at beginning of year	$ 36,535	$ 36,430	$ 36,265
Par value of shares issued under stock option plans	82	105	165
Balance at end of year	36,617	36,535	36,430
Additional paid-in capital:			
Balance at beginning of year	30,450	27,489	23,484
Stock option transactions	2,170	2,961	4,005
Balance at end of year	32,620	30,450	27,489
Retained earnings:			
Balance at beginning of year	910,663	811,155	732,080
Net earnings	189,565	167,038	139,015
	1,100,228	978,193	871,095
Cash dividends paid	(73,183)	(67,530)	(59,940)
Balance at end of year	1,027,045	910,663	811,155
Stockholders' equity at end of year	$1,096,282	$977,648	$875,074
Cash dividends per share of common stock	$ 2.00	$ 1.85	$ 1.65

II. ANALYSIS OF FINANCIAL STATEMENTS

When analyzing financial statements, one must keep in mind the purpose of the analysis. Since different analysts are interested in different aspects of the corporation's performance, no single analytical technique is correct for all situations. However, there are several general considerations that the analyst should bear in mind in reviewing the data on the financial statements.

First, all of the financial statement data are historic. Although one may make projections based on the financial statement data, the accuracy of these projections depends on both the forecaster's ability and the continued pertinence of historical relationships to current or future operations.

Second, the historical data were collected and reported on the basis of some accounting conventions. These accounting principles and rules may vary among countries; and even within a country, several approaches to specific issues may be allowed. Although the notes to the financial statements may summarize some of the significant accounting policies, the analyst should be aware of the impact these policies have on the reported performance of the company.

Third, because of the variability of seasonal funds flows and requirements, the timing of the reporting period should be considered. For companies in highly seasonal or cyclical industries, comparisons of different reporting periods should be approached cautiously.

Despite these concerns, an analyst can develop an insightful examination of the corporation's financial performance. The most common method of analyzing financial statements is with the use of ratios. These ratios, which show the relationship between various items, are simple mathematical calculations. Thus, the analytical skill is not in the computation of the ratios but in the determination of which ratios are important and in the interpretation of the results. The ratios by themselves are relatively meaningless. Only by comparing ratios and by determining the underlying causes of the differences among them does ratio analysis become useful. Proper interpretation of the ratios depends on the perspective of the analyst, the company's industry, its maturity, and its susceptibility to change.

The various ratios can be categorized into six groups: profitability, liquidity, asset-usage, capitalization, coverage, and market ratios.

1. Profitability Ratios

This group of ratios depicts the relative profitability of the corporation. Although the following discussion deals with several of the most common ratios, it is not intended to be inclusive. Each situation will have individual items that need to be included in the profitability analysis.

Margin ratios. A useful type of comparison relates various expense items to revenue or sales. Two common ratios use the relationship of the cost of goods sold or total expenses to revenues or sales. Using the data from the 1984 Whirlpool Corporation annual financial statements,[1] the first of these two ratios, *gross margin,* is calculated as follows:[2]

$$\text{Gross margin} = \frac{\text{Net sales} - \text{Cost of goods sold}}{\text{Net sales}}$$

$$= \frac{\$3{,}137{,}482 - \$2{,}476{,}235}{\$3{,}137{,}482}$$

$$= .21 \text{ or } 21\%$$

The second ratio is called the *net profit margin* or *profit margin.*

$$\text{Profit margin} = \frac{\text{Net income}}{\text{Total revenue}}$$

$$= \frac{\$189{,}565}{\$3{,}207{,}812}$$

$$= .06 \text{ or } 6\%$$

---

[1]The 1984 Whirlpool financial data will be used in the remainder of the chapter to illustrate the calculation of the ratios.

[2]Since the financial statements are given in thousands of dollars, the calculations are done in thousands.

Profitability related to investment ratios. Another common concern is the company's ability to generate income from the available resources. A satisfactory return on the resources is critical if the corporation is to raise additional funds for growth. Two ratios commonly used to assess this performance are the following:

$$\text{Return on assets} = \frac{\text{Net income}}{\text{Average total assets}}$$

$$= \frac{\$189{,}565}{[(\$1{,}565{,}015 + \$1{,}466{,}503)/2]}$$

$$= .125 \text{ or } 12.5\%$$

$$\text{EBIT to assets} = \frac{\text{Earnings before interest and taxes}}{\text{Average total assets}}$$

$$= \frac{\$338{,}422}{[(\$1{,}565{,}015 + \$1{,}466{,}503)/2]}$$

$$= .223 \text{ or } 22.3\%$$

The first ratio is frequently termed the *return on investment* (ROI) or *return on assets* (ROA). The second ratio, *EBIT to assets,* is sometimes used to eliminate any distortions that might occur because of unusual tax assessments or interest expenses. Since these ratios use the depreciated assets as reported by the corporation, the analyst must use caution in interpreting the results. A company with older machinery and equipment will have a smaller asset base than a comparable company utilizing newer facilities. In addition, the analyst must take care when comparing the ratios of companies with considerable fixed assets and those whose primary productive assets (for instance, skilled employees) do not appear as a fixed asset on the balance sheet.

Return on owners' equity ratios. Most equity holders in the corporation are concerned about the return that the company is earning on their investment. Their return on investment is usually calculated using the *return on equity ratio.*

$$\text{Return on equity} = \frac{\text{Net income available to shareholders}}{\text{Shareholders' equity}}$$

$$= \frac{\$189{,}565}{\$1{,}096{,}282}$$

$$= .173 \text{ or } 17.3\%$$

2. Liquidity Ratios

These ratios reflect the ability of the company to meet its short-term liabilities and obligations. Short-term obligations are defined as those that are due within one year. The purpose of these ratios is to measure the company's ability to pay the liabilities as they become due. The financial resources that can be used to meet these obligations are usually the company's short-term assets. In assessing the liquidity of the company, analysts normally calculate two ratios.

$$\text{Current ratio} = \frac{\text{Current assets}}{\text{Current liabilities}}$$

$$= \frac{\$912{,}432}{\$375{,}754}$$

$$= 2.43$$

$$\text{Acid test} = \frac{\text{Cash} + \text{Short-term investments} + \text{Accounts receivable}}{\text{Current liabilities}}$$

$$= \frac{\$22{,}535 + \$288{,}086 + \$199{,}476}{\$315{,}754}$$

$$= 1.36$$

The first ratio is referred to as the *current ratio.* The higher the ratio, the more liquid the corporation. However, it is obvious that a company with a higher percentage of current assets in cash is more liquid than a company with most of its current assets in the form of inventories. This concern is addressed with the second ratio, known as the *acid-test ratio* or the *quick ratio.* The acid-test ratio includes only the asset items that are assumed to be most readily convertible into funds to use in paying short-term liabilities.

Determining what is a good or bad level of liquidity depends on who is analyzing the ratio. A banker who has made a short-term loan would like a high current or quick ratio. This indicates that the company has sufficient current assets to pay all current liabilities including the banker's loan. On the other hand, the company's manager might prefer a lower quick ratio, suggesting that the company has minimized the funds invested in current assets, which may have lower returns.

3. Asset-Usage Ratios

These ratios, often called "turnover" ratios, measure the company's effectiveness in using its resources.

One of the most common concerns is the quantity of the company's credit sales. The ratio of accounts receivable to net sales indicates the relative proportions of credit and cash sales. This ratio is used to determine the *days' sales outstanding* or the *receivable collection period.* Companies that sell their products on credit, such as furniture manufacturers, will have a long collection period.

$$\text{Days' sales outstanding} = \frac{\text{Accounts receivable}}{\text{Net sales}} \times 365 \text{ days}$$

$$= \frac{99{,}476}{\$3{,}137{,}482} \times 365 \text{ days}$$

$$= 23.2 \text{ days}$$

Creditors of the company may be concerned with how promptly the company is paying its obligations. To determine this, the accounts payable are analyzed by measuring the *payables payment period.* This period should be very short for companies with relatively low purchases of materials; e.g., radio and TV broadcasters.

$$\text{Payables payment period} = \frac{\text{Accounts payable}}{\text{Cost of goods sold}} \times 365 \text{ days}$$

$$= \frac{\$195{,}613}{\$2{,}476{,}235} \times 365 \text{ days}$$

$$= 28.8 \text{ days}$$

In measuring the length of time the firm takes to pay for its purchases, it is more appropriate to use the amount of purchases that the company made as the denominator in this ratio. However, since the purchase data is normally not available to outside analysts, the cost of goods sold is typically used as an approximation.

Another measure of asset utilization is the *inventory turnover.* A high ratio indicates that the company is using financial resources efficiently by maintaining low inventories. The nature of some companies (for example, aircraft manufacturers) makes achieving high inventory turnovers difficult.

$$\text{Inventory turnover} = \frac{\text{Cost of goods sold}}{\text{Average inventory}}$$

$$= \frac{\$2{,}476{,}235}{[(\$359{,}726 + \$264{,}480)/2]}$$

$$= 7.93$$

This ratio indicates the number of times that the company's inventory was sold and replaced during the reporting period. It is important to note that this formulation assumes that inventories are valued at cost as is the normal practice. If inventories are carried at market value then sales should be the numerator in the ratio.

Another ratio, sometimes called the *asset turnover,* is used to examine the effectiveness of the company in utilizing all of its assets in generating sales. As with inventory turnover, a higher ratio is generally preferred. For service companies with relatively low asset investments, such as advertising and consulting, high asset turnover is easier to achieve than for manufacturing companies.

$$\text{Asset turnover} = \frac{\text{Total revenues (or sales)}}{\text{Average total assets}}$$

$$= \frac{\$3{,}207{,}812}{[(\$1{,}565{,}015 + \$1{,}466{,}503)/2]}$$

$$= 2.12$$

The asset turnover ratio can be combined with the net income ratio (or profit margin) to develop the *return on investment.*

$$\text{Return on investment} = \frac{\text{Net income}}{\text{Total revenues (or sales)}} \times \frac{\text{Total revenues (or sales)}}{\text{Average total assets}}$$

$$= \frac{\$189{,}565}{\$3{,}207{,}812} \times \frac{\$3{,}207{,}812}{[(\$1{,}565{,}015 + \$1{,}466{,}503)/2]}$$

$$= .125 \text{ or } 12.5\%$$

By analyzing both the asset turnover and the net income ratios, the analyst can more precisely examine the component elements of the return on investment. In this manner, the analyst can determine whether the return on investment is changing because of changes in profit margin or in asset turnover.

4. Capitalization Ratios

The capitalization ratios provide information about the long-term sources of financing that the company has used. Since the long-term financing sources are either debt or equity funds, the capitalization ratios involve various combinations of these accounts. Three of the most common ratios are the *long-term debt to equity* ratio, the *long-term debt to total assets* ratio, and *total liabilities to assets* ratio.

$$\text{Debt to equity} = \frac{\text{Total long-term debt}}{\text{Total stockholders' equity}}$$

$$= \frac{\$52{,}751}{\$1{,}096{,}282}$$

$$= .048 \text{ or } 4.8\%$$

$$\text{Debt to assets} = \frac{\text{Total long-term debt}}{\text{Total assets}}$$

$$= \frac{\$52{,}751}{\$1{,}565{,}015}$$

$$= .034 \text{ or } 3.4\%$$

These two ratios indicate how the company has provided its long-term capital. They show the percentage of long-term debt used to finance the company; this is termed the financial leverage. For companies that use significant amounts of short-term debt, these ratios may not be adequate. In this case, the total liabilities-to-assets ratio may be preferable.

$$\text{Total liabilities to assets} = \frac{\text{Total liabilities}}{\text{Total assets}}$$

$$= \frac{\$375{,}754 + \$92{,}979}{\$1{,}565{,}015}$$

$$= .30 \text{ or } 30\%$$

In determining the long-term debt of the corporation, the analyst must decide which items to include. If the decision is made to include deferred taxes, long-term contingent liabilities, or other long-term liabilities, these items should be included consistently in the analysis.

As with the liquidity ratios, the appropriate capitalization ratio depends on the perspective of the analyst, the nature of the company, and the situation it is in. Lenders such as bondholders and bankers would prefer lower debt ratios, which would provide greater security for their loans. Equity investors generally prefer that the company take on more debt. If the company operates profitably, the equity holders benefit from an increased return on equity provided by the increased leverage. Issues involved in determining the appropriate capital structure will be discussed in Chapter 6.

5. Coverage Ratios

The coverage ratios provide information about the ability of the company to pay its financial obligations. Debt financing carries a contractual obligation to pay interest and repay the amount borrowed. A frequently calculated ratio is the *earnings interest coverage* ratio.

$$\text{Earnings interest coverage} = \frac{\text{Earnings before interest and taxes}}{\text{Interest expense}}$$

$$= \frac{\$338{,}422}{\$4{,}892, + \$1{,}665}$$

$$= 51.61$$

Because depreciation is a noncash expense, the company may have more cash available for paying interest than is shown by the earnings before interest and taxes (EBIT) figure. Often, the depreciation amount is added to the EBIT in the ratio calculation as a means of approximating the cash availability. Cash is important because debt payments must be made with cash.

Since companies also must make principal payments, sometimes referred to as sinking-fund payments, analysts are interested in whether the company is generating sufficient funds to make these payments as well. Since principal repayments are not a deductible expense for tax purposes, the principal repayments must be paid with after-tax funds. Therefore, in calculating the *debt service coverage ratio,* the payments must be adjusted to a before-tax basis.

$$\text{Earnings debt service coverage} = \frac{\text{Earnings before interest and taxes}}{\text{Interest} + [\text{Sinking fund}/(1 - \text{Tax rate})]}$$

$$= \frac{\$338{,}422}{\$6{,}557 + [\$8{,}448/(1 - .46)]}$$

$$= 15.24$$

The sinking-fund obligations and marginal tax rates can be found in the notes to the financial statements. For purposes of brevity, the notes to the 1984 Whirlpool annual report have not been reproduced here.

For the debt service coverage ratio, the EBIT could be replaced by the cash flow amount (earnings increased by the depreciation) to better approximate the availability of cash to meet the payment obligations. In addition, other financial obligations, such as lease payments, could be included with a tax adjustment similar to that done for the sinking-fund payments.

6. Market Ratios

In addition to the ratios that are calculated using only the data from the financial statements, analysts often calculate ratios using information from the stock market. These ratios facilitate analyzing the company's financial market performance. Since investors purchase shares of equity or stock of a company, most market analysis is performed on a per share basis rather than using total amounts. A typical starting point for market analysis is the *earnings per share* or *EPS.*

$$\text{Earnings per share} = \frac{\text{Net income}}{\text{Number of common shares outstanding}}$$

$$= \frac{\$189{,}565{,}000}{36{,}585{,}557}$$

$$= \$5.18$$

Other ratios are based on the market price for a share of common stock. In May 1985, the share price for Whirlpool was $41. Using this price, several useful ratios can be calculated.

$$\text{Price-earnings ratio} = \frac{\text{Market price per share}}{\text{Earnings per share}}$$

$$= \frac{\$41.00}{\$5.18}$$

$$= 7.9$$

$$\text{Dividend yield} = \frac{\text{Dividends per share}}{\text{Market price per share}}$$

$$= \frac{\$2.00}{\$41.00}$$

$$= .049 \text{ or } 4.9\%$$

Both of these ratios are used to evaluate the relative financial performance of the stock. The *price-earnings or PE ratio* indicates how much investors are willing to pay for a dollar of the company's earnings. It is a scale factor that allows market value comparisons between companies with different earnings levels. Typically, investors expect high-PE companies to have more rapid increases in market prices than companies with low PE's.

The *dividend yield* indicates the return on the stock investment provided by the dividend payment. Of course, the dividend return is only part of the expected return from an investment in common stock; the other part comes through potential increases in the share price. Usually companies with higher dividend yields are expected to have lower increases in market price.

The percentage of the company's net income that is paid to the shareholders as dividends is indicated by the *dividend payout ratio.*

$$\text{Dividend payout ratio} = \frac{\text{Dividends per share}}{\text{Earnings per share}}$$

$$= \frac{\$2.00}{\$5.18}$$

$$= .386 \text{ or } 38.6\%$$

The percentage of net earnings retained for reinvestment in the company, the *retention ratio,* is calculated by subtracting the payout ratio from 1. Having a high retention ratio means the company retains more of its earnings to reinvest in its business. Such a situation may allow a company greater flexibility in financing its capital needs; however, equity investors are interested in having dividends paid out to increase their investment return. Dividend policy will be discussed in Chapter 6.

Another frequently calculated ratio is the *market-to-book ratio.* This ratio is based on the relationship of the market value per share of common stock to the book value or net worth per share. Often this ratio is used as a measure of whether management has created value for the shareholders. A ratio greater than 1.0 indicates that shareholders are willing to pay a premium over the book value per share. The book value per share of a company is calculated by dividing the retained earnings on the financial statements by the number of shares outstanding.

$$\text{Market-to-book} = \frac{\text{Market value per share}}{\text{Book value per share}}$$

$$= \frac{\$41.00}{\$1{,}096{,}282{,}000 \,/\, 36{,}585{,}557}$$

$$= 1.37$$

The analyst should keep in mind that book values result from specific accounting conventions that require the use of historic values for assets. When historic values do not reflect the underlying economic value or earning potential of these assets, the use of replacement cost or inflation-adjusted valuations may result in a more meaningful market-to-book ratio. The market-to-book value and price-earnings ratios for a number of industries are shown in Exhibit 1–5.

This discussion of ratios is not intended to be all-inclusive. Rather, these are only illustrations of the types of ratios that may be calculated to provide the analyst or manager with insights into the performance of the corporation. Any number of ratios can be computed; the important considerations are to determine what information is relevant to the problem at hand and then to undertake the appropriate ratio analysis.

7. Percentage Analysis

In addition to these types of ratios, the analyst might undertake another type of ratio analysis called *percentage analysis.* There are two general methods of percentage analysis—percentage change and component percentage.

Percentage change is used to compare the same item over a series of reporting periods. The objective is to determine the relative change in the item (expense, income, asset, or liability) over time, since the magnitude of raw data can mask the changes. The analyst then compares these percentage changes with the changes in the related items over the same time period.

Component percentages are used to examine the composition of the various items on the financial statements. A percentage breakdown of the statement of earnings is common and facilitates a comparison of trends over time.

III. COMPARATIVE RATIO ANALYSIS

Calculating the ratios or the percentages is relatively simple. The critical ingredient in a useful analysis is the analyst's interpretation of these figures. To interpret the ratios, analysts generally (1) compare performance from various time periods, (2) compare the firm's performance with that of one or more companies in the industry, and (3) compare the firm's performance with the average performance of the industry. To be valid, the financial statements used to prepare the various ratios must be based on comparable accounting procedures or statements adjusted to ensure comparability of the results. Further, the analyst must thoroughly understand the firm and the industry—the products, marketing techniques, organization, and the like—if he or she is to explain the differences in performance among various time periods and companies.

Using the Whirlpool Corporation as an example, Exhibits 1–6, 1–7, and 1–8 illustrate the three types of comparative ratio analysis.

EXHIBIT 1-5 Market-to-Book Value and Price-Earnings Ratios (industry averages, 1983)

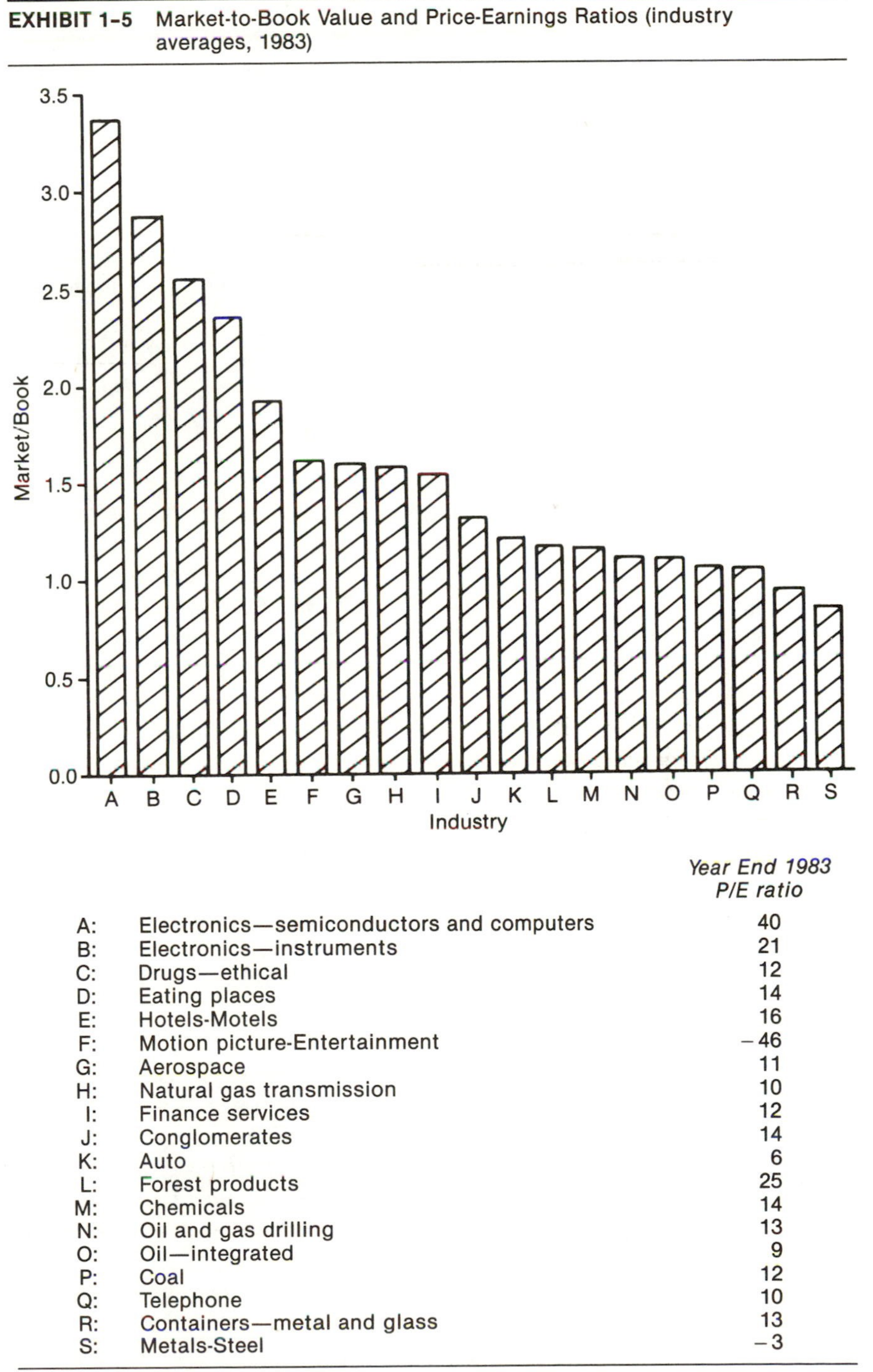

		Year End 1983 P/E ratio
A:	Electronics—semiconductors and computers	40
B:	Electronics—instruments	21
C:	Drugs—ethical	12
D:	Eating places	14
E:	Hotels-Motels	16
F:	Motion picture-Entertainment	−46
G:	Aerospace	11
H:	Natural gas transmission	10
I:	Finance services	12
J:	Conglomerates	14
K:	Auto	6
L:	Forest products	25
M:	Chemicals	14
N:	Oil and gas drilling	13
O:	Oil—integrated	9
P:	Coal	12
Q:	Telephone	10
R:	Containers—metal and glass	13
S:	Metals-Steel	−3

SOURCE: Standard and Poor's Compustat Services, *Industry Composite.*

EXHIBIT 1–6

WHIRLPOOL CORPORATION
Percentage Components for the Statement of Earnings

	1984	*1983*	*1982*	*1981*	*1980*
Income:					
Net Sales	97.8%	97.6%	97.1%	97.3%	98.2%
Equity in net earnings of affiliated companies	.9	.6	1.1	.9	.5
Other	1.3	1.8	1.8	1.8	1.3
Gross income	100.0%	100.0%	100.0%	100.0%	100.0%
Deductions from income:					
Cost of goods sold	77.2%	76.9%	78.0%	79.0%	79.5%
Selling and administrative expenses	12.1	11.3	11.6	11.2	11.6
Interest on long-term debt	.2	.2	.2	.2	.3
Other interest expense	—	—	—	—	.1
Provision for plant closings	.2	.8	—	—	—
Income taxes	4.4	4.8	4.2	4.2	3.9
Total expenses	94.1%	94.0%	94.1%	94.6%	95.4%
Earnings from continuing operations	5.9	5.9	5.8	5.4	4.6
Gain (loss) from discontinued operations	—	.1	.1	(.4)	(.1)
Net earnings	5.9%	6.0%	5.9%	5.0%	4.5%

1. Historic Comparisons

Exhibit 1–6 shows a historic comparison of the component percentages drawn from the statements of earnings over a five-year period. The purpose of this comparison is to determine if any significant changes have occurred during these years. The analysis shows that the cost of products sold was the largest component of the company's expenses. During the five-year period, Whirlpool managed to reduce the cost of its products sold from 79.5% of total revenues to 77.2% in 1984.

Offsetting this favorable trend was an increase in selling and administrative expenses from 11.6% to 12.1% of revenues. The company's history explains this increase. Whirlpool for many years produced most of its products for sale under private labels, primarily for Sears, a major international retailer. In recent years, Whirlpool has attempted to become less dependent on Sears and has begun marketing a greater percentage of its products under its own name. This change, in turn, caused an increase in advertising and other sales expenses.

The net profit margin, net income as a percentage of sales, increased from 1980 to 1984. In 1983, the percentage was at 6.0%, slightly higher than in 1984.

EXHIBIT 1-7 Comparison of 1984 Whirlpool Corporation Financial Data with the Maytag Company

	Whirlpool	*Maytag*
Income statement as percent of net sales:		
Cost of goods sold	77.2%	64.7%
Selling and administrative expenses	12.1	16.8
Interest expense	.2	.6
Income taxes	4.4	8.2
Net income	5.9	9.7
Financial factors in percentages:		
Inventory to current assets	39.4%	43.9%
Net income to net worth	17.3	27.6
Return on investment	12.5	19.2
Retained earnings to net income	61.4	35.3
Financial ratios:		
Current ratio	2.4	3.4
Quick ratio	1.4	1.8
Inventory turnover	7.9	5.5
Long-term debt to equity	—	.1
Asset turnover	2.1	2.0
Days' sales outstanding	23.2 days	26.7 days

2. Comparisons between Companies

Another type of comparison analysis, contrasting two companies within the same industry, is shown in Exhibit 1-7. The 1984 financial data for the Maytag Company, another company in the household appliances industry, is compared with the 1984 Whirlpool performance. Because financial requirements and uses of funds differ among industries, it is important that companies chosen for comparison be limited to those within the same industry.

There are a few significant differences between Maytag and Whirlpool. Maytag is known as a premium-priced manufacturer: it attempts to present its products as being of premium quality and therefore worth a higher price. This strategy is reflected in Maytag's lower costs of goods sold percentage. Since a lower cost of goods sold could result from either efficiencies in operations or higher prices for the product, understanding the differences in operating and marketing policies is crucial to providing a relevant analysis. Maytag's policy also means higher selling and administrative expenses, which are confirmed by Exhibit 1-7. Whirlpool's selling and administrative expenses were 12.1% of net sales, while Maytag's were 16.8%

The net income percentage also shows a marked difference between the two companies. Maytag has apparently been successful in its strategy, since its 9.7% profit margin is considerably higher than Whirlpool's 5.9%.

Another significant difference between the two companies is the greater liquidity of Maytag. This is shown by the higher current and quick ratios for Maytag. However, both of the companies have very low debt levels.

Because of its higher net income percentage, Maytag's return on equity, or net income to net worth percentage, was also higher than Whirlpool's—27.6% as compared to Whirlpool's 17.3%. The higher profit margin was also the factor underlying the significant difference between the return on investment figures for the companies. Maytag's return on investment, 19.2%, is greater than Whirlpool's return of 12.5%.

3. Comparisons within an Industry

The comparisons can be expanded from only one company to several. Typically, industry-wide comparisons are based on industry averages. These averages are available from several sources that collect and publish the data. Exhibit 1-8 compares the 1984 Whirlpool data with 1984 industry averages. Because of financial differences among companies of differing sizes, analysts commonly select from the industry a sample of companies that correspond in size to the target company. This selection was made in preparing Exhibit 1-8.

An analysis of the data in Exhibit 1-8 indicates that Whirlpool's performance compares very favorably with that of the industry. Although Whirlpool's cost of goods sold percentage of 77.2% was higher than that of the industry, the net profit before tax, 10.3%, was much higher than the industry average of only 1.8%.

Whirlpool was more liquid than the industry and had a greater inventory turnover. It was capitalized with a lower percentage of debt than the industry average, and the return on equity of 17.3% was significantly higher than the industry average of 9.7%. Whirlpool also retained a greater percentage of its net income, which means that its dividend payout on common equity was lower than the industry average.

IV. SUMMARY

Using the primary external sources of financial information, the financial statements, an analyst can learn a great deal about the financial performance of a company through the techniques of ratio preparation and comparative ratio analysis. Calculating a ratio is not a difficult skill. It is in the assessment of which ratios to use and the interpretation of the results that analytical skills are required.

Proper interpretation requires an understanding of the company as well as the environment. Critical issues that need to be included are the general economic conditions, the competitive situation, and the business and financial strategy of the company. Each of these factors, individually and in combination, affects the financial results of the company.

A critical element in the general economic environment is inflation. During periods of unstable prices, historical comparisons are much more difficult than during periods of stability. The recent requirement in the United

EXHIBIT 1-8 Comparison of 1984 Whirlpool Corporation Financial Data with Household Appliance Manufacturing Industry

	Whirlpool Corporation	*Industry Average for Companies over $250 Million in Assets**
Operating factors as percent of net sales:		
Cost of goods sold	77.2%	68.8%
Interest	.2	2.2
Net profit before tax	10.3	1.8
Financial ratio:		
Current ratio	2.4	1.9
Quick ratio	1.4	.9
Inventory turnover	7.9	3.4
Total liabilities to net worth	.4	1.3
Financial factors in percentages:		
Inventory to current assets	39.4%	47.0%
Net income to net worth	17.3	9.7
Retained earnings to net income	61.4	45.4

*SOURCE: Data from Leo Troy, *Almanac of Business and Industrial Ratios,* 1984 ed. (Englewood Cliffs, N.J.: Prentice-Hall, 1984), p. 155.

States for inflation-adjusted financial statements is a step in the direction of providing better external data to assess the effects of inflation on the company. The recognition of the need for better data demonstrates the need for analytical skill through the inclusion of all relevant data for a company.

SELECTED REFERENCES

Sources of industry data and financial ratios are:

Dun & Bradstreet. *Industry Norms and Key Business Ratios.*

Robert Morris Associates. *Annual Statement Studies.*

Troy, Leo. *Almanac of Business and Industrial Ratios.* Englewood Cliffs, N.J.: Prentice-Hall.

An in-depth example of the use of financial ratios is found in:

Backer, Morton, and Martin L. Gosman. "The Use of Financial Ratios in Credit Downgrade Decisions." *Financial Management,* Spring 1980, pp. 53–56.

For further discussion on using financial ratios, see:

Brealey, Richard, and Stuart Myers, *Principles of Corporate Finance.* 2d ed. New York: McGraw-Hill, 1984, chap. 25.

Fraser, Lyn M. *Understanding Financial Statements: Through the Maze of a Corporate Annual Report.* Reston, Va.: Reston Publishing, 1985.

Pringle, John J., and Robert S. Harris. *Essentials of Managerial Finance.* Glenview Ill.: Scott, Foresman and Company, 1984, chap.7.

Seitz, Neil. *Financial Analysis: A Programmed Approach.* 3d ed. Reston, Va.: Reston Publishing, 1984, chap. 1.

Van Horne, James C. *Financial Management Policy.* 6th ed. Englewood Cliffs, N.J.: Prentice-Hall, 1985, chaps. 27–28.

Weston, J. Fred, and Eugene F. Brigham. *Managerial Finance.* 7th ed. Hinsdale, Ill.: The Dryden Press, 1981, chap. 7.

STUDY QUESTIONS

1. The financial analyst from the Arlington Manufacturing Company had been assigned the task of reconstructing the 1985 financial statements of Hopper, Ltd., a privately owned company and one of Arlington's main competitors. All he had available was the following data, published by Hopper in a newsletter to their stockholders: (*a*) Return on equity for the period was 10%; (*b*) net income was 3% of sales; (*c*) cost of goods sold was 77% of sales; (*d*) long-term debt was 80% of equity; (*e*) the current ratio was 2; (*f*) there were 35 days' sales outstanding in accounts receivable and 30 days' outstanding in accounts payable; (*g*) inventory turnover was 6 times based on ending inventories; (*h*) asset turnover was 1.5 times based on ending assets; and (*i*) retained earnings at the end of the period was $62,000. Additionally, the analyst knew that Hopper had 40,000 shares of common stock outstanding with a par value of $1.00.

   The analyst laid out the balance sheet and income statement shown below and settled down to work.

Income Statement

Sales	______
Cost of goods	______
Other expenses	______
Profit after tax	______

Balance Sheet

Cash	______	Accounts payable	______
Accounts receivable	______	Other short-term liabilities	______
Inventories	______	Total current liabilities	______
Net plant and equipment	______	Long-term debt	______
		Common stock	40,000
		Retained earnings	62,000
		Total long-term debt and equity	______
Total assets	______	Total liabilities and equity	______

2. Compute the component and percentage changes over time for the Marvel Company using the historical income statements shown below. What does their strategy appear to have been? Were they successful?

	1980	*1981*	*1982*	*1983*	*1984*
Sales	$27,000	$28,350	$29,654	$31,344	$33,852
Cost of goods sold	23,490	24,098	24,613	25,075	27,082
Advertising	540	510	652	1,254	2,031
Interest expense	270	340	415	408	508
Other expenses	1,620	1,616	1,601	1,599	1,659
Profit before taxes	$ 1,080	$ 1,786	$ 2,373	$ 3,008	$ 2,572

3. Below you have ratios for PBJ, Inc., and its industry. Evaluate PBJ, Inc.'s position relative to the industry, citing specific ratios and trends as evidence to support your conclusions.

	PBJ, Inc.		*Industry*
	1983	*1984*	*1984*
Current ratio	2.7	2.3	2.1
Acid-test ratio	1.5	0.9	1.0
Inventory turnover	2.1	2.5	3.0
Days' sales in accounts receivable	40.0	45.0	32.0
Days' payables	30.0	32.0	30.0
LTD/equity	70%	75%	72%
Gross profit margin	16%	17%	15%
Profit before tax/sales	9%	8%	11%
ROE	20%	21%	19%

Managing Working Capital

Although much attention has recently been devoted to long-term financial strategy and planning, most financial managers find that a significant amount of their time is spent dealing with "brush fires"—short-term problems or opportunities. The development of a long-term financial strategy in conjunction with a corporate business strategy is important for the long-term growth of the company. However, the financial manager must ensure that the corporation can successfully cope with short-term contingencies. Otherwise, the long-term plan has no value.

A major source of short-term problems is the need for working capital for the company. Working capital refers to the current assets of the corporation and therefore includes inventories, accounts receivable, cash, and marketable securities. These resources are directly involved in the production and sales of the company. Successful management of the corporate working capital requires the management and financing of those assets that are required for the corporation's immediate activities.

I. THE WORKING-CAPITAL CYCLE

The term *working-capital cycle,* or *production-sales cycle,* refers to the ebb and flow of funds through the company in response to the changes in the level or rate of activity in manufacturing and sales. When the company decides to manufacture a product, funds are needed to purchase the raw materials, pay for the production process, and maintain the inventory. If the product is sold on credit, the company requires funds to support the accounts receivable until the customer ultimately reimburses the company for the product.

The term *cycle* refers to the difference between the time that production expenses are due for payment and the time that the customer pays for the product. If the company received payment for the product at the same time it was required to pay for the expenses of producing the product, there would

EXHIBIT 2–1 Graph of Working-Capital Cycle

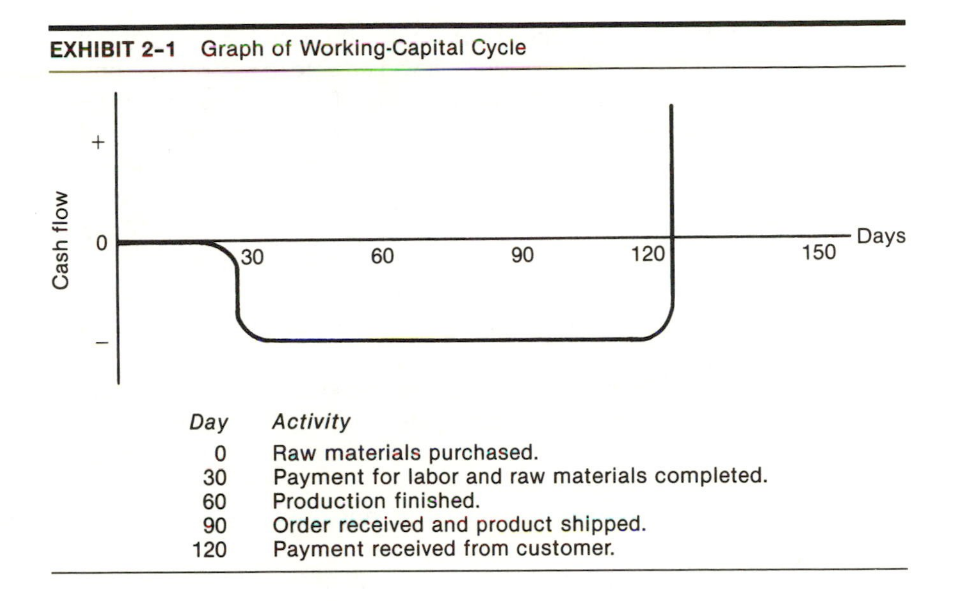

Day	*Activity*
0	Raw materials purchased.
30	Payment for labor and raw materials completed.
60	Production finished.
90	Order received and product shipped.
120	Payment received from customer.

be no working-capital cycle, nor would firms have difficulty managing working capital.

This timing difference can be illustrated with a simple graph, as shown in Exhibit 2–1. In this highly simplified, hypothetical cycle, the company orders the raw materials required for production at Day 0. The materials arrive and production begins. As production proceeds, the company begins to pay for the labor and by Day 30 has paid for all labor involved in the production process as well as for the materials. The product is completed on Day 60 and is put into finished goods inventory. A customer order is received on Day 90, and the product is sold. Payment is received from the customer on Day 120. In this example, the working-capital cycle is a total of 120 days or four months.

From a cash flow standpoint, the company would have made all of the cash payments for the labor and raw material costs by Day 30 and would have received no cash payment from the customer until Day 120. Consequently, the company would have required some type of financing for more than 90 days.

The working-capital cycle can vary significantly among different companies. Two extreme examples are wine producers and grocery retailers. The wine producer typically must store the wine for several years to attain proper aging. There may be several years between the cash outflows for production and the receipt of cash from sales to customers. The grocery retailer usually has a very rapid inventory turnover and makes mostly cash sales. In this case, the working-capital cycle is very short.

Most companies do not produce only one unit at a time. Many units are produced, and all are at various stages in the production-sales cycle at any given point in time. Thus, once a company is able to successfully complete the start-up phase of operations, it will be able to rely on the continuous flow of products through the cycle to provide funds for its needs. The company can use the cash from previous sales to pay for the expenses of producing current units. If the company were in a stable environment with no inflation, no sales growth, and no changes in customer demand, it would be able to deal with the working-capital cycle without difficulty. All of these factors exist, however, and combine to cause managerial problems.

1. The Impact of Inflation

In an inflationary environment, the cost of producing each unit increases over time. Thus, by the time the company has collected the cash from its early sales, the production costs on the subsequent units have increased. Unless the company was able to price the units with sufficient profit margins, it may not be able to meet the subsequent production costs with the revenues from the prior production.

To illustrate this problem, we will examine a simplified production cycle for a steel company with a $1,000 beginning cash balance, as shown in Exhibit 2–2. Assume that the company can produce a ton of steel for $400 and charges the customer $430 per ton to allow for a profit. If the working-capital cycle is about four months, the company will not receive any cash payment for the first ton of steel until four months after the production begins. In the interim, production of the second ton of steel commences.

If the inflation rate is 20% annually, the costs of producing the second ton of steel six months later will have increased to $440. Thus, when the company receives the cash payment for the steel billed at $430 per ton, its current production costs will be $440 per ton. The company will require some additional financing to allow it to meet the increased production costs, which, in this example, exceed the revenues received from the previous sales. Without financing, the cash balance will continually be reduced until it reaches zero.

Of course, the company will probably increase the price of the steel to maintain the profit margin. In this example, the price would probably be about $473 per ton. However, by the time the steel company collects this amount, inflation will have continued to increase the cost of the next ton produced.

This example is obviously highly simplified. Continual production and multiple products with varying working-capital cycles and exposures to inflation complicate the analysis. Nevertheless, the conceptual framework for analyzing the increased working-capital requirements caused by inflation is the same.

2. The Impact of Sales Growth

The effect of sales growth on working-capital needs is similar to that of inflation. In the case of sales growth, the problem is not caused by an increasing

EXHIBIT 2-2 Impact of Inflation on the Working-Capital Cycle

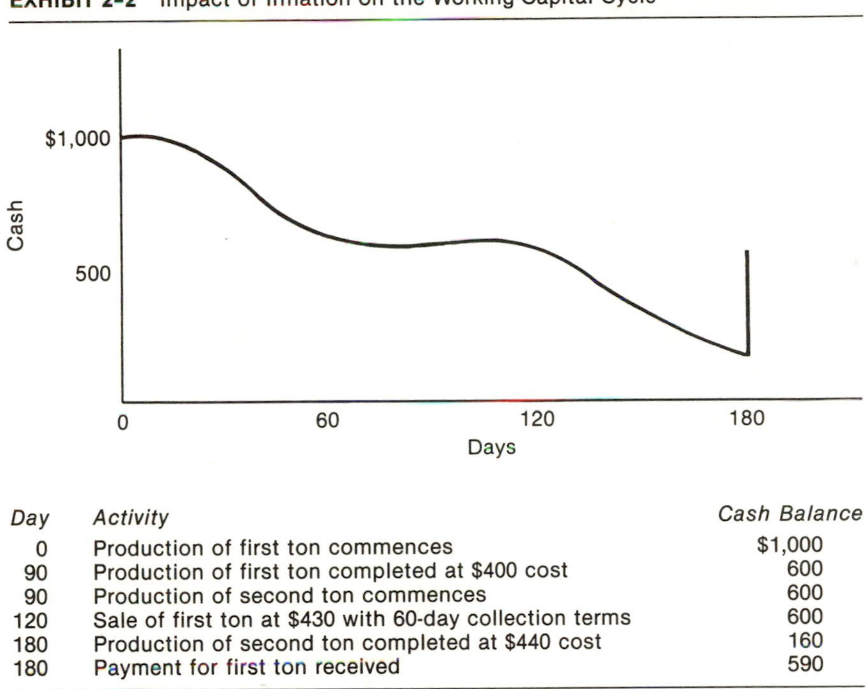

Day	*Activity*	*Cash Balance*
0	Production of first ton commences	$1,000
90	Production of first ton completed at $400 cost	600
90	Production of second ton commences	600
120	Sale of first ton at $430 with 60-day collection terms	600
180	Production of second ton completed at $440 cost	160
180	Payment for first ton received	590

per-unit cost but by an increasing number of units. Although the cost per unit may be stable, the total costs are increasing because of the increased volume.

For example, a microcomputer producer may have been very successful in developing a market for its products. Assume that the company can produce microcomputers for a cost of $700 each. The company produces and sells 500 units at $800 each during a particular month. The company extends credit of 30 days to the buyers of the microcomputers. During the ensuing month, the demand for the microcomputers is such that the company produces 600 units. At production costs of $700 per unit, the company will incur a total production cost of $420,000. However, the sales revenue collected from the sales of the previous month will be only $400,000 (500 × $800).

Thus, even if the company continues to charge $800 per unit, a price that allows a profit margin of 12.5%, the growth in sales will cause a working-capital problem. The company will have insufficient cash inflow each month to meet the expenses incurred for the production of the next units.

In this situation, the problem is not that the company has priced its products inappropriately. The company's prices allow an adequate profit margin above the costs of production. The problem stems from the timing differences between the payment of production expenses and the receipt of payment from the sales of the products.

This illustrates a problem that growing companies face. In order to grow, companies require funds to support that growth. The inability to provide the required funding may restrict the potential growth of the company. The maximum growth rate that a company can fund with its existing financing policies is termed the sustainable growth rate. Sustainable growth depends on the profitability of the company, the need for assets to support sales growth as measured by the asset turnover ratio, and the financing of the company as indicated by the dividend payout and debt to assets ratios. The relationship between sustainable growth and financial strategies is discussed in Chapter 8.

3. The Impact of Variable Sales Demand

The other major factor that can cause working-capital problems is a varying level of sales. Changes in sales activity are of three types:

1. *Seasonal:* The peak demand occurs during particular periods of the year; snow-skiing equipment is a seasonal product.
2. *Cyclical:* The peak demand occurs during different phases of the business cycle; the demand for building materials is cyclical.
3. *Secular:* Demand fluctuates over a long period of time; radio broadcasting revenues have been secular.

All three cycles differ in duration but have similar effects on the working capital of the company. For simplicity's sake, we will focus on the seasonal cycle, since its impact on working-capital needs is easier to trace because of its shorter duration.

In a seasonal industry, the company may not have sold the completed units before it is necessary to incur the costs of producing the next units. To illustrate the problem, we will use the example of the snow-skiing equipment manufacturer. This business is highly seasonal; peak consumer demand occurs during the fall and winter. The producer's peak sales period, however, occurs in the late summer and early fall when retailers place their orders to have the equipment for sale during the peak snow-skiing months.

The peak sales period for the manufacturer is not, however, the peak production period. It would be very inefficient to attempt to produce the skiing equipment as the orders from the retailers were received. To do so, the manufacturer would need to have a large production capacity, which would be idle for most of the year. New workers would have to be hired and trained for each production season. During the peak production period, the work force would be required to work overtime; at the conclusion of the period, the workers would be laid off. All in all, this would be a very inefficient and expensive production method.

To avoid these problems, the ski-equipment manufacturer may utilize a level production approach. During the slack sales months, in the late winter and spring, production is continued, but little equipment is actually sold to the retailers. The manufactured equipment is stored in inventory. The growing inventory will be used by the company to fill the sales orders as they arrive in the late summer and early fall. During this period of inventory buildup, the company still incurs the costs of the raw materials and labor associated with the production of the skiing equipment.

As the retailers begin to place orders in the late summer, the manufacturer ships the equipment from the inventory. During this period, the manufacturer starts to draw on the finished goods inventory if the orders exceed the continuing production level. However, the manufacturer still has not received payment for any of the equipment. The retailers buy from the manufacturer on credit with perhaps 30 or 60 days in which to pay for the equipment. During this period of high but decreasing inventories, continuing production, and increasing accounts receivable, most seasonal companies experience the greatest working-capital needs.

As the selling season progresses, additional orders will be received by the manufacturer. As these orders are filled, the large inventory is used much more rapidly than it is being replenished from the continuing production. While the receivables increase from the credit sales, the company begins to receive some payment for the shipments made in the late summer.

By the end of the fall selling season, the company's inventory is depleted, and all of its receivables should have been collected. At this point, the company should have a large amount of cash ready to begin the cycle of inventory buildup, receipt of orders, increase in accounts receivable, and collection of funds.

The seasonal cycle requires an infusion of cash to begin the cycle. Once the cycle starts, the funds cycle through different balance sheet accounts. Initially cash is invested in inventory in anticipation of future sales. Then, as orders are placed and goods shipped, the inventories are reduced and the capital is transferred to accounts receivable. As payments for the accounts receivable are received, the working capital is returned as cash, which is invested in production for inventory in preparation for the next selling season. This cycle is shown in Exhibit 2–3.

Even though the total amount of funds invested in inventories and accounts receivable does not change over the cycle, the company must still provide for the cash funds required at the beginning of the working cycle. From a cash standpoint, cash is spent on production at the outset of the cycle, and cash is received at the end of the cycle.

This pattern of inflow and outflow of funds might occur for several seasonal peaks during a year, over a business cycle, or over a long-term secular trend. In any of these situations, the pattern of working-capital needs would be similar. The primary difference among these situations is the duration of the cycle.

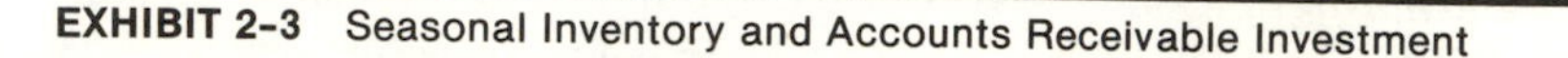

EXHIBIT 2-3 Seasonal Inventory and Accounts Receivable Investment

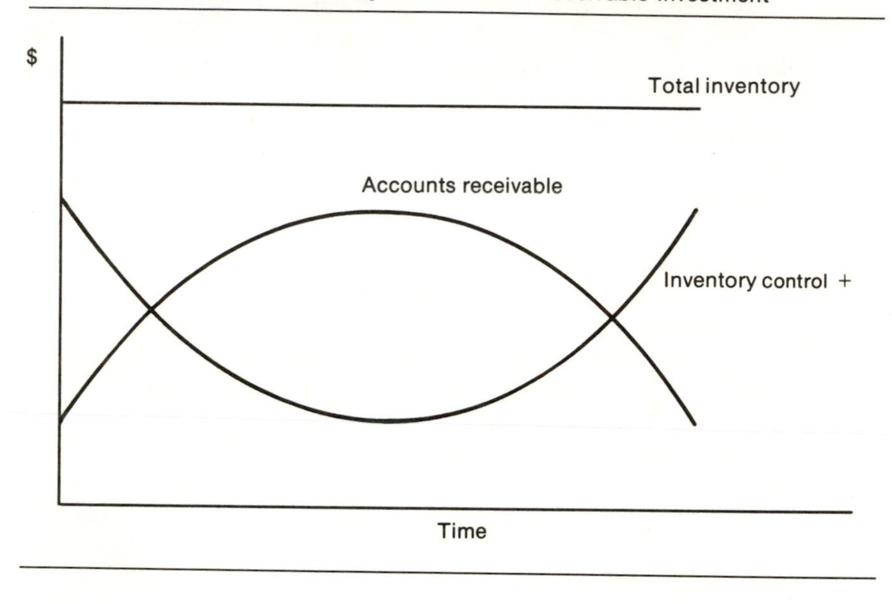

II. CASH MANAGEMENT

Because financial obligations must be paid in cash, the most important resource in the working-capital cycle is cash. Corporate managers need to ensure that sufficient cash is available to meet their obligations. This need has led to the development of sophisticated techniques to manage the cash availability in companies. These techniques have three objectives: accelerate the speed of cash receipts, decelerate the speed of cash disbursements, and maximize the return through investment of cash balances. In recent years, high interest rates have emphasized the importance of managing cash, while the development of computers has allowed managers access to the information needed for close monitoring of cash balances.

1. Managing Receipts

The process of managing cash receipts involves collecting the funds as quickly as possible and concentrating them in accounts so that the financial manager can control them.

Lockboxes. The use of lockboxes speeds the collecting, processing, depositing, and reporting of payments received through the mail. A lockbox is a special post office box to which the company's customers have been instructed to mail payments. The box is checked several times daily in the processing operation, which is usually operated by a bank. The checks are immediately entered into the check-clearing process to be converted into available funds for the company.

Preauthorized checks. Preauthorized checks (PACs) are preprinted, unsigned checks. For fixed, repetitive payments, companies authorize their creditors to draw checks on their accounts. The creditor sends the PAC to the bank, which then deposits the funds into the creditor's account.

Deposit concentration. Because it is difficult to control funds in many different banks, most receipt management systems provide for transferring funds through electronic or wire transfers into a few or even one large account. Central accounts can be more closely managed.

2. Managing Disbursements

The goal in managing disbursements is to delay payments in order to keep funds in use as long as possible.

Managed balance account. A managed balance account is a special checking account that has a zero balance. As checks are presented to this account, a negative balance is created. Funds are then automatically transferred from a control or master account to bring the account back to zero or another predetermined balance. In this way, all funds are centralized, and no idle balances remain in the disbursing account.

Controlled disbursement system. The purpose of this system is to maximize the time it takes for checks to clear a corporation's account. By making payments through geographically remote banks, the clearing time or "float" is increased. This postpones the date when the company must provide funds to cover the checks and allows funds to remain in interest-earning assets or delays the need to borrow.

3. Managing Cash Balances

By carefully managing the cash accounts, a financial manager can minimize the cash that the corporation must maintain. This increases the amount of funds available for investment in productive assets, such as inventories or plant and equipment, and reduces the need to raise additional capital.

The ultimate success in minimizing cash would be to have a zero balance in all accounts. Despite the efforts to control and predict disbursements, however, there may be some unforeseen need for disbursements or a slowdown in receipts. Therefore, corporations typically maintain some cash balances.

Having these balances sitting idly in checking accounts is an unproductive use of funds. Managers attempt to maximize the return on these cash balances by investing in short-term assets available in the money market.

The money market consists of borrowers and lenders of short-term funds. Although technically money market instruments could have a maturity of up to one year, most have much shorter maturities. The money market is highly liquid in that there are many buyers and sellers. Furthermore, the borrowers in this market are institutions with high credit ratings. These factors allow any investment to be quickly converted into cash if needed. Money market investments include Treasury bills (T-bills), short-term notes issued by the U.S. government; commercial paper, short-term notes issued by corporations; and certificates of deposits, short-term notes issued by banks. Although the returns from these short-term investments may be relatively low compared to longer-term, less liquid investments, it is still better than having no earnings from idle cash balances.

In order to invest in these instruments, the financial manager must know how much cash is available to invest. Cash management systems are designed to provide daily information about the amount of funds available. Managers can use this information to decide how much to invest in money market instruments. In many cases, investments will be made for periods as short as overnight to maximize the return available from the cash balances.

III. MANAGING OTHER WORKING-CAPITAL REQUIREMENTS

Cash by itself is not a productive asset. Most corporations are in business to make and sell a product. In order to be successful, companies need to invest their cash in the other elements of working capital—inventories and accounts receivable. Just as cash must be managed, the other working-capital investments must be managed as well. Similarly, managing these accounts is based on minimizing the working-capital investment and providing the resources that are required.

1. Minimizing Working-Capital Needs

The two components of working-capital needs are accounts receivable and inventories. The task of minimizing working capital, then, is one of reducing the company's investments in these two accounts.

The size of a company's accounts receivable is, to a large extent, determined by its competitive environment. If competitors are selling goods on credit, the company may be forced to follow the practice to remain competitive. The company has little control over the magnitude of the credit sales. The only method of reducing the accounts receivable is to ensure that credit collections are prompt. If goods are sold on 30-day terms, the company should vigorously attempt to ensure that payment is received within the 30-day period. Any lapse beyond this period represents an extension of noninterest-bearing credit by the manufacturer. Because of the expenses associated with the company's financing of its working-capital needs, any unnecessary increases in accounts receivable must be recognized as an extraneous expense for the manufacturer.

In an environment in which a company can independently determine its accounts receivable policy, the critical factor to be considered is the relationship between sales and accounts receivable. By reducing the financing that it is willing to offer buyers, a company may be eliminating some potential buyers. Thus, the accounts receivable may be reduced, but only at a cost of reducing the total revenues of the company.

On the other hand, extending more credit to buyers may have the effect of reducing the inventory that the company must bear. With easier credit terms, buyers may be willing to purchase more goods, thereby assuming some of the costs of inventory maintenance from the manufacturer. However, while the company's investment in inventory would decline, the investment in accounts receivable would increase.

An increased volume of credit sales also exposes the company to the additional risk of uncollectible accounts. The potential cost of bad debts must be weighed against the potential incremental profits resulting from the sales generated by the easier credit terms.

Like accounts receivable, inventory is directly related to sales volume. While maintaining too much inventory is expensive, it will have no impact on sales volume; however, too little inventory may cause stock-outs and lost sales. Maintenance of the appropriate inventory level has become so significant that sophisticated inventory models have been developed. The objective of these models is to determine the relationship between the inventory levels and the sales levels, so that the company can determine the inventory level that will maximize the return to the company.

In sum, from the standpoint of reducing the need for working capital, the company should attempt to reduce its investment in accounts receivable and inventories. However, the company risks the loss of sales revenues if these accounts are reduced inordinately. The managerial task is to ascertain the appropriate level for each of these accounts.

2. Financing Working-Capital Needs

Having determined the minimum level of working capital needed by the company to carry out the production and sales cycle, the manager must then select the most appropriate method of financing the needs. Not surprisingly, an important consideration is the cost of the various sources of financing.

Two immediate sources of funds are the cash and marketable securities accounts of the company. One of the first methods of financing that companies typically use is to reduce their cash to the minimum practical amount. To minimize their cash holdings, companies use the cash-management techniques previously described. Minimizing the cash account reduces the need for funds or allows for a larger investment in inventory or accounts receivable.

Another significant source of internal funding is the profit margin on sales. If the competitive environment allows, the company may be able to price its products so that there is sufficient profit to fund the working-capital requirements internally. For example, in an inflationary environment, the company might attempt to increase its prices in excess of the inflation rate in order to finance the working-capital needs caused by the inflating production costs. The company's ability to adjust its prices in this manner naturally depends on the competitive situation. In a highly competitive environment, the company may not have much latitude in its pricing and is likely to be an industry follower in pricing.

Having used these readily available sources of financing, the company may turn to the accounts payable for funding. In other words, the company takes longer to pay its bills.

The two major nonfinancial-institution creditors for most corporations are suppliers of raw materials and the government. Obviously, a company that extends its accounts payable (e.g., delays payment) to the various suppliers of its materials faces the risk that they will refuse to ship the materials needed for production. Similarly, while government entities may allow a temporary deferral of taxes, nonpayment of the amounts due is a punishable offense. Thus, although some additional financing may be available through the expansion of the accounts payable and other obligations, there are limitations on these sources.

The primary external source of working-capital funding is short-term bank debt. For corporations that face a seasonal working-capital cycle, short-term bank debt provides the resources needed, with the company's expected cash flows providing the debt's liquidation. Since the financing needs are short-term, short-term debt is considered to be appropriate. For this reason, a company's net working capital is often defined as current assets less current liabilities.

It is often suggested that long-term debt is a more appropriate method to fund working-capital needs caused by inflation, sales growth, and cyclical or secular trends. In these situations, the financing requirements are longer term, and a reliance on short-term debt might be inappropriate. In keeping with the concept that long-term needs should be financed with long-term sources, it is often suggested that long-term debt be utilized in this situation.

It is, of course, possible for a company to utilize short-term debt to fund these needs. The risk is that the company will continually need to refinance its debt, exposing itself to continuing interest-rate fluctuations as well as the potential unavailability of funds. If the company is willing to accept these risks, it might benefit from the lower interest costs normally associated with short-term as compared to longer-term debt.

The other external source of financing available to the company is the sale of additional equity. While equity capital is usually the most expensive form of financing, the company benefits from the fact that there are no restrictions or contractual obligations associated with it as there are with debt.

All of these sources of financing will be discussed in greater detail in Chapters 5 and 6.

IV. SUMMARY

Through the normal course of business operations, companies require current assets or working capital. These assets, inventories, accounts receivable, and cash, are needed to allow the company to manufacture and sell its products. However, because of the timing differences between the cash outflow for the costs of production and the cash inflow from the sale of the products, companies require some financing for these working-capital needs.

Because of the magnitude of the amounts required, companies can make a significant impact on their profitability through skillful management of their working capital. Thus, management may reduce the needed working capital by shortening the working-capital cycle or eliminating unneeded assets. Using cash management techniques, companies can reduce the amount of cash needed, which frees funds for investment in other assets. In assessing the working-capital needs, managers are required to analyze the trade-off between reducing working capital and reducing sales. Having achieved an appropriate working-capital level, management's remaining responsibility is to finance this in the least costly manner.

SELECTED REFERENCES

For further discussion of cash-management systems, see:

Serraino, William J.; Surrendra S. Singhvi; and Robert M. Soldofsky. *Frontiers of Financial Management*. 4th ed. Cincinnati: South-Western Publishing, 1984, part VI.

Stone, Bernell K., and Ned C. Hill. "Cash Transfer Scheduling for Efficient Cash Concentration." *Financial Management,* Autumn 1980, pp. 35–43.

For discussion of inventory and accounts receivable management, see:

Halloran, John A., and Howard P. Lanser. "The Credit Policy Decision in an Inflationary Environment." *Financial Management,* Winter 1981, pp. 31–38.

Scott, David., Jr.; Arthur J. Keown; John D. Martin; and J. William Petty III. *Readings in Financial Management*. New York: Academic Press, 1982, sec. 2.

For additional information on the money markets, see:

Brick, John R., ed. *Financial Markets: Instruments and Concepts*. Richmond, Va.: Robert F. Dame, 1981, sec. I.

For a more detailed explanation of working-capital management in general, see:

Brealey, Richard, and Stewart Myers. *Principles of Corporate Finance*. 2d ed. New York: McGraw-Hill, 1984, chaps. 27–30.

Seitz, Neil. *Financial Analysis: A Programmed Approach*. 3d ed. Reston, Va.: Reston Publishing, 1984, chap. 4.

VanHorne, James C. *Financial Management and Policy.* 6th ed. Englewood Cliffs, N.J.: Prentice-Hall, 1983, chaps. 13–16.

Weston, J. Fred, and Eugene F. Brigham. *Managerial Finance.* 7th ed. Hinsdale, Ill.: Dryden Press, 1981, part 3.

STUDY QUESTIONS

1. The W&H Manufacturing Company was very satisfied with their 1984 performance. The company had only begun operations the prior year, and as a result, sales had been slow. However, things had picked up considerably in 1984 with sales more than doubling in volume. W&H had changed none of its business practices during the year and had managed to hold its cost of goods sold to 78% of sales. All sales were made on credit, and payment was required within 30 days of the sale. The company paid for its purchases in 30 days and maintained a cash balance of 20% of sales. The only thing that had changed during the year was the company's inventory turnover, which had jumped from 3 to 6. While W&H's management was enthusiastic about the company's increased level of sales, it was concerned about the possible necessity of increasing its short-term debt. In order to assess the situation, the company was in the process of completing the financial statements shown below.

   Complete the forms given. For 1984, use other short-term liabilities as the balancing account (a "plug").

	1983	*1984*
Income statement:		
Sales	$250,000	$510,000
Cost of goods sold	195,000	
Gross margin	55,000	
Other expenses	40,000	40,000
Profit before tax	15,000	
Taxes @ 40%	6,000	
Profit after tax	$ 9,000	
Balance sheet:		
Cash	$ 50,000	
Accounts receivable	20,548	
Inventory	65,000	
Total current assets	135,548	
Net property, plant, and equipment	80,000	76,000
Total assets	$215,548	
Accounts payable	$ 16,027	
Other short-term liabilities	30,521	
Total current liabilities	46,548	
Long-term debt	60,000	60,000
Common stock	100,000	100,000
Retained earnings	9,000	
Total long-term debt and equity	169,000	
Total liabilities and equity	$215,548	
Net working capital:		
Current assets		
Current liabilities		
Net working capital		

2. In looking down the road toward 1985, the W&H Manufacturing Company anticipated that some changes would be required to continue their growth. Management anticipated that the 1984 level of sales was the maximum they could expect under their current credit terms. However, management also felt that W&H could retain its 1984 customers, each of whom would continue to pay within 30 days, regardless of whether or not the company changed its credit terms. W&H anticipated that it could increase its 1984 sales level by 30% by extending its credit terms to 45 days. W&H management thus anticipated 1985 sales to increase to $663,000 with credit terms of 45 days.

   Unsure of the effect these new credit terms would have on their financial statements, W&H management laid out the forms shown below. All operating conditions were expected to remain the same as they had been in 1984: (*a*) cost of goods sold at 78% of sales; (*b*) purchases to be paid within 30 days; (*c*) cash to be maintained at 20% of sales; and (*d*) inventory turnover to be six.

   Calculate the revised statements for 1985 and use the data for 1984 (calculated in answer to question 1) as the basis for comparison. Explain your findings.

	1983	*1984*
Income statement:		
Sales	$510,000	$663,000
Cost of goods sold		
Gross margin		
Other expenses	40,000	40,000
Profit before tax		
Taxes @ 40%		
Profit after tax		
Balance sheet:		
Cash		
Accounts receivable		
Inventory		
Total current assets		
Net property, plant, and equipment	76,000	72,000
Total assets		
Accounts payable		
Other short-term liabilities		
Total current liabilities		
Long-term debt	60,000	60,000
Common stock	100,000	100,000
Retained earnings		
Total long-term debt and equity		
Total liabilities and equity		
Net working capital:		
Current assets		
Current liabilities		
Net working capital		

3. W&H management also wants you to assess the possible ramifications of the following scenario:

   a. Credit terms were extended to 60 days and sales jumped to $700,000.

   b. Payment was never received for 2% of the sales.

c. All purchases were paid for within 30 days.
d. The balance in the cash account was held at 20% of sales.
e. An inventory turnover of six times was maintained throughout the year.
f. Cost of goods sold was held at 78% of sales.

Unlike some companies which established a reserve for bad debts, W&H followed a conservative account practice and deducted their losses from their profits as they occurred. Complete the form shown below and analyze the result.

	1985 Alternative scenario
Income statement:	
Sales	$700,000
Bad debt losses	
Net sales	
Cost of goods sold	
Gross margin	
Other expenses	40,000
Profit before tax	
Taxes @ 40%	
Profit after tax	
Balance sheet:	
Cash	
Accounts receivable	
Inventory	
Total current assets	
Net property, plant, and equipment	72,000
Total assets	
Accounts payable	
Other short-term liabilities	
Total current liabilities	
Long-term debt	60,000
Common stock	100,000
Retained earnings	
Total long-term debt and equity	
Total liabilties and equity	
Net working capital:	
Current assets	
Current liabilities	
Net working capital	

CHAPTER 3

Forecasting Future Needs

Most analysts are concerned about the company's future performance. Although an analysis of past performance can provide useful insights into the operation of a company, the historical data are most valuable for use in developing forecasts for the company's future. Sophisticated techniques, most of which are beyond the scope of this book, have been developed to forecast a company's future. Despite the level of quantitative and statistical sophistication involved, however, all forecasting techniques are essentially projections of historical relationships and results. The accuracy of forecasts is therefore contingent on proper interpretation of historical data as well as the continued pertinence of the identified relationships. The manager must bear in mind that the application of sophisticated quantitative analysis should not give the forecasts an unwarranted aura of veracity.

All forecasts are necessarily based on certain assumptions—assumptions about the relationships between past and future performance and about the relationships among the variables that are being forecast. These assumptions are critical and therefore should be explicit. The fact that forecasts are based on assumptions will not invalidate the results: rather, the inability to recognize that assumptions have been made and the failure to test them will result in tenuous forecasts.

Although technically similar, basic approaches to forecasting vary depending on the planned use of the results. The purpose of the forecast suggests the appropriate methods and variables to be used. External analysts typically make forecasts to determine a company's expected performance. For example, they may try to determine the returns from an equity investment in a company or whether a company will generate sufficient cash to remain solvent and repay its obligations. Internal analysts, on the other hand, are concerned with forecasting the need for financial resources so that managers can plan future operations and investments. The remainder of this chapter will focus on the types of analyses typically used by inside analysts.

In forecasting funding needs, analysts usually use two methods of analysis. For short time periods, a method known as cash budgeting is most often employed. For longer periods of time, pro forma financial statements are typically developed. We will discuss each of these methods in turn. We will then describe the means of testing the assumptions used to prepare the forecasts.

I. CASH BUDGETS

The cash-budget approach to forecasting financial needs focuses specifically on the cash account of the company. This approach differs significantly from the more common method of accounting, the accrual method. Accrual accounting attempts to match the revenues earned during a specific period with the expenses incurred without regard to actual cash receipts or disbursements. For cash budgeting, the objective is to identify whether sufficient cash will be available to meet financial needs as they occur. This is done by comparing cash receipts with cash disbursements. The difference between cash receipts and disbursements will reveal either an excess of or need for additional cash.

The cash-budget cycle is similar in many respects to the working-capital cycle discussed in Chapter 2. Like working-capital problems, the cash problems of a company are typically caused by timing differences between receipts and payments. Assuming that the company is adequately pricing its products, it would have no cash problems if the cash payments for its sales were received at the same time that payments for its production costs are required. However, credit sales, seasonal demand, and other factors combine to cause delays between receipts and disbursements.

In drawing up a cash budget, the analyst's first step is to choose an appropriate time period for analysis. Usually, cash budgets are developed by analyzing monthly cash flows. In industries with highly volatile cash flows or during times of high interest rates, the cash budgets may be based on weekly or daily cash flows. In some highly inflationary environments, companies have been known to prepare cash budgets for hourly cash flows. The analyst's second step is to choose a suitable forecast horizon date. The forecast horizon for the cash budget also depends on the firm's situation. If monthly cash budgets are used, the company would typically prepare a 12- or perhaps a 24-month forecast. Cash budgets based on shorter time periods would usually be developed for correspondingly nearer forecast horizons.

After the appropriate time period and forecast horizon have been chosen, the next step is to determine which variables will be used as the bases for the forecast's critical underlying assumptions. Most forecasts begin with an assumption about sales volume during the period. Predictions for all other variables are based on the forecasted level of sales. The assumed relationships between sales and the other variables are, of course, important and need to be explicitly stated.

EXHIBIT 3–1 Assumptions for Murphy's Apparel, Cash Budget 1985–1986

1. Sales would be seasonal, peaking in the summer. In general, sales would increase by 10% annually.
2. About 10% of sales would be for cash. Credit terms during summer peak months would be eight weeks; off-season collections would be four weeks.
3. Suppliers would require payment within 30 days.
4. The bank would not allow more than the current $50,000 credit line.
5. The expected purchase of new equipment would require a $15,000 payment in May 1986.
6. Cost of sales would be 79% of sales.
7. Selling and administrative expenses would be 9% of sales.
8. Fixed operating costs would be $5,400 a month, including $500 depreciation expense.
9. The monthly lease and interest payments would be $3,000. This is a simplifying assumption since interest costs would depend on the actual amount borrowed.
10. No taxes would be paid because of a tax loss carryforward.

The cash budgets developed for Murphy's Apparel, a wholesale distributor of tennis and swimming clothing and accessories will serve as examples for forecasting the cash position. Although Murphy's Apparel sustained some losses during its initial operations, management expected that continuing operations would be profitable. The company had only been in existence for two years, and the owner had relied on a bank loan of $50,000 to offset the financial drain caused by the early losses. Although sales were expected to increase annually by 10%, the necessity of extending long credit during the peak summer sales season caused severe cash problems. To determine the severity of these problems, a monthly cash budget, commencing on September 1, 1985, and extending through mid-1986 was prepared.

Starting with the assumed sales growth of 10%, analysts prepared a set of assumptions for the cash budget. These are listed in Exhibit 3–1. Using these assumptions, the analysts forecast the expected sales volume, cash sales, accounts receivable collections, and purchases of merchandise for each of the 12 months of the cash-budget period. These forecasts are shown in Exhibit 3–2.

On the basis of these data, the monthly cash receipts and cash disbursements were calculated. The results are shown in Exhibit 3–3. For each month, the cash payments for expenses and merchandise were subtracted from the cash generated by cash sales and from collections of previous credit sales. On a cumulative basis, an excess of receipts over disbursements increased the cash balance, while a shortfall reduced it.

Using the cash budget, managers determined that the firm would need cash in June and July. The cash need of $3,000 in June 1986 and $28,000 in July is less than the $50,000 credit line already arranged with the bank. Even though Murphy's would need to draw on the credit line, the cash-budget forecast indicates no significant cash problems because of the large cash amounts accumulated early in the year. With these cash reserves, Murphy's

EXHIBIT 3-2 Forecast of Net Sales, Purchase, and Collections, Murphy's Apparel, 1985-86 (in thousands)

	Net Sales	*Cash Sales (10%)*	*Credit Sales*	*Collections from Accounts Receivable*	*Purchase of Merchandise**
1985:					
September	$ 95	$10	$ 85	$111	$ 67
October	75	8	67	144	51
November	55	6	49	137	40
December	45	5	40	51	32
1986:					
January	35	4	31	41	32
February	45	5	40	32	45
March	70	7	63	39	69
April	105	11	94	61	99
May	145	15	130	16	128
June	180	18	162	85	136
July	165	17	148	117	119
August	135	14	121	159	95

*Purchases calculated from half of current month expected sales plus half of next month.

would be able to fund most of its cash needs without resorting to additional borrowing from the bank.

Of course, a company's need for cash also depends on its need for liquidity. This, in turn, is determined by the company's environment. Companies in a more volatile environment, with greater uncertainty about sales, collections, costs, etc., need to maintain a higher cash balance than those operating in a more stable environment. The more difficult it is to forecast future events, the greater the need to maintain a high cash reserve to provide for unforeseen needs. The cash budget also provides a benchmark that may be used to measure the company's performance. If the cash account fell below the level forecasted for a particular month, the company would have an early warning of potential cash problems. Therefore, the cash budget is not only a planning tool but a control device as well.

II. PRO FORMA FINANCIAL STATEMENTS

The cash budget describes the flow of cash during the forecast period: pro forma financial statements, like normal financial statments, provide aggregate information for the forecast period. Pro forma financial statements are essentially summaries of the information provided by the cash budget. Cash budgets provide the details while the pro forma financial statements provide summaries in the more familiar financial statement format. Pro forma income statments forecast earnings and expenses for the period; pro forma balance sheets forecast the assets and liabilities at the conclusion of the forecast period; and pro forma sources and uses of funds statements forecast the

EXHIBIT 3-3 Monthly Cash Budget 1985-86, Murphy's Apparel (in thousands)

	1985				1986							
	Sept.	*Oct.*	*Nov.*	*Dec.*	*Jan.*	*Feb.*	*Mar.*	*Apr.*	*May*	*June*	*July*	*Aug.*
Receipts:												
Beginning accounts receivable	$246	$220	$143	$ 55	$ 44	$ 34	$ 42	$ 66	$ 99	$213	$290	$321
Credit sales	85	67	49	40	31	40	63	94	130	162	148	121
Less: Collections	111	144	137	51	41	32	39	61	16	85	117	159
Ending accounts receivable	$220	$143	$ 55	$ 44	$ 34	$ 42	$ 66	$ 99	$ 213	$290	$321	$283
Cash sales	$ 10	$ 8	$ 6	$ 5	$ 4	$ 5	$ 7	$ 11	$ 15	$ 18	$ 17	$ 14
Collections	111	144	137	51	41	32	39	61	16	85	117	159
Total receipts	$121	$152	$143	$ 56	$ 45	$ 37	$ 46	$ 72	$ 31	$103	$134	$173
Disbursements:												
Beginning accounts payable	$ 84	$ 67	$ 51	$ 40	$ 32	$ 32	$ 45	$ 69	$ 99	$128	$136	$119
Purchases	67	51	40	32	32	45	69	99	128	136	119	95
Less: Payments	84	67	51	40	32	32	45	69	99	128	136	119
Ending accounts payable	$ 67	$ 51	$ 40	$ 32	$ 32	$ 45	$ 69	$ 99	$ 128	$136	$119	$ 95
Payments	$ 84	$ 67	$ 51	$ 40	$ 32	$ 32	$ 45	$ 69	$ 99	$128	$136	$119
Administrative and selling expenses	9	7	5	4	3	4	6	9	13	16	15	12
Fixed costs	5	5	5	5	5	5	5	5	5	5	5	5
Lease and interest	3	3	3	3	3	3	3	3	3	3	3	3
New equipment	0	0	0	0	0	0	0	0	15	0	0	0
Total disbursements	$101	$ 82	$ 64	$ 52	$ 43	$ 44	$ 59	$ 86	$ 135	$152	$159	$139
Receipts less disbursements	$ 20	$ 70	$ 79	$ 4	$ 2	$ (7)	$ (13)	$ (14)	$(104)	$(49)	$ (25)	$ 34
Cumulative cash flow	20	90	169	173	175	168	155	141	37	(12)	(37)	(3)
Monthly cash change:												
Beginning cash	9	29	99	178	182	184	177	164	150	46	(3)	(28)
Change in cash	20	70	79	4	2	(7)	(13)	(14)	(104)	(49)	(25)	34
Ending cash	$ 29	$ 99	$178	$182	$184	$177	$164	$150	$ 46	$ (3)	$ (28)	$ 6

funds availability during the period. Although pro forma financial statements could be prepared weekly or monthly, as are cash budgets, they are usually developed for annual forecasts. A typical five-year forecast would consist of a series of annual pro forma financial statements.

Like cash budgets, pro formas require the definition of one or more critical variables (again, usually the sales forecast) and the definition of the relationships of other variables to the basic independent variable. These assumed relationships should be explicitly stated.

1. Developing Pro Formas from Cash Budgets

Since the cash budget forecasts require the same information as the pro forma financial statements, it is possible to develop a set of pro formas using the cash budget. The only additional information needed is the balance sheet as of the beginning of the forecast period. Using the data from the cash budget, one can calculate a pro forma income statement. Then, using the pro forma income statement, the cash budget, and the beginning balance sheet, the analyst can develop a pro forma balance sheet and sources and uses of funds statement.

The data from the cash budget for Murphy's Apparel have been used to develop a pro forma income statement for the period from September 1, 1985, to August 31, 1986. This income statement is shown in Exhibit 3–4. The balance sheet for August 31, 1985, the beginning of the forecast period, and the pro forma balance sheet for August 31, 1986, are included in Exhibit 3–5. The exhibit also details the changes which were forecast to occur in the various accounts during the forecast period. These changes are also included in Exhibit 3–6, the pro forma sources and uses of funds.

Although the pro formas do not provide the detail of the ebbs and flows in the cash account during the period, they do show precisely the same cash balance at the end of the forecast period. Thus, they do indicate the company's financing needs at the end of the period. For companies that do not experience a significant change in cash during a year, the pro forma approach to forecasting funds needs is usually adequate. Since cash budgets are more time-consuming to prepare, managers of most companies elect to develop the pro forma financial statements directly, rather than on the basis of cash budgets.

2. Developing Pro Formas Directly

To develop pro formas directly, analysts use an extension of ratio analysis. First, the historic relationships among the financial statements' accounts for previous years are determined. These relationships, expressed as ratios, are then adjusted to account for expected future events and trends. Finally, pro forma accounts are forecast on the basis of adjusted ratios. As is the case with cash budgets, the first projection made is usually sales. The balances in the other accounts are then forecast on the basis of their expected relation-

EXHIBIT 3-4

Murphy's Apparel
Pro Forma Income Statement
September 1, 1985 to August 31, 1986
(in thousands)

Net sales	$1,150
Cost of goods sold	909
Gross profit	241
Expenses:	
Selling and administrative expense	103
Fixed operating costs	60
Depreciation	6
Lease and interest expense	36
Net profit*	$ 36

*As noted on Exhibit 3-1, Murphy's Apparel has a tax loss carryforward which exceeds the expected profit and, therefore, has no tax liability.

EXHIBIT 3-5

Murphy's Apparel
Balance Sheet
(in thousands)

	August 31, 1985 Actual		*August 31, 1986 Pro Forma*
Assets		**Changes**	
Cash	$ 9	From cash budget	$ 6
Accounts receivable	246	From cash budget	283
Inventories	89	+913 (Purchases from cash budget) −909 (Cost of goods sold from income statement)	93
Total current assets	344		382
Equipment	42	+15 (New equipment from cash budget) −6 (Depreciation from income statement)	51
Total assets	$386		$433
Liabilities and Equity			
Notes payable	$ 10		$ 10
Accounts payable	84	From cash budget	95
Total current liabilities	94		105
Long-term debt	100		100
Equity	192	+36 (From income statement)	228
Total liabilities and equity	$386		$433

EXHIBIT 3-6

Murphy's Apparel
Pro Forma Sources and Uses of Funds Statement
September 1, 1985 to August 31, 1986
(in thousands)

Sources:	
Decrease in cash	$ 3
Increase in accounts payable	11
Net profits	36
Depreciation	6
Total sources	$ 56
Uses:	
Increase in accounts receivable	$ 37
Increase in inventories	4
Increase in working capital	41
Increase in equipment	15
Total uses	$ 56

ships with sales. Forecasts are made for each account, with the exception of a balancing or "plug" account on the pro forma balance sheet.

An easy way to calculate the required balancing amount is to include a "net financing need" liability account in the pro formas. If the balancing amount in this account is positive, it means that the assets exceed the liabilities and equity and additional financing will be needed. If the net financing need is negative, the liabilities and equity are greater than the assets. In this case, funds are available for additional investment in assets.

Since these forecasts are derived directly from specified relationships among the various accounts, the assumptions embedded in the analysis may be more obvious than those used in cash budgets. Nevertheless, it is critical to realize that the pro forma's reliability depends on the validity of the assumptions.

The pro forma financial statements for the Monson Company, a distributor of surveying, drafting, and architectural supplies, appear in Exhibits 3-7, 3-8, and 3-9. The company was organized as a partnership. The majority equity investment was provided by a silent partner. The minority equity owner was the manager of the company; the silent partner was not involved in any of the company's operations. The silent partner considered his equity position in Monson strictly as an investment. He was willing to have the minority partner buy out his equity position at a price that would provide an adequate return on his investment. The minority owner and manager of the company hoped that the Monson Company would provide sufficient funds to allow him to buy out his silent partner in the near future.

To determine whether adequate funds would be available to do this, the minority owner develped a five-year forecast. Exhibit 3-7 shows the income statements for the previous three years, the five-year pro forma income state-

EXHIBIT 3-7

THE MONSON COMPANY
Income Statements
(in thousands)

	Actual			Pro Forma				
	1982	*1983*	*1984*	*1985*	*1986*	*1987*	*1988*	*1989*
Sales	$1,094	$1,360	$1,402	$1,612	$1,854	$2,132	$2,452	$2,820
Cost of goods sold	792	980	984	1,128	1,298	1,492	1,716	1,974
Gross profit	302	380	418	484	556	640	736	846
Operating expenses	244	290	351	376	402	430	460	492
Profit before tax	58	90	67	108	154	210	276	354
Taxes	15	30	14	36	51	69	91	117
Net income	$ 43	$ 60	$ 53	$ 72	$ 103	$ 141	$ 185	$ 237

Assumptions for pro forma:
- Sales will grow at 15%.
- Gross margin will be 30%.
- Operating expenses will grow at the expected 7% inflation rate.
- Taxes will be 33% of profit before tax.

EXHIBIT 3-8

THE MONSON COMPANY
Balance Sheets
(in thousands)

	Actual			Pro Forma				
	1982	*1983*	*1984*	*1985*	*1986*	*1987*	*1988*	*1989*
Assets								
Cash	$ 45	$ 54	$ 60	$ 64	$ 68	$ 73	$ 78	$ 83
Accounts receivable	118	168	165	177	204	235	270	310
Inventory	309	320	365	403	464	533	613	705
Other current assets	46	52	75	80	86	92	98	105
Total current assets	518	594	665	724	822	933	1,059	1,203
Fixed assets (net)	13	19	14	14	14	14	14	14
Total assets	$531	$613	$679	$738	$836	$947	$1,073	$1,217
Liabilities and Equity								
Accounts payable	$ 41	$ 61	$ 73	$ 81	$ 93	$107	$ 123	$ 141
Other current liabilities	3	5	6	6	6	6	6	6
Total current liabilities	44	66	79	87	99	113	129	147
Common stock	350	350	350	350	350	350	350	350
Retained earnings	137	197	250	322	425	566	751	988
Net financing need				(21)	(38)	(82)	(157)	(268)
Total liabilities and equity	$531	$613	$679	$738	$836	$947	$1,073	$1,217

Assumptions for pro forma:
Receivables will be 11% of sales.
Inventory will be 25% of sales.
Cash, other current assets, and liabilities will increase at the expected 7% inflation rate.
New fixed asset investment will equal depreciation expense.
Accounts payable will be 5% of sales.

EXHIBIT 3–9

THE MONSON COMPANY
Sources and Uses of Funds Statement
(in thousands)

	Actual		*Pro Forma*				
	1983	*1984*	*1985*	*1986*	*1987*	*1988*	*1989*
Sources:							
Increase in accounts payable	$20	$12	$ 8	$ 12	$ 14	$ 16	$ 18
Increase in other current liabilities	2	1	0	0	0	0	0
Net income	60	53	72	103	141	185	237
	82	66	80	115	155	201	255
Net financing need	—	—	(21)	(17)	(44)	(75)	(111)
Total sources	$82	$66	$59	$ 98	$111	$126	$144
Uses:							
Increase in cash	$ 9	$ 6	$ 4	$ 4	$ 5	$ 5	$ 5
Increase in accounts receivable	50	(3)	12	27	31	35	40
Increase in inventory	11	45	38	61	69	80	92
Increase in other current assets	6	23	5	6	6	6	7
Increase in working capital	76	71	59	98	111	126	144
Increase in fixed assets	6	(5)	0	0	0	0	0
Total uses	$82	$66	$59	$ 98	$111	$126	$144

Note: A negative entry as a use means that amount was a source of funds. A negative entry as a source of funds means that it was actually a use.

ments, and the assumptions used in developing the pro formas. Exhibit 3–8 provides similar information on the balance sheets and Exhibit 3–9 for the sources and uses of funds.

From the pro formas, it did not appear that the company would generate sufficient funds during the five years to allow the manager to buy out the silent partner. However, the pro formas did indicate that the company would accumulate significant excess funds during the forecast period as indicated by the negative net financing need account. These funds could be paid out in dividends, and the manager could use his portion to purchase some of the equity from the majority owner. Another alternative might be to borrow the required funds from a lending institution, using the future proceeds from the operations of the company to repay the loan.

III. ANALYZING ASSUMPTIONS

As has been stated repeatedly, any projection requires underlying assumptions. If the assumptions are not valid, then the subsequent forecasts are valueless. Since the true validity of an assumption is recognizable only after the fact, several procedures have been developed to assist in analyzing the reasonableness of assumptions beforehand.

1. Historical Comparisons

An obvious place to begin in examining assumptions is to compare them to recent actual relationships. If an assumption differs significantly from actual results, additional analysis of that assumption is warranted.

Since the relationships are typically stated as ratios, this evaluation of the assumptions is another use of the ratio analysis described in Chapter 1. Just as ratios are used to examine the historical performance of a company, they can be used to test whether assumptions about future performance are reasonable.

Comparisons of the assumed relationships with those that exist for other companies will also provide a check for the appropriateness of the assumptions. As with any ratio analysis, the comparison companies should be analogous. This means that the companies should be in similar industries and have similar operating and marketing strategies. If such strictly comparable companies cannot be found for evaluation, then the analyst should adjust the comparison companies' ratios as needed.

Another means of using historical data to forecast future relationships is regression analysis. This statistical technique allows the analyst to mathematically project the pro forma relationships based on several past periods of data. While this method provides the security of quantitative rigor, it may be a false security if the analyst has good reason to expect future relationships between various financial accounts to differ from their historical patterns.

Using the Monson Company's pro formas as examples, Exhibit 3–10 is a simple comparison of some of the assumptions used in developing the pro forma financial statements with the actual relationships for the prior years.

Two of the assumptions may be cause for concern. The actual sales growth rate from 1982 to 1983 exceeded the forecast rate, but the growth in sales from 1983 to 1984 was significantly below the forecast. A greater departure from past experience is shown by the operating expense forecast. The forecast is based on operating expenses increasing at the 7% inflation rate. Since sales are increasing at 15%, this means that operating expenses would be decreasing as a percentage of sales. The historical data suggest that operating expenses have been between 20% and 25% of sales for the past three years. It appears that the forecast may have been overly optimistic.

To examine the effects of an increase in the operating expenses, the pro formas were recalculated with operating expenses at 25% of sales. This provided a 15% annual increase in operating expenses, the same growth rate as sales. The revised results are shown in Exhibits 3–11, 3–12, and 3–13.

Using the revised operating expense forecast, the Monson Company's outlook is much different. Profits continue to grow, although at a slower rate. However, instead of generating excess funds, the revised pro formas indicate an increasing need for additional funding each year. This illustrates how a changed assumption may greatly affect the projected results.

EXHIBIT 3-10 Comparison of Pro Forma Assumptions to 1983 and 1984 Actual Results, The Monson Company

Relationships	*Assumptions for Pro Forma*	*Actual 1984*	*Actual 1983*
Sales growth	15%	3%	24%
Receivables as a percentage of sales	11	12	12
Inventory as a percentage of sales	25	26	24
Payables as a percentage of sales	5	5	4
Gross margin	30	30	28
Operating expense as a percentage of sales	decreasing	25	21
Operating expense increase over previous year	7	21	25

EXHIBIT 3-11

THE MONSON COMPANY
Pro Forma Income Statements with Changed Assumption
(in thousands)

	Actual	*Pro Forma*				
	1984	*1985*	*1986*	*1987*	*1988*	*1989*
Sales	$1,402	$1,612	$1,854	$2,132	$2,452	$2,820
Cost of goods sold	984	1,128	1,298	1,492	1,716	1,974
Gross profit	418	484	556	640	736	846
Operating expenses	351	403	464	533	613	705
Profit before tax	67	81	92	107	123	141
Taxes	14	27	30	35	41	47
Net income	$ 53	$ 54	$ 62	$ 72	$ 82	$ 94

Assumptions for pro forma:
Sales will grow at 15%.
Gross margin will be 30%.
Operating expenses will be 25% of sales.
Taxes will be 33% of profit before tax.

2. Sensitivity Analysis

A second means of analyzing the assumptions is called *sensitivity analysis.* This process examines the forecast's sensitivity to changes in the assumptions. If changing a particular assumption has little impact on the pro formas, then the assumption is not considered critical. If changing an assumption causes a major change in the pro forma financial statements, then it is considered a critical variable that warrants further analysis and careful monitoring.

It should be obvious that, although sensitivity analysis is a fairly simple concept, it is rather time-consuming to execute properly. If the pro formas incorporate many assumptions, a considerable number of pro formas would need to be calculated to adequately examine the sensitivity of the results to

EXHIBIT 3-12

THE MONSON COMPANY
Pro Forma Balance Sheets with Changed Assumption
(in thousands)

	Actual	*Pro Forma*				
	1984	*1985*	*1986*	*1987*	*1988*	*1989*
Assets						
Cash	$ 60	$ 64	$ 68	$ 73	$ 78	$ 83
Accounts receivable	165	177	204	235	270	310
Inventory	365	403	464	533	613	705
Other current assets	75	80	86	92	98	105
Total current assets	665	724	822	933	1,059	1,203
Fixed assets (net)	14	14	14	14	14	14
Total assets	$679	$738	$836	$947	$1,073	$1,217
Liabilities and Equity						
Accounts payable	$ 73	$ 81	$ 93	$107	$ 123	$ 141
Other current liabilities	6	6	6	6	6	6
Total current liabilities	79	87	99	113	129	147
Common stock	350	350	350	350	350	350
Retained earnings	250	304	366	438	520	614
Net financing need		(3)	21	46	74	106
Total liabilities and equity	$679	$738	$836	$947	$1,073	$1,217

Assumptions for pro forma:
Receivables will be 11% of sales.
Inventory will be 25% of sales.
Cash, other current assets, and liabilities will increase at the expected 7% inflation rate.
New fixed asset investment will equal depreciation expense.
Accounts payable will be 5% of sales.

changes in each variable. To ease this process, analysts attempt to simplify the assumptions and to estimate which factors will have critical impact on the results. The sensitivity analysis is then confined to these limited factors.

A frequently used technique is to use three different values for the assumption, the most likely, an optimistic, and a pessimistic value. Since the original projection is usually based on the most likely relationship, the analyst should then project the other two outcomes. It is important to understand that the optimistic and pessimistic forecasts are not the same as the absolute best and worst cases. The likelihood of an extremely favorable or undesirable outcome is probably remote. Therefore, it makes more sense to focus on outcomes with a greater likelihood of occurring.

Some analysts only analyze the negative outcomes. Their reasoning is that while optimistic relationships may occur and create problems, those problems are easier to deal with than the problems that pessimistic outcomes create. By focusing only on the "downside" risks, they forecast the range of potential negative results. In some cases, however, the negative results arise from "upside" factors. For example, a large increase in sales may appear positive, but it could also mean an increased need for working-capital financing.

EXHIBIT 3-13

THE MONSON COMPANY
Pro Forma Sources and Uses of Funds Statement with Changed Assumption
(in thousands)

	Actual	*Pro Forma*				
	1984	*1985*	*1986*	*1987*	*1988*	*1989*
Sources:						
Increase in accounts payable	$12	$ 8	$12	$ 14	$ 16	$ 18
Increase in other current liabilities	1	0	0	0	0	0
Net income	53	54	62	72	82	94
	66	62	74	86	98	112
Net financing need		(3)	24	25	28	32
Total sources	$66	$59	$98	$111	$126	$144
Uses:						
Increase in cash	$ 6	$ 4	$ 4	$ 5	$ 5	$ 5
Increase in accounts receivable	(3)	12	27	31	35	40
Increase in inventory	45	38	61	69	80	92
Increase in other current assets	23	5	6	6	6	7
Increase in working capital	71	59	98	111	126	144
Increase in fixed assets	(5)	0	0	0	0	0
Total uses	$66	$59	$98	$111	$126	$144

Note: A negative entry as a use means that amount was a source of funds. A negative entry as a source of funds means that it was actually a use.

The risk of this simplification is that some critical assumptions might be ignored. Computer-based financial modeling systems have been developed that greatly increase the analyst's ability to undertake sensitivity analysis. Not only can the modeling systems do the calculations rapidly, they also facilitate the use of probability analysis.[1]

3. Probability Analysis

Probability analysis is an extension of sensitivity analysis. The analyst first forecasts a range of possible values for any given variable and then estimates the likelihood that each of the values may occur. For example, the analyst may estimate that a 7% growth in sales has a probability of 45%; a 10% sales growth, 70%; and a 15% sales growth, 30%. By combining these probabilities with those estimated for other variables—such as cost of goods sold and rates of inflation—the computer can calculate the overall probabilities of all possible net financial outcomes. This series of calculations, called a *simulation,* provides more useful information than do pro formas relying on a single or "point" estimate for each variable.

[1]The use of these modeling systems is explained in Appendix A.

IV SUMMARY

Using historic relationships, analysts can project the future performance of a company. The historic pattern must be adjusted for changes in the environment and/or changes in the company. Based on these assumptions, managers can estimate future cash needs through the technique of cash budgets and future financial statement results through pro forma statements. The appropriate method depends on the needs of the analyst.

Any projections are only as useful as the validity or reasonableness of the underlying assumptions. An important part of any forecast is the testing of the assumptions through sensitivity analysis. In so doing, the manager becomes aware of the critical assumptions and is forewarned about areas needing additional analysis and special monitoring.

SELECTED REFERENCES

For discussions on the impact of inflation on funds forecasting, see:

Seed, Allen H., III. "Measuring Financial Performance in an Inflationary Environment." *Financial Executive,* January 1982, pp. 40–50.

Vancil, Richard F. "Funds Flow Analysis During Inflation." *Financial Analysts Journal,* March–April 1976, pp. 43–56.

For an examination of various quantitative forecasting techniques, see:

Vatter, Paul A.; Stephen P. Bradley; Sherwood Frey, Jr.; and Barbara B. Jackson, *Quantitative Methods in Management.* Homewood, Ill.: Richard D. Irwin, 1978, chaps. 7–9.

For additional discussions of forecasting financial needs, see:

Pringle, John J., and Robert S. Harris. *Essentials of Managerial Finance.* Glenview, Ill.: Scott, Foresman, 1984, chap. 8.

VanHorne, James C. *Financial Management and Policy.* 6th ed. Englewood Cliffs, N.J.: Prentice-Hall, 1983, chap. 28.

Weston, J. Fred, and Eugene F. Brigham. *Managerial Finance.* 7th ed. Hinsdale, Ill.: Dryden Press, 1981, chap. 8.

For a discussion of simulation, see:

Hertz, David B. "Risk-Analysis in Capital Investment." *Harvard Business Review,* September–October 1979, pp. 169–81.

STUDY QUESTIONS

1. The SUN Company sold swimwear and other summer-related goods. As a result, sales peaked in the second quarter of the year, just prior to the onset of the summer season. The projected sales for the 1985 season are shown on the next page. Complete the SUN cash budget using the following assumptions:
   a. Payment for 20% of its sales is received in cash. Payment for the remainder is received in 30 days.
   b. Cost of goods sold, which equaled 74% of sales, represented 100% of the company's purchases. Because of short delivery schedules, SUN was able to

1985 SUN Company Cash Budget (in thousands)

	Jan.	*Feb.*	*Mar.*	*Apr.*	*May*	*June*	*July*	*Aug.*	*Sept.*	*Oct.*	*Nov.*	*Dec.*
Sales	65	70	90	100	115	125	150	175	130	110	80	70
Receipts:												
Beginning accounts receivable	70											
Credit sales												
Less: Collections												
Ending accounts receivable												
Cash sales												
Collections												
Total receipts												
Disbursements:												
Beginning accounts payable	51											
Purchases												51
Less: Payments												
Ending accounts payable												
Payments												
Selling and administrative costs												
Fixed costs												
Lease and interest												
Total disbursements												
Receipts less disbursements												
Cumulative cash flow												
Monthly cash change:												
Beginning cash balance	11											
Change in cash												
Ending cash												

purchase its goods one month in advance of their anticipated need. In order to provide themselves a cushion, management traditionally ordered 5% more goods than their sales projections indicated they would need. All purchases were paid for in one month.

c. Selling and administrative expenses were projected to be 7% of sales.

d. Fixed operating costs were projected at $6,000 per month, excluding $3,000 depreciation per month.

e. Monthly lease and interest payments would be $3,000.

f. No taxes would be paid due to a tax loss carryforward.

Assuming the SUN company meets its short-term cash shortfalls with short-term debt, in what month will the company's borrowing be the greatest? How much will it be borrowing? What is the company's cumulative cash flow for the year?

2. Use SUN's forecasted cash budget to develop a pro forma income statement for 1985.

Sales	
Cost of goods sold	______
Gross margin	
Selling and administrative	
Fixed costs	
Depreciation	
Lease and interest payments	______
Net income	======

3. Using the forecasted cash budget, pro forma income statement, and SUN's 1984 balance sheet, complete the pro forma balance sheet shown below.

	1984 Actual	*1985 Pro Forma*
Assets		
Cash	11	
Accounts receivable	70	
Inventories	60	
Total current assets	141	
Property, plant, and equipment	540	
Total assets	681	
Liabilities and Equity		
Accounts payable	51	
Notes payable	89	
Total current liabilities	140	
Equity	541	
Total liabilities and equity	681	

Net Working Capital	*1984*	*1985*
Current assets	141	
Current liabilities	140	
Net working capital	1	

Capital Budgeting

In the last chapter, we discussed some simple methods of forecasting future financing needs. Most of these techniques used the history of the business to create forecasts for the future. While most of these techniques are useful for examining the financial effects of corporate strategy and policy, they assume that a specific strategy has been decided on and will be undertaken. What we did not discuss is how managers choose among different investments and strategies. In this chapter, we will examine the process by which managers choose among different courses of action. This process of making investment decisions is called *capital budgeting*.

There are two kinds of corporate investments. Chapter 3 discussed the increases and decreases in current assets that can occur in businesses whose sales are seasonal or cyclical. Most of these changes could be called *spontaneous* since they do not occur as a consequence of managers' actions but are instead the normal results of changing sales levels. For instance, during a cyclical upturn, a manufacturing firm whose sales are made on credit would need funds for both increased inventories and larger accounts receivable. Both of these increases are investments—that is, they are outlays of funds on which management expects a return. The return, of course, comes from the profit on the expected sales increase.

Spontaneous investments often have short-term benefits and are usually categorized as changes in working capital rather than as investments. Typically, an investment is thought of as having potential benefits extending over a longer period of time, usually more than one year. Investments characterized by these longer-term benefits are called *capital investments*. They include such things as permanent additions to working capital (such as an increase in accounts receivable due to a change in the company's credit policy); purchase of land, buildings, or equipment to expand capacity; and the costs associated with advertising campaigns or research and development programs. Since capital investments are often irreversible, or the redeployment of assets comes only at considerable loss of time, money, and managerial effort, capital investments should be and are evaluated more formally than are spontaneous investments.

In most firms, the capital-budgeting process consists of six steps:

1. Generating and gathering investment ideas.
2. Analyzing the cost-benefit of proposed investments.
   a. Forecasting the costs and benefits for each investment.
   b. Evaluating the costs and benefits.
3. Ranking the relative attractiveness of each proposed investment and choosing among investment alternatives.
4. Implementing the investments chosen.
5. Evaluating the implemented investments.

Of course firms continuously repeat these five steps. In this chapter, we will concentrate on steps 2 and 3, the steps in which financial analysts are most involved: estimating and evaluating the costs and benefits and choosing among the alternative investments.

I. COST-BENEFIT ANALYSIS OF PROPOSED INVESTMENTS

The goal of investing is to create value for the owners of the firm. If an investment is to create value for the firm, the expected returns from the investment must exceed its costs. In economic terms, we say that the marginal or incremental benefits—the benefits deriving solely from the investment—must exceed the marginal or incremental costs. There are several hidden difficulties with this first step. First, when we say incremental we must ask, incremental to what? The second difficulty is how to measure costs and benefits.

In estimating the value of an investment, we are measuring the costs and benefits that would not have occurred if the firm had not undertaken this particular project. In some instances, the project may be charged with a portion of the ongoing expenses of the firm—the overhead. This is an accounting allocation of costs, and if this investment neither increases nor decreases these expenses, they are neither costs nor benefits for the purposes of the investment analysis. Only incremental, new expenses or benefits are relevant. To estimate the investment's benefits and costs, the analyst forecasts the cash associated with the investment at the time that it will be received or disbursed. The analyst does not measure income and expenses as they are recorded by the firm's accountants.

The benefits and costs of an investment are measured by the receipt and disbursement of cash. Most U.S. corporations use the accrual method of accounting: sales are recorded when an order is received and obligations recorded when incurred. Accrual accounting can trick the investment analyst. For instance, many firms record sales before the payment is received. In some industries, the payment for purchased products typically lags behind the shipment of the order by several months. Thus the real benefit the firm derives, the cash, also lags by several months. It is the receipt or disbursement of cash that affects the firm, and cash is what concerns the investment analyst.

1. Cash Benefits

Four sources of cash benefits or receipts may be derived from an investment:

1. Cost reductions when a more efficient process is substituted for a more costly one.
2. Profits or revenues from increased sales.
3. Cash received when replaced equipment is sold.
4. Cash received from the salvage value of the new plant or equipment at the end of its useful life.

Let's illustrate these benefits by analyzing a shipping company's investment in a sail-assisted tanker. The shipping firm's managers are considering replacing one of their diesel-fueled, oceangoing tankers with a tanker that has auxiliary metal sails to take advantage of the wind. The firm might benefit from this investment in several ways. First, the wind-assisted ship will use less fuel and thus be less expensive to operate than the diesel-powered vessel. This cost reduction will lower the operating costs for every year that the ship is in operation. Furthermore, if the new ship is faster or has a larger cargo space, the tonnage carried by the ship should exceed that carried by the old tanker. This increase in tonnage will yield increased yearly revenues. In addition to the benefits from reduced operating expenses and increased sales, the firm may also sell the old diesel-powered ship for cash and gain favorable tax treatment as a result of the sale. Finally, at the end of its useful life, the salvage value of the sail-assisted ship itself and any favorable tax effects would also be benefits.

This single example shows that most investments offer a variety of benefits at various times throughout their useful lives. The analyst's responsibility is to identify the magnitude and timing of all benefits.

2. Cash Payments

The cash payments or costs associated with any investment fall into three categories:

1. The initial cost (capital cost) of the investment.
2. Capital improvements made during the life of the project.
3. Operating costs.

Capital costs include the initial price of making an investment as well as any subsequent major outlays of cash required to extend the life of the project or equipment. In the example of the shipping company, the capital costs would include the cost of obtaining the new ship and the costs of subsequent major engine replacements or other major repairs needed to extend the life of the vessel. Operating costs are those recurring annual cash outlays that are required once the investment becomes a part of the firm's operations. With the purchase of the tanker, cash would be needed to cover such annual operating costs as wages, fuel, taxes, and maintenance.

Any cash already expended on the investment, such as research done to develop the sails, would not be a relevant cost in this investment analysis. Instead, this type of expense is considered a *sunk cost:* it represents a past outlay of funds that has no bearing on this decision. The manager's concern is not to recover sunk or irreversible costs but to create value from subsequent investments. In other words, any investment being considered must have a positive marginal return.

Tax benefits and costs also will be incurred by the company as a result of making an investment. Unfortunately the exact effect tax laws will have over the life of a given project may not be known at the time an investment is made. If current tax laws were to continue in effect during the life of the project, the impact of taxes on the costs and benefits could be determined. However, over the last decade in the United States, we have had two major changes in the tax code, and another has been proposed and is currently being debated. Since 1981, the Accelerated Cost Recovery System (ACRS) has been in use, and this is the one that we will use in evaluating the projects described in this book. In brief, ACRS affects the way an investment is depreciated and the amounts, if applicable, of the investment tax credit that can be taken at the time the investment is made. Exhibit 4–1 provides the depreciation or cost recovery schedules appropriate for the four categories of non-real estate property. Since the tax code and its effect on the project's costs and benefits are sources of uncertainty, the impact of changes in the code should be assessed. Later in the chapter, we will describe several methods for incorporating uncertainty into the analysis.

To identify and estimate the size of the costs and benefits associated with any investment, the analyst will call on experts in marketing, engineering, accounting, and operations to provide the needed forecasts.

II. EVALUATING INCREMENTAL COSTS AND BENEFITS

Once the costs and benefits have been itemized, the analyst's major task is to determine the marginal or incremental effect that the investment will have on the firm as a whole. An incremental cost or benefit is one derived exclusively from the investment and one that would not otherwise occur. To evaluate incremental costs and benefits, many analysts group investment proposals into categories that help them examine each proposal in terms of its relation to the firm's business as a whole.

The most useful scheme is to group projects according to the degree of independence of their costs and benefits from the costs and benefits of the

EXHIBIT 4–1 ACRS Cost Recovery Percentages (for nonreal estate property placed in service after December 31, 1980)

	*Class of Investment**			
Ownership Year	*3-Year*	*5-Year*	*10-Year*	*15-Year Utility Property*
1	25%	15%	8%	5%
2	38	22	14	10
3	37	21	12	9
4		21	10	8
5		21	10	7
6			10	7
7			9	6
8			9	6
9			9	6
10			9	6
11				6
12				6
13				6
14				6
15				
	100%	100%	100%	100%

**ACRS Classification*	*Asset Description*
3-Year Property	Autos, trucks, research and development equipment, and special tools.
5-Year Property	Most machinery and equipment.
10-Year Property	Most real estate, coal conversion boilers, and railroad tankcars.

firm and its other investments and projects: (1) *Independent investments* are projects that could be accepted or rejected, regardless of the action taken on any other investment, now or later. (2) *Mutually exclusive investments* are projects that preclude one another; once one project is accepted, the others become unavailable or inappropriate. Often mutually exclusive projects are designed to solve the same problem or to serve the same function. For example, managers often must choose among alternate means of adding plant capacity, or among advertising programs, or among several new product lines.

There are two types of mutually exclusive and independent investments—replacements and investments in new products and processes. Replacement investments are made to modernize an existing process or to revitalize an old product line. Because estimating the net effect on the company of replacing a process or product can be especially difficult, analysts often place these investments in a separate category. They are, however, just an especially troublesome type of mutually exclusive or independent investment.

To show the advantage of these categories, we will use them to estimate the incremental costs and benefits of two investment proposals being considered by the management of Consumer, Inc., one of the largest franchisers of fast foods in the West. Consumer, Inc., sold a variety of hamburgers, soft drinks, and french fries through its 500 restaurants. Consumer management was considering two investments—opening their restaurants for breakfast or adding salad bars to their existing lunch and dinner menus. Because of the management effort needed to implement either project, management considered these investments as mutually exclusive—they would choose one or the other but not both projects.

1. The Breakfast Proposal

The Consumer, Inc., restaurants were open from 11 A.M. to 11 P.M. Since many of Consumer's competitors had begun to serve breakfast, Consumer's managers were considering opening from 6:30 to 11:00 A.M. to serve breakfast. While the same buildings and equipment could be used, the longer serving hours would increase overhead expenses. There would be added costs for ingredients, salaries of managers and employees, and advertising. Together, incremental overhead and operating expenses for all 500 restaurants were expected to total $14.25 million per year. In addition, since breakfast was a new product, management planned an extensive employee-training program. The program, to be completed before the company started offering breakfast, would cost $1.75 million. Consumer, Inc., would benefit from an estimated $15 million increase in sales per year to be made from the breakfast service. The estimated costs and benefits of this project are detailed in Exhibit 4–2. Since management expected no inflation the costs and benefits are in real dollars. The costs and benefits were forecast for six years because management believed that the equipment used in the operation had a useful life of six years. The format used in this exhibit is very useful and often employed by financial analysts.

2. Salad Bar Proposal

Managers at Consumer, Inc., were also considering adding salad bars, all-you-can-eat salad buffets, to their existing lunch and dinner menus. They had already spent $600,000 in developing the salad bar concept and in limited test marketing. To introduce the product into all of their restaurants, they estimated that during the first year personnel would have to be trained at a cost of $832 per restaurant and that display cases would have to be bought and installed at $2,800 per salad bar. The managers expected that the display cases would be scrapped in six years and that the scrap would have a total value of $50,000. Incremental (marginal) operating expenses would include the cost of ingredients, additional refrigeration, and the salary of one additional employee per restaurant to stock the salad bar. On the basis of test-market results, the marketing staff estimated sales of salad would be $15 million per year.

The diverse effects that these two proposals would have on Consumer, Inc., illustrate the usefulness of categorizing investments as independent or mutually exclusive. Managers considered the two proposed investments to be

EXHIBIT 4–2 Consumer Breakfast Proposal—Marginal Costs and Benefits (thousands of real dollars)

	Period						
	0	*1*	*2*	*3*	*4*	*5*	*6*
Capital investment	$ 0						
Investment tax credit	0						
Salvage value							$ 0
Training costs*	(1,750)						
Incremental sales		$ 15,000	$ 15,000	$ 15,000	$ 15,000	$ 15,000	15,000
Operating expenses		(14,250)	(14,250)	(14,250)	(14,250)	(14,250)	(14,250)
Depreciation		0	0	0	0	0	0
Pre-tax profit	(1,750)	750	750	750	750	750	750
Taxes (40%)	700	(300)	(300)	(300)	(300)	(300)	(300)
Profit after tax	(1,050)	450	450	450	450	450	450
Noncash charges†	0	0	0	0	0	0	0
Net cash flow	$(1,050)	$ 450	$ 450	$ 450	$ 450	$ 450	$ 450

*Using the current tax code, the training expenses (as well as installation and transportation costs for new equipment) could be expensed or capitalized and depreciated. In this case, we have expensed them in the first year. Thus there is a reduction in the taxes for Consumer, Inc., in year 0 as a result of this investment.

†Ordinarily, noncash charges (e.g., depreciation and net new investment) would be added back to the profit after tax to determine the cash flow associated with the project. Since training costs were expensed, there are no depreciable capital costs in this project.

mutually exclusive as they did not feel that they could adequately oversee both projects at the same time. The breakfast option would be independent of Consumer's existing businesses since it would extend the existing product line. The salad bar, however, would be a partial replacement since it would affect existing sales of hamburger meals at lunch and dinner. In fact, the marketing staff estimated that half of the salad bar's sales would come from customers who would otherwise have purchased hamburgers and french fries. Thus, while total salad sales would be $15 million, incremental sales would be only $7.5 million per year.

The salad bar's status as a partial replacement was responsible not only for the lower net cash receipts but also for lower incremental overhead and operating expenses. Unlike the breakfast option, the salad bar would add less to the current overhead and operating expenses since it would be served during existing hours and manned by existing employees. If the analyst did not realize that the salad bar would be a replacement investment, he or she might erroneously include a portion of the costs of buildings and equipment as part of the salad bar's incremental costs or use the total salad bar sales of $15 million rather than the $7.5 million incremental sales as a benefit. The net cash flow for the salad bars is the net profit plus any noncash charges that were deducted from profit before taxes for the purpose of calculating taxes.

The details of this evaluation of the net benefits of the salad bar appear in Exhibit 4–3. Note, the $600,000 in expenses that were incurred in developing and test marketing the salad bar concept are not included. They are sunk costs, cash already spent and not relevant in making this new decision.

Now that the incremental costs and benefits for the two projects have been estimated, Consumer's management must decide whether to accept one or the other of the plans or to reject both projects and seek other opportunities. To make these decisions, the managers need a method to measure the relative value of the two proposals.

III. CHOOSING AMONG INVESTMENTS

There are a number of different ways to rank the relative attractiveness or value of investments. Each method has advantages and disadvantages.

1. Simple Valuation Methods

Benefit/cost ratio. The easiest way to compare two investments is to compare their benefit/cost ratios. If the benefits of an investment exceed the costs—if the benefit/cost ratio is greater than 1.0—the project would be deemed acceptable using this measure. To choose among several acceptable investments, managers would select the project with the highest benefit/cost

EXHIBIT 4-3 Consumer Salad Bar Proposal—Incremental Costs and Benefits (thousands of real dollars)

	Period						
	0	*1*	*2*	*3*	*4*	*5*	*6*
Equipment*	$(1,400)						
Investment tax credit†	112						
Salvage value							$ 50
Training costs ‡	(416)						
Incremental sales		$ 7,500	$ 7,500	$ 7,500	$ 7,500	$ 7,500	7,500
Operating expenses		(6,972)	(6,972)	(6,972)	(6,972)	(6,972)	(6,972)
Depreciation‡		(210)	(308)	(294)	(294)	(294)	0
Pre-tax profit	(416)	318	220	234	234	234	578
Taxes (40%)	166	(127)	(88)	(94)	(94)	(94)	(231)
Profit after tax	(250)	191	132	140	140	140	347
Noncash charges (depreciation or net new investment)	(1,288)	210	308	294	294	294	(0)
Net cash flow	$(1,538)	$ 401	$ 440	$ 434	$ 434	$ 434	$ 347

*Note, the $600,000 spent in test marketing and development of the concept is not included in the analysis since it constitutes a sunk cost.

†Investment tax credit is a direct reduction to taxes. The credit is 8% of the initial cost of the equipment. Under ACRS tax rules, a maximum of 10% may be taken; however, 2% of the credit must either act as a reduction of the depreciable investment, or the credit must be reduced to 8%. In this example, we have reduced the credit to 8%.

‡Depreciation is taken on the investment of $1,400. Training costs are expensed in the year they are incurred (ACRS allows the company to capitalize and depreciate such expenses if desired).

ratio. For the proposed investment in breakfast service, the benefit/cost ratio would be calculated as follows:

$$\text{Benefit/cost ratio} = \frac{\text{Net benefits}}{\text{Investment}}$$

$$= \frac{\$(450 \times 6)}{\$1{,}050}$$

$$= \$2{,}700/\$1{,}050$$

$$= 2.57$$

A comparable analysis of the salad bar proposal yields a ratio of 1.62 ($2,490/$1,538).

Payback. A similar measure, and one that is more widely used, is called *payback*. Quite simply, payback measures the number of years before the annual net benefits of the project equal its initial cost. For the breakfast proposal, the payback would be calculated as follows:

$$\text{Payback} = \frac{\text{Investment}}{\text{Yearly net benefit}}$$

$$= \$1{,}050/\$450$$

$$= 2.3 \text{ years}$$

A similar analysis of the salad bar proposal yields a payback of 3.6 years.

Whether a payback of just over two years is adequate or not is a decision for Consumer's managers. Ordinarily, the managers would set a limit on the length of the payback period they would allow and reject those investments that exceed it. To choose among several projects with acceptable payback periods, managers would select the project with the lowest payback.

Payback can be useful as a quick approximation of a project's relative attractiveness or to indicate whether a firm can recover the project costs in time to make another planned investment. The method ignores, however, all benefits that are derived after the payback date; thus, it can arbitrarily exclude potentially attractive investments that have longer lives.

This points out an obvious problem with both the benefit/cost ratio and the payback methods of analysis. Neither method takes the timing of the cash flows into account. The benefit/cost ratio treats cash received at all points in time as equivalent. We know, however, that investors prefer equivalent amounts of cash received sooner to those received later. The payback method, on the other hand, attempts to incorporate the investors' preference for the timing of cash flows into account by ignoring cash flows beyond the payback period. But we know that cash flows across time are neither equally attractive to the investor nor are later cash flows irrelevant. The benefit/cost ratio and the payback method evaluate investments solely on the size of their returns, and thus neither adequately incorporates the investor's time value of money.

2. Dealing with the Timing of Cash Flow: Discounting Techniques

Investors want to be rewarded for waiting for future returns. They need a method of evaluating investments that will take into account their time value of money and will compensate them for temporary lack of liquidity by giving priority to investments that offer earlier rather than later returns. To give priority to earlier returns, we can use a method called *discounting*. If one applies a discount factor (R) of 5% to cash flows five years hence, a single dollar at that time would be worth 78% of the value of a dollar today. In formula form we can calculate the discount factor thus:

$$\begin{aligned} \text{Discount factor} &= (1 + R)^n \\ &= (1 + .05)^5 \\ &= 1.28 \end{aligned}$$

The discounted value, called the *present value,* of the $1.00 cash flow (CF) would be

$$\begin{aligned} \text{Present value} &= \frac{CF_n}{(1 + R)^n} \\ &= \frac{\$1.00}{1.28} \\ &= \$0.78 \end{aligned}$$

For $5.00 the present value would be $3.91, which is 78% of $5.00 (3.91/5.00 = .78).

Compounding is simply the reverse of the discounting process. For instance, if you put $3.91 in a savings account today at a 5% annual compound rate of return, in five years you would have $5.00. This *future value* would be calculated as follows:

$$\begin{aligned} \text{Future value} &= (1 + R)^n \times (CF) \\ &= (1 + .05)^5 \times (\$3.91) \\ &= 1.28 \times \$3.91 \\ &= \$5.00 \end{aligned}$$

Fortunately one does not have to go through the laborious process of calculating present value factors. Lists of present value factors are available in most finance textbooks. They are not included here because all but the simplest modern calculators perform compounding and discounting functions quite painlessly, rendering the direct use of discount factors an unnecessary step.

Present value payback. The most simplistic use of this discounting approach is the present value payback. To calculate a present value payback,

EXHIBIT 4–4 Breakfast Proposal—Present Value Payback

Year	*Cash Flow*	*Present Value Cash Flow*	*Remaining Investment*
0	$(1,050)	$\frac{(\$1,050)}{(1.05)^0}$ = ($1,050.00)	($1,050.00)
1	450	$\frac{450}{(1.05)^1}$ = 428.57	(621.43)
2	450	$\frac{450}{(1.05)^2}$ = 408.16	(213.27)
3	450	$\frac{450}{(1.05)^3}$ = 388.73	175.46

*The total present value payback would be 2.55 years. The .55 is calculated thus:

$$\frac{\$213.27}{\$388.73} = .55 \text{ years}$$

one first discounts each net cash flow to its equivalent present value. These discounted present values are summed until the total equals the amount of the original investment. Exhibit 4–4 provides the data needed to calculate the discounted payback for the breakfast project. Using 5% as the equivalent time value of money, the discounted payback value of the breakfast is 2.6 years. The salad bar option's discounted payback is 4.1 years.

While including the time value of money, the discounted payback still ignores the cash flows beyond the payback period. This is a particularly critical fault when projects with large future returns such as new products are being considered. It is neither necessary nor appropriate to arbitrarily discriminate against projects with longer-term returns.

The *net present value* and the *internal rate of return* are two frequently used discounting techniques that take all cash flows into consideration. Either method provides a better measure of value than do the more simplistic ranking methods. We will describe and point out the advantages and disadvantages of each method.

Net present value. The net present value—that is, the value as a lump sum today—is the present value of all the future benefits less the present value of all current and future costs. The net present value could also be described as the present value of the net worth that an investment will contribute to a firm by the end of its useful life. Net present value (NPV) is calculated by means of a discount rate. The discount rate is used to adjust each year's returns according to that year's distance from the date of the initial investment. Net present value is calculated as follows.

$$NPV = \frac{NCF_1}{(1 + R)^1} + \frac{NCF_2}{(1 + R)^2} \cdots\cdots + \frac{NCF_n}{(1 + R)^n} - I$$

where

NCF = The net cash flow *per year* (cash flow benefits minus cash flow costs)
R = Discount rate
1,2,....,N = Years from the date of original investment
I = Amount of initial investment

For Consumer, Inc., using 5% as a discount rate, the net present value of the salad bar would be calculated as follows:

$$\text{NPV} = \frac{\$450{,}000}{(1 + .05)^1} + \frac{\$450{,}000}{(1 + .05)^2} + \frac{\$450{,}000}{(1 + .05)^3} + \frac{\$450{,}000}{(1 + .05)^4} + \frac{\$450{,}000}{(1 + .05)^5} + \frac{\$450{,}000}{(1 + .05)^6} - \$1{,}050{,}000$$

$$= \$1{,}234{,}061$$

The net present value of $1,234,061 is the present value of the net worth that the breakfast project will contribute to Consumer by the end of the investment's six-year life. The NPV of the salad bar project is $573,943 at a 5% discount rate. The process is quite simple when a calculator with a net present value function is used.

The NPV approach offers a logical method of evaluating investments. It takes into account the timing of cash flows by placing a higher value on those received immediately and a lower value on those to be received in the future. Once the timing of the cash flows has been taken into account, acceptable investments are those with a NPV equal to or greater than zero.

Present value index. Some managers prefer to use the profitability or present value index (PVI) rather than the net present value. The PVI is simply an adaptation of the benefit/cost ratio:

$$\text{Present value index} = \frac{\text{Present value of net benefits}}{\text{Cost}}$$

The process of calculating the present value index is simple and straightforward. Using the breakfast option as an example, and a 5% discount rate,

$$\text{Present value index} = \left[\frac{\$450{,}000}{(1 + .05)^1} + \frac{\$450{,}000}{(1 + .05)^2} + \frac{\$450{,}000}{(1 + .05)^3} + \frac{\$450{,}000}{(1 + .05)^4} + \frac{\$450{,}000}{(1 + .05)^5} + \frac{\$450{,}000}{(1 + .05)^6}\right] \Big/ \$1{,}050{,}000$$

$$= 2.18$$

This means that for each dollar of investment, the breakfast proposal returns a present value of $2.18 of benefits. The present value ratio for the salad bar project is 1.37. As is the case with any method utilizing a discount rate, the magnitude of the present value index will change if the discount rate is changed.

Internal rate of return. A second discounted cash flow technique is the internal rate of return (IRR). This method is used to measure the average rate of return that will be earned over the life of the project. To calculate the IRR, the same formula as that for calculating net present value is used except we set the net present value equal to zero and we solve for R.

Solving for R is somewhat more difficult than solving for the NPV. To do so we must use a trial-and-error method. We start by choosing an arbi-

EXHIBIT 4–5 Salad Bar and Breakfast Projects (net present value profile)

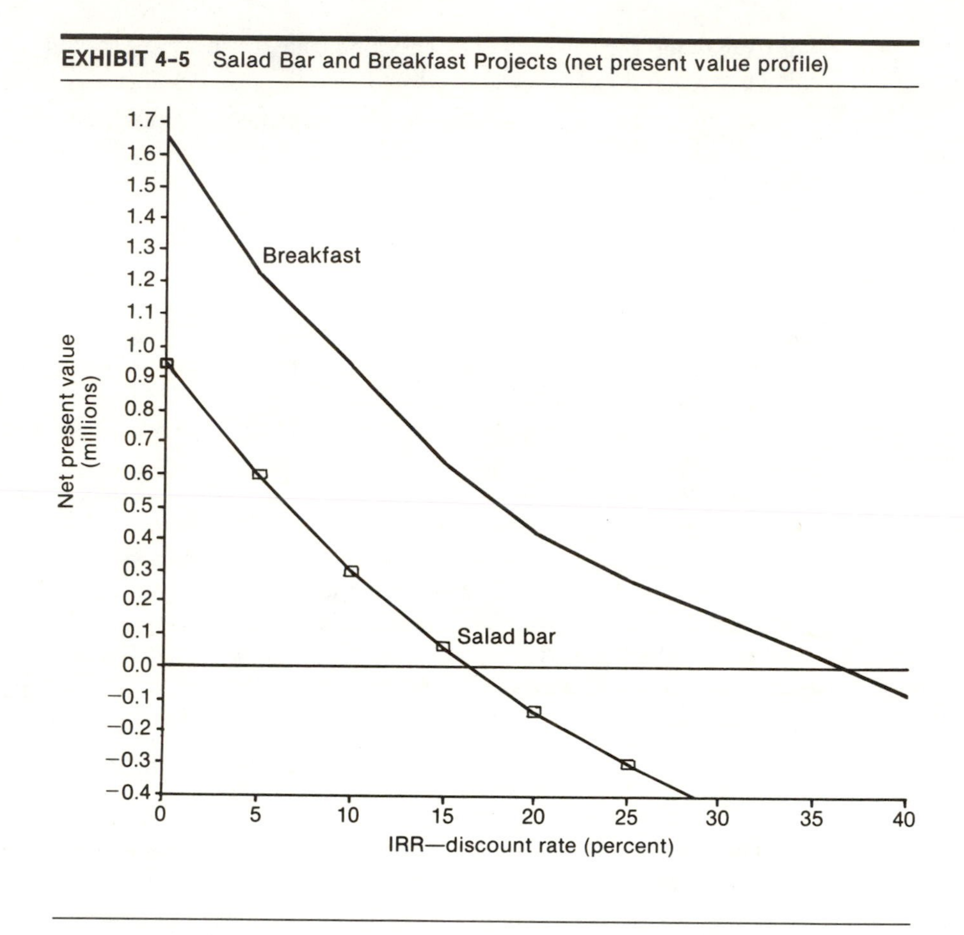

trary discount rate (say 5%), calculate the NPV, and see if the NPV is zero. If the NPV is positive, a higher discount rate is next selected, and the NPV recalculated. We continue to choose discount rates until we find the discount rate that yields an NPV of 0. With the Consumer, Inc., breakfast project, the IRR is obviously larger than 5% since at 5% the NPV is equal to $1,234,061. Exhibit 4–5 provides a graph of the results of the trial-and-error approach. Rates above 5% were chosen until the IRR of 36.1% was found. The graph is also called a *net-present-value profile* since it depicts the project's net present value at various discount rates. Note that at a discount rate of zero, the net present value is the simple sum of the undiscounted cash flows. For the salad bar project, the IRR is 16.0% and at all discount rates, it provides a lower NPV than does the breakfast project. An acceptable IRR for a risk-free project would be a return that compensated the investor for his or her time value of money. Here we have used 5%.

While the IRR method is purported to be equivalent to the net present value method, it poses special problems for the user. If the investments are of quite different sizes, if the timing of the cash flows is different for each project under consideration, or if negative and positive net cash flows alternate over the life of the project, the internal rate of return can give results that are misleading or difficult to interpret. For instance, in evaluating our sail-assisted tanker project, we noted there would be significant investments at several points over the useful life of the tanker. First, the tanker would be purchased, and later, extensive engine overhauls would be needed. Thus, the net cash flows would be negative in the first year and at several points in the future. During the intervening years, the cash flows would be positive. As a result of alternating positive and negative net cash flows, several different discount rates allow the NPV to equal zero. In other words, the project would have several IRRs. Most simple computer models and calculators are designed to solve for one IRR. Thus, the analyst with one IRR may erroneously believe he or she has the complete information necessary to analyze the project. For these and other reasons, the net present value technique is the preferred approach.

We have summarized in Exhibit 4–6 the result of using the four ranking methods for Consumer's two projects. The benefit/cost ratio and payback take the size of the cash flows, but not their timing, into account. The net present value and internal rate of return take into account both the size and timing of cash flows. Fortunately for Consumer, Inc., all of our methods indicate that the breakfast option is the most attractive.

3. Ranking Projects

So far we have assumed that if an investment creates value it should be accepted. In doing so, we assume the firm has enough capital to invest in all attractive projects. If that were not true, investments would be ranked by their relative value, and the firm would continue to invest in those with the greatest values until its investment resources were exhausted. In most circumstances, that means investing first in those investments with the highest relative values.

For the manager with more projects than cash, the projects must be ranked from highest to lowest in value. Our preference is the use of the net present value method or the profitability index to rank projects. These approaches provide a ranking consistent with the assumption that managers are attempting to maximize the value of the firm. But what about risk? Since rational investors require larger returns to compensate them for uncertain cash flows, relative value also depends on the risk being taken when making an investment.

4. Dealing with Risk

What do we mean by risk? By risk we mean that our cash flow forecasts might be wrong. Over- or underestimated cash flows result in lower or higher than expected returns. Investors, in addition to preferring larger, rapid re-

EXHIBIT 4–6 Breakfast versus Salad Bar Option

	Benefit Cost Ratio	*Payback*	*Present Value Payback*	*Net Present Value (in thousands)*		*Present Value Index*	*Internal Rate of Return*
				At Discount Rate of 10%	*At Discount Rate of 5%*	*At Discount Rate of 5%*	
Breakfast	2.57	2.3 years	2.6	$910	$1,234	2.18	36.1%
Salad bar	1.62	3.6 years	4.1	$278	$574	1.37	16.0%
Decision rule	B/C ≥ 1.0	Payback ≥ Management minimum	PV payback ≥ Management minimum	NPV ≥ 0		PVI ≥ 1.0	IRR ≥ Hurdle rate

turns, also prefer certain returns—they do not like to take a risk. To induce the typical risk-averse investor to invest in risky projects, larger returns must be anticipated. The higher the risk, the larger the return premium required.

Of all the problems facing the investment analyst, risk is the most troublesome. To date we have not found the ideal method for incorporating risk into the measurement of an investment's value. However, there are several methods currently being used by managers. None of these methods is flawless—all are tentative attempts at dealing with a very complex problem.

In most analyses, we assume that the risk of the project is the same as the risk of the firm. That is, the cash flows for the project are as predictable (or unpredictable) as the cash flows from the firm's current business. Once that assumption is made, we can use, as a discount rate, the firm's average cost of capital.

We can use this as a discount rate because the cost of capital is the marginal return required by the firm's providers of capital (creditors and stockholders). These investors require a return for the time value of their investment and for the risk they are taking by allowing the firm the use of their money. Instead of directly estimating the return required for the risk being taken by the firm, we often use the firm's marginal cost of capital as an indication of the fair return as determined by the capital markets. In Chapter 5, we will discuss how this cost is calculated. Meanwhile, we can use the firm's cost of capital as a discount rate if all the firm's investments are of equal risk to that of the firm.

As the hurdle rate increases—that is, as investors require greater returns as compensation for greater risks—the net present value of an investment diminishes dramatically. Exhibit 4–5 illustrates this decline. When the discount rate is 5%, the breakfast and salad bar options provide net present values of $1,234,060 and $573,940, respectively. If a hurdle rate of 10% is substituted for the discount rate, the net present values diminish to $909,867 and $278,032 as shown in Exhibit 4–6.

Even discounting the cash flows at a higher rate, the breakfast project still offers the greatest value to Consumer's shareholders. But these calculations again assume that the risks of the projects are equivalent. To the contrary, opening for breakfast is more risky than adding salad bars. New employees must be hired, a new advertising campaign must be undertaken, new food items will be offered, and a large unrecoverable investment in training is required. Consumer, Inc., management could be wrong in their forecasts of the potential sales and costs of the breakfast option. Salad bars, on the other hand, add little to the risk of the firm. The initial investment is small and a portion of it is recoverable, training costs are low, and few additional employees must be hired. The two projects have different levels of risk. How can these differences in risk be included in the comparison?

So far, neither academics nor businessmen have answered that question very well, although several techniques are currently being used. One approach is to present the problem of risk directly to the managers. Using the cost of capital as a discount rate, managers can determine for themselves whether the net present value compensates for the risk of the project. For instance, the net present value of the breakfast option at a discount rate of 10% is greater by $631,835 than that of the salad bars. Is this amount adequate, in the managers' view, to compensate for the differences in risk between the two investments? It is up to them to decide.

This approach, however, is often too ad hoc for managers who prefer a more structured approach. Another method is to modify the hurdle rate according to the apparent risk of the investment. For example, new products may be considered to have greater risks than the risk of the firm as a whole. Consequently, management would set a higher hurdle rate for new products than the firm's marginal cost of capital. A scheme such as the one shown in Exhibit 4–7 is used by many firms to categorize investments.

Managers who use this scheme believe that investments in cost reductions are less risky than their average and that new products are more risky. Using this scheme, Consumer's management might discount the salad bar's cash flows at the cost of capital, 10%. But since breakfast is a new product, it may be considered riskier, and its cash flows may be discounted at a higher rate.

While this scheme is often used, it leads to predictable results—new products are less attractive, whereas cost-reduction projects are usually acceptable. These conclusions may or may not be appropriate for the specific firm or investment. Furthermore, it is difficult to determine the appropriate changes to make to the hurdle rate.

Managers with a number of divisions or lines of business have attempted to adapt their corporate hurdle rate for the specific risks of the division or product line. Since the cost of capital for a division is not available, a number of methods are used to estimate the appropriate discount rate. Most often the rate is calculated by using the average of the costs of capital for a number of publicly traded proxy firms—firms with similar characteristics. These proxy methods are imprecise but hold more promise than using a single rate for businesses with very different risks in their various projects.

In addition to varying the discount rate for risk, some suggest that manipulating the cash flows is more appropriate. The most simplistic method of revising the cash flows for risk is conservative forecasting. Conservative forecasting typically involves overestimating the costs and underestimating the revenues. Rather than being conservative, it is wrong. Such cash flows permit an inaccurate picture of the real potential (upside and down) of the project. While such conservatism is broadly practiced, the good analyst will seek the most accurate forecasts and analyze risk using a different method.

Another method of adjusting cash flows is used and can be useful. The investor, or the manager on the investor's behalf, examines the forecasted net cash flow for each year of the project's life. The manager then determines the certainty equivalent for each of those cash flows and discounts them at the time value of money. A certainty equivalent is an estimate of an absolutely

EXHIBIT 4–7 Risk Categories

Investment Category	*Risk Level*	*Hurdle Rate*
Cost reduction	Less than firm's average risk	Lower than the firm's marginal average cost of capital
Plant expansion	Average risk	Marginal average cost of capital
New products	Higher than average risk	Higher rate than the marginal average cost of capital

risk-free amount that the investor would take for the uncertain cash flow that is actually forecast. For instance, in the breakfast project, management forecast a cash flow of $450,000 in the first year. However, they are very uncertain about the success of the project. Sales or costs could exceed or be considerably below expectations. The actual net cash flow might be as low as $80,000 and as high as $936,000. Instead of masking the risk, management would assess the certainty equivalent. In this case, it might be $450,000—the certain amount that would induce management on behalf of the shareholders to give up the chance of higher returns and avoid lower ones as well. The certainty equivalent—the risk-free sum—is then discounted at the risk-free rate, the time value of money.

The certainty equivalent includes the risk preference of the individual manager determining the sum. Thus, while theoretically appealing, the problems with certainty equivalents are obvious—who will make the judgment on the shareholders' behalf?

Finally, there are two methods for incorporating risk directly into investment valuation. Both are based on the analyst forecasting several probable outcomes (costs and benefits), multiple scenarios, for an investment. The analyst then incorporates this information into the investment analysis.

In the simple use of multiple-scenario analysis, an analyst forecasts just three alternative outcomes—optimistic, pessimistic, and most likely—for each of the project's costs and benefits. The result of this analysis is three forecasts and three sets of measures of value for each investment. For instance, management of Consumer, Inc., might decide that the breakfast proposal has a possibility of much greater success as well as real potential for failure. Its success or failure will depend on whether the customer will perceive a fast-food restaurant as a place for breakfast. The forecasts that Consumer management made for the breakfast project shown in Exhibit 4–2 were their most likely estimates—but management was quite uncertain about what would occur if they opened their restaurants for breakfast. If the sales from their new breakfast menu exceed their most likely estimate of $15 million, they expect operating costs will be slightly lower since some costs, for instance maintenance, will not increase with sales. Likewise, if sales are lower than expected, the operating costs will not decrease as fast as sales, and the net profit will be lower. Exhibit 4–8 provides the annual cash flows for opti-

EXHIBIT 4-8 Consumer Breakfast Proposal—Annual Cash Flow (in thousands of real dollars)

	Pessimistic	*Most Likely*	*Optimistic*
Incremental sales	$ 3,300	$ 15,000	$ 26,000
Operating expenses*	(3,170)	(14,250)	(24,440)
Depreciation	0	0	0
Pre-tax profit	130	750	1,560
Taxes (40%)	(52)	(300)	(624)
Profit after tax	78	450	936
Noncash charges	0	0	0
Net cash flow	$ 78	$ 450	$ 936
Net present value (5%)	$ (654)	$ 1,234	$ 3,701

*Operating expenses are projected by management to decline as sales increase—to be 96,95, and 94% of sales, respectively.

mistic, most likely, and pessimistic scenarios for the breakfast proposal. The net present value for each scenario is listed at the bottom of the exhibit. The investment cost of $1.75 million before taxes would remain the same regardless of the success of the project. Quite obviously, if the breakfast project is not successful, the value to Consumer is negative—costs exceed the benefits. Using a higher discount rate would make the net present value even lower. However, if customers find the new breakfast menu appealing, the project could be quite a boon to Consumer and their shareholders—the net present value would be very attractive. To decide whether to proceed with the breakfast proposal, management must decide on the likelihood of the pessimistic scenario occurring and whether the most likely and optimistic scenarios could create enough value to offset this danger.

Most managers who use this three-scenario analysis implicitly presume that each scenario is equally likely, and they use the information contained in the analysis to decide whether the company could afford the project if the pessimistic scenario were the one that occurred. Note that in making these forecasts, the analyst must take care that all three sets of forecasts are probable, not just possible. If the analyst were to take the worst (or best) outcome possible for every cost and benefit, the outcome would be a forecast that is possible, but not very probable. Possible but not probable forecasts give managers very little information on which to base decisions.

Managers do not need to believe that each of the scenarios is equally likely to happen. Using the breakfast proposal as an example, the management of Consumer might think it most likely that, based on the experience of other fast-food restaurants in introducing a breakfast menu, the breakfast proposal will have sales of $15 million as predicted in Exhibit 4-2. While the $15 million is a good estimate of the expected sales, there is a reasonable chance that the innovative menu Consumer management is planning will be very successful. The analyst could estimate the likelihood, or probability that each of the

EXHIBIT 4-9 Probabilistic Analysis—Breakfast Proposal (in thousands of real dollars)

Probability	*Net Present Value*	*Weighted Value*
15%	$ (654)	$ (98.1)
20	850	170.0
30	1,234	370.2
20	1,620	324.0
15	3,993	598.9
Expected value (weighted average)		$1,365.0

three scenarios shown in Exhibit 4–8 will occur. In fact, the analyst could estimate the probabilities of more than three likely outcomes occurring. Instead of only three scenarios, the analyst might estimate five or more. In Exhibit 4–9, the analyst has estimated five alternative outcomes for the breakfast proposal and the likelihood that each will occur.

To put the forecasts into perspective, the analyst would weight the net present values for each of the scenarios by the probability it will occur to obtain what is called an expected value—the probability-weighted net present value. Exhibit 4–9 provides the result of such an analysis. While the net present value of $1,365,000 is not one that the analyst explicitly forecast, it represents a sort of average for the project. The analyst also could compute a standard deviation to obtain a measure of risk.

In a more complex investment analysis, where there are numerous costs and benefits for which an analyst could assess a probability distribution, computer-assisted analysis, especially simulation, provides a good means for analyzing these complex data and estimating the expected value and standard deviation for a project.

One word of caution in the use of multiple-scenario, expected value, analysis. The veracity of this method depends on the company engaging in a number of projects at the same time, or over time, for the net present value to represent the average net present value the firm will receive from its projects. If only one project is undertaken, only one outcome can occur—no other projects exist to average the results. Thus probabilistic analysis can yield rich information for a knowledgeable user and dangers for the naive.

Simulation analysis is used by an increasing number of companies. Managers find that the discipline of deciding what might occur for each of the various costs and benefits keeps their assumptions reasonable and makes the analysis useful. However, this technique (simulation) is time-consuming and requires a computer. The increasing use of microcomputers has made multiple-scenario, not simulation, analysis, more accessable and useful for managers. As computer simulation models become readily available for use on the microcomputer, simulation may also become a widely used method of risk assessment.

None of these available risk-adjustment methods is completely satisfactory. New methods for incorporating risk into capital-investment decision making are being developed. Some firms assign different hurdle rates to divisions or strategic business units that are exposed to different levels of risk. Other firms attempt to quantify risk differences for each individual investment. Still other firms are using statistical techniques, such as probabilistic simulation analysis, to estimate directly the riskiness of investments. To date, risk is the most difficult problem in assessing value.

IV. OTHER CONSIDERATIONS IN CREATING VALUE

Not all investments are as complex or as risky as these two examples. Some are simple replacements of old, antiquated, or technologically inferior equipment. The analysis of one of these replacement investments will allow us to examine the impact of such things as different methods of depreciation and the effect of taxes. Consumer, Inc., management is considering just such a replacement investment—microwave ovens.

Currently each of Consumer's restaurants uses conventional electric ovens to heat some of its sandwiches and desserts. Such ovens are large, take an average of 10 minutes to heat the food, and, since they warm up slowly, must be kept hot whether they are being used or not.

Microwave ovens have been proposed to replace these ovens. They are small, cook much more rapidly, and, since the method of heating and cooking is totally different, need only be turned on when actually in use. Thus, the primary savings would be in the expense for electricity.

Management has made the following estimates of the costs and benefits associated with each new oven.

1. The microwave ovens can be purchased, fully installed, for $630.
2. The old ovens can be sold to a used equipment dealer for their book value of $25 each.
3. While annual usage and costs of electricity vary from restaurant to restaurant, the average cost per year per oven had been $300. The new ovens would use about one third the electricity for a cost of $100 per oven per year.
4. The new ovens are expected to be fully useful for five years. After that time, the ovens would be obsolete or in need of substantial repair. Management believes the ovens would have no salvage value at the end of the fifth year. Management used ACRS depreciation.

This is a very straightforward problem. As you can see in Exhibit 4–10, we treat reduced costs the same as increased income. Using ACRS depreciation, the IRR is 12.5% and the NPV (at a 10% discount rate) is $39.65 per oven, seemingly a reasonable investment opportunity.[1]

---

[1]The result of the analysis for ovens for all 500 restaurants would be the same IRR of 12.5% but an NPV of $19,825 (500 × $39.65).

EXHIBIT 4-10 Investment Analysis per Oven (microwave oven investment)

	Year					
	0	*1*	*2*	*3*	*4*	*5*
Costs:						
Investment in microwave oven	$(630)					
Salvage value—old oven	25					
Salvage value—new oven						$ 0
Net new investment	(605)					
Yearly costs and benefits:						
Electricity:						
Old oven		$(300)	$(300)	$(300)	$(300)	$(300)
New oven		(100)	(100)	(100)	(100)	(100)
Net decrease in expenses		200	200	200	200	200
Noncash charges:						
Old oven depreciation		0	0	0	0	0
New oven depreciation		95	139	132	132	132
Net increase in depreciation		95	139	132	132	132
Net increase in profit before tax		105	61	68	68	68
Profit after tax (tax = 40%)		63	37	41	41	41
Yearly net cash flow	$(605)	$ 158	$ 176	$ 173	$ 173	$ 173

IRR = 12.5%
NPV (@10%) = $39.65

However, there are changes within management's discretion that can increase the value of the investment. As an example, under certain tax laws, management could elect to use straight-line or a more rapid method of depreciation. Methods such as sum-of-the-years' digits or double-declining balance accelerate the rate of depreciation although still fully depreciating the asset by the end of the fifth year. Let's examine the effect of using other depreciation methods on the value of the microwave oven investment.

The yearly depreciation changes that would result from using other methods of depreciation are shown in Exhibit 4–11. The effect on the net cash flow of using other methods is shown in Exhibit 4–12. The double-declining-balance method yields the largest increase in the project's value.

At first glance, this may seem like numerical black magic, but it is, in fact, a real change in the value of the project to the firm. While the same total depreciation is taken, the amount taken in each year is different and thus the timing of the taxes paid by the firm is different. Since the discounting process deems earlier cash flows as more valuable and accelerated depreciation methods provide earlier cash flows, the method of depreciation chosen by management can create value.

At least in part because of the differences in tax liabilities, resulting from these depreciation approaches, Congress decided to standardize the depreciation allowances in the Economic Recovery Tax Act of 1981. The act estab-

EXHIBIT 4–11 Yearly Depreciation Charge—Different Depreciation Methods (microwave oven investment)

Year	*Straight Line**	*Double-Declining Balance†*	*Sum-of-Years' Digits‡*	*ACRS*
1	$126	$252	$210	$ 95
2	126	151	168	139
3	126	91	126	132
4	126	54	84	132
5	126	82	42	132
Total	$630	$630	$630	$630

*The depreciation rate is calculated by dividing 100% by number of years. In this case, the depreciation rate would be 100/5 = 20% per year. To determine yearly depreciation, multiply the purchase price, minus the salvage value, by the depreciation rate.

†Double the straight-line depreciation rate is multiplied by the full *undepreciated* value of the asset. In the final year, the remaining depreciation, less the salvage value, is taken.

‡To calculate the sum-of-the-years' digits factor:

a. Sum the numbers of the years, in this case 5 + 4 + 3 + 2 + 1 = 15.
b. For each year divide the number of remaining years by the summed years. In this case, the depreciation factor for the first year would be 5/1 + 2 + 3 + 4 + 5 or .33.
c. Multiply the depreciable value by this factor.

lished a new system of depreciation, the accelerated cost recovery system (ACRS). Corporations no longer have the option of selecting which depreciation method to use. Rather, the act prescribes specific depreciation rates according to five classes of capital assets. Each asset is assigned to a specific class with a prescribed depreciation life and schedule. If management decides not to use the depreciation allowance prescribed by ACRS, straight-line depreciation must be used.

This change in the tax laws illustrates the impact that external factors can have on the operations and decisions of the company. With the tax shield having a significant impact on the attractiveness of a project, the analyst should be informed of not only the current tax regulations but pending legislation as well. This concern for being informed of the economic, social, and political environment is essential for properly analyzing managerial decisions.

There is one last problem that analysts and managers must consider every time they analyze the value of an investment—inflation. You will notice that all the cash flows that Consumer management forecast were in real terms—they did not include inflation. Inflation can have a positive or negative effect on the value of a project depending on whether managers can pass on their costs in the form of prompt price increases. If the cost increases can be passed on immediately and fully, the relative value of the project will remain the same. If, however, there is a lag between the time the company's costs increase and when it can raise its prices, inflation can have a very negative effect on the value of a project.

Inflation can have yet other effects. Revenues themselves may rise or fall depending on the rate of inflation. For instance, if more people eat breakfast at fast-food restaurants than at traditional restaurants when inflation and

EXHIBIT 4–12 Changes in Net Cash Flow, IRR, and NPV—Depreciation Methods*

	Year					
Item	*0*	*1*	*2*	*3*	*4*	*5*
Accelerated cost recovery system:						
Net costs and benefits after tax, excluding depreciation	$(605)	$120	$120	$120	$120	$120
Depreciation tax shield	0	38	56	53	53	53
Net cash flow	$(605)	$158	$176	$173	$173	$173
IRR = 12.5%						
NPV (@ 10%) = $39.65						
Straight line:						
Net costs and benefits after tax, excluding depreciation	$(605)	$120	$120	$120	$120	$120
Depreciation tax shield	0	50	50	50	50	50
Net cash flow	$(605)	$170	$170	$170	$170	$170
IRR = 12.5%						
NPV (@ 10%) = $39.43						
Double-declining balance:						
Net costs and benefits after tax, excluding depreciation	$(605)	$120	$120	$120	$120	$150
Depreciation tax shield		101	60	36	22	33
Net cash flow	$(605)	$221	$180	$156	$142	$183
IRR = 14.9%						
NPV (@ 10%) = $72.49						
Sum-of-years' digits:						
Net costs and benefits after tax, excluding depreciation	$(605)	$120	$120	$120	$120	$150
Depreciation tax shield		84	67	50	34	17
Net cash flow	$(605)	$204	$187	$170	$154	$167
IRR = 14.8%						
NPV (@ 10%) = $71.60						

*Based on the microwave oven analysis in Exhibit 4–10.

prices rise, Consumer, Inc., may find that its revenues rise in both real (more customers are eating breakfast) and nominal terms (prices rise to account for the increased costs of producing the same number of breakfasts). The effects of these increases should be well understood by the manager. Exhibit 4–13 provides a forecast for the salad bar proposal that Consumer, Inc., management is considering. In this example, there is no increase in revenues greater than that driven by the 10 percent expected inflation: the unit sales remain the same.

You will note in looking at Exhibit 4–13 that inflation does not affect depreciation. As the rate of inflation increases, the taxes that are deferred by the depreciation tax shield decrease, making the investment less valuable. This is one of the insidious costs of inflation, a cost that occurs in countries where the depreciation schedules for capitalized property are calculated on the basis of historical cost, as is done in the United States. In other countries, particularly those with high inflation, companies are allowed to increase the

EXHIBIT 4-13 Consumer Salad Bar Proposal—Incremental Costs and Benefits with Inflation of 10 Percent

	Period						
	0	*1*	*2*	*3*	*4*	*5*	*6*
Equipment	$(1,400)						
Investment tax credit*	112						
Salvage value							$ 88
Training costs (after tax)	(416)						
Incremental sales		$ 8,250	$ 9,075	$ 9,983	$ 10,981	$ 12,079	13,287
Operating expenses		(7,669)	(8,436)	(9,280)	(10,208)	(11,228)	(12,351)
Depreciation†		(210)	(308)	(294)	(294)	(294)	0
Pre-tax profit	(416)	371	331	409	479	556	1,024
Taxes (40%)	166	(148)	(132)	(164)	(192)	(223)	(410)
Profit after tax	(250)	223	199	245	287	334	614
Noncash charges (depreciation or net new investment)	(1,288)	210	308	294	294	294	(0)
Net cash flow	$(1,538)	$ 433	$ 507	$ 539	$ 581	$ 628	$ 614

*Investment tax credit is a direct reduction to taxes. The credit is 8% of the initial cost of the equipment. Under ACRS tax rules a maximum of 10% may be taken; however, 2% of that credit must either act as a reduction of the depreciable investment, or the credit must be reduced to 8%.

†Depreciation is taken on the investment of $1,400. Training costs are expensed in the year they are incurred.

book value of fixed assets, and hence the depreciation, with increases in inflation. Because of this, profits actually increase at a rate comparable to inflation.

Exhibit 4-13 is a simple example of the effect that inflation can have on the value of an investment. Using as an example the salad bar proposal shown in Exhibit 4-3, the costs and benefits (except for depreciation) have been increased to reflect a 10% inflation. Of course, individual costs and revenues could increase at rates slower or faster than inflation. However, note that with a simple increase in inflation to 10%, the net present value is reduced to $224,663 from $278,032 shown in Exhibit 4-6. That is due to two factors. First, the depreciation tax shield declines in real terms, and second, while the cash costs and benefits increase with inflation, so must the rate at which the net cash flows are discounted. Here we have added the 10% rate of inflation to the real, inflation-free discount rate—in this example estimated to be 10%. This is because providers of corporate capital require a return to offset risk and inflation. Thus the cash flows in Exhibit 4-13 are discounted at 20% to account for the value of money at a real rate of 10% and inflation of 10%.

V. SUMMARY

Good investments are critical to the future of the firm. The analyst's job is to gather and analyze the relevant information and present it in such a way that the future is adequately foreseen. Analysts have three major problems in assessing potential investments. First, the appropriate cash costs and benefits must be determined. That process, as we have suggested, can be difficult, particularly when evaluating replacement investments. The analyst's second problem is to evaluate the relative attractiveness of the investment's net marginal benefits. We suggest that the net present value method is the most appropriate technique to use in measuring this value. Third, the problem of incorporating risk into the evaluation of any investment is a particularly vexing one. If all of the investments are of a risk similar to that of the firm, an appropriate method is to use the firm's marginal cost of capital for a hurdle rate. If the investment is more or less risky than the firm, the analyst may leave it to the managers to decide subjectively whether the return is adequate to compensate for the risk or if they should use one of the hurdle rate adjustment techniques. However, until risk analysis is refined, we are left with methods that do not fully satisfy our needs.

SELECTED REFERENCES

For comprehensive reviews of the capital budgeting process, see:

Bierman, Harold, Jr., and Seymour Smidt. *The Capital Budgeting Decision.* 5th ed. New York: MacMillan, 1980.

Levy, Haim, and Marshall Sarnot. *Capital Investment and Financial Decisions.* Englewood Cliffs, N.J.: Prentice-Hall International, 1978.

For an analysis of the capital budgeting and planning process in one firm, see:

Bower, Joseph. *Managing the Resource Allocation Process: A Study of Corporate Planning and Investments.* Homewood, Ill.: Richard D. Irwin, 1970.

For descriptions of various approaches to risk analysis, see:

Bower, Richard S., and J. M. Jenks. "Divisional Screening Rates." *Financial Management,* Autumn 1975, pp. 42–49.

Hertz, David B. "Risk Analysis in Capital Investment." *Harvard Business Review,* September–October 1979, pp. 169–81.

Hull, J. C. *The Evaluation of Risk in Business Investment.* Elmsford, N.Y.: Pergammon Press, 1980.

Weston, J. Fred. "Investment Decisions Using the Capital Asset Pricing Model." *Financial Management,* Spring 1973, pp. 25–33.

STUDY QUESTIONS

1. The Marvel Corporation was considering the development of a new assembly line. The necessary machinery was estimated to cost $800,000. Although the accelerated cost recovery system would allow the equipment to be depreciated in 5 years, the company decided to depreciate the equipment over its useful economic life of 20 years. The ACRS therefore required that straight-line depreciation be used. Marvel management estimated that the costs associated with owning and running the machinery (gas, minor repairs, etc.) would be constant over time and total $200,000 over the equipment's estimated life. Thirty people would be required to work the assembly line. These would be new employees earning an average salary of $15,000 a year. Sales from the new assembly line were estimated to total $1.25 million a year with raw materials representing 37% of that amount. No other costs specific to the project were anticipated. The Marvel Corporation had a 42% tax rate and a required payback period of four years on all new projects. Should they develop the assembly line? What is the project's benefit/cost ratio?

2. The SUN Company was considering an investment which would cost $200,000 initially. The new equipment was estimated to have a useful life of five years but would require an additional investment of $60,000 in year 2 for specialized equipment. The initial investment would be in the five-year ACRS class which would allow 15% depreciation in the first reporting year, 22% in the second year, and 21% for each of the three remaining years. The second investment would meet the guidelines for the ACRS three-year class and would be depreciated 25%, 38%, and 37% for the respective years. Sales specific to the project were forecasted at $120,000 in year 1, increasing 15% a year to $209,881 in year 5. Necessary raw materials, labor, etc., were estimated at 39% of sales. Compute the project's net present value using a 10% discount rate and a 40% tax rate.

   What is the major factor creating the project's net present value?

3. The Kertin Company was trying to decide between the two capital projects described below. Evaluate each of the projects on the basis of their payback period, benefit/cost ratio, and net present value. Which project would you recommend Kertin Company undertake? Why?

Project 1: Expand existing production by acquiring new machinery costing $800,000:

a. Incremental sales = $500,000/year.
b. Cost of goods sold = $49% of sales.
c. Advertising = Constant $50,000 a year.
d. Depreciation computed on the ACRS recovery allowance for 10-year class assets.

Project 2: Expand product line by undertaking a project estimated to cost $600,000 for production facilities and $200,000 for production training for employees. Kertin management had already funded $100,000 worth of market research which had documented the product's sales potential. Kertin hoped to recoup this outlay through further sales.

a. Sales in year 1 estimated to be $350,000, increasing 10% a year in years 2–4, 15% a year in years 5–7; and 10% a year in years 8–10.
b. Cost of goods sold projected at 50% of sales for first three years, declining to 42% thereafter.
c. Advertising to be 25% of sales for first three years and to level off at $100,000 thereafter.

Kertin had a 45% tax rate and used a 10% discount rate to evaluate all projects.

Year	*Discount Factors at 10%*	*ACRS Depreciation*
1	1.100	8%
2	1.210	14
3	1.331	12
4	1.464	10
5	1.611	10
6	1.772	10
7	1.949	9
8	2.144	9
9	2.358	9
10	2.594	9

CHAPTER 5

The Cost of Capital

In Chapter 4, we followed the financial analyst through the evaluation of investment opportunities for Consumer, Inc. We used two projects to describe incremental cash flow analysis and to demonstrate several methods for evaluating the value of those investments. We said that the net present value technique is both intuitively acceptable and superior to the other methods since any investment with a positive net present value would be expected to create value. Those with a zero net present value could neither create nor destroy value. Those with a negative NPV should be rejected and available investment funds returned to the shareholders: the shareholders could do better for themselves by investing those funds in other securities in the capital markets than by allowing Consumer, Inc., to use the funds on their behalf.

To evaluate investments using the net present value method, we needed two estimates: (1) the cash flows expected over the life of the project and (2) a rate at which to discount those cash flows. We first used a discount rate designed to compensate investors for the timing of the cash flows. We later augmented this rate in order to compensate investors for risk as well. This second discount rate, called a *hurdle rate,* we set at an amount equal to Consumer's cost of capital. The use of the firm's cost of capital as the hurdle rate is acceptable so long as the investments being considered are as risky as the firm itself.

What determines the cost of capital? First, since the lender or shareholder is inconvenienced by no longer having funds available to spend at will, he or she requires a rate of return to compensate for illiquidity—not having the money readily available. Second, because there is some possibility that the funds will never be regained (the loan may not be repaid or the stock's price may fall), the investor requires compensation for risk. The cost of any type of capital is the investor's compensation for these two factors, illiquidity and risk. The riskier the investment, the higher must be its expected returns. That is why common stocks have higher expected returns than debt or preferred stock, both of which have claims on the firm's assets that supersede the claims of common shareholders.

To better understand the cost of capital and how investors determine what return they expect on their investment, it will be helpful to briefly discuss the capital markets. It is in these markets that the users of funds (the corporations) and the providers of funds (the investors) meet.

I. CAPITAL MARKETS

The financial market for long-term funds for the corporation is called the capital market. The capital market differs from the money market discussed in Chapter 2 by the nature of the funds that are invested. Money market funds are short-term investments—investments under one year. Capital market funds are long-term investments, exceeding one year. In addition to debt obligations, capital markets include equity funds that have no stated maturity.

Capital markets exist on two levels, the primary market and the secondary market. Primary market transactions occur when companies issue securities to investors. Typically these securities are sold through investment bankers, who, through their relationship with brokers, act as agents for the companies selling the instruments. The proceeds from the sale of the financial instruments minus the investment bankers' commission are paid to the issuing company. The primary market is the source of capital for companies.

After the securities have been sold initially, the purchaser of the securities, stocks or bonds, may then trade them in the secondary market. The financial instruments are traded between individuals or institutions who may have no relationship with the original issuing company. The company, however, is not indifferent to the activities in the secondary market. The trading of securities in this market gives rise to the market prices that are used to assess the market value of a company and its securities. The prices for securities that are reported in various publications reflect the trading in the secondary market.

In recent years, several new instruments such as options and futures have been introduced in the financial markets. These instruments, which are designed to provide a means of protecting investors against price movements in the capital market, are all secondary market instruments. They are not a source of capital for corporations.

Trading in capital market instruments can take place in organized market exchanges or "over-the-counter." Organized exchanges such as the New York Stock Exchange (NYSE) and the American Stock Exchange (AMEX) allow trading only in listed securities. To achieve listed status, companies must meet specific qualifications of the exchange including such things as the size of the company, the total market value of the publicly traded shares, and the amount of trading in the company's securities. Trading on these exchanges can only be done by members of the exchange who own one of a limited number of "seats." Members of the exchange are typically brokerage companies who buy and sell securities for their customers.

Unlike the exchanges, which have a specific location where trading takes place, the over-the-counter market consists of numerous traders located throughout the country. These traders "make a market" in one or several securities. Brokerage firms are market makers. A computerized network called NASDAQ that is sponsored by the National Association of Securities Dealers ties these various market makers together. There are many more securities traded over-the-counter than on the exchanges. The average trading volume for the securities listed on the exchanges is much greater, however.

In addition to the public markets, capital can be raised through private placements. Public issues are regulated by the Securities and Exchange Commission (SEC), which requires the issuing company to disclose specific information about the company's business activities and the financial instrument being issued. Such disclosure provides the public with information that facilitates subsequent trading on the secondary market. Private placements are direct placements of the securities with investors—for instance, large insurance companies. These private placements are not registered with the SEC and therefore cannot be traded in the secondary market. However, because the issuer can directly negotiate with the investor, private placements allow more complicated and specialized financial arrangements between borrower and lender than are available in the public market.

Private institutional investors such as mutual funds, insurance companies, and pension funds are also the largest investors in the public markets. Although precise data are difficult to obtain, estimates suggest that well over half of the publicly traded securities are owned by these institutions. Individual shareholders account for the remainder of investments.

Two primary types of securities used by companies to raise long-term capital are debt and equity. In addition, some instruments combine the two types through "convertible" provisions. Convertible instruments typically allow the investor to convert a debt instrument or preferred stock into equity, usually common stock, at a specified conversion price or ratio.

1. Debt Markets

Long-term instruments are frequently called bonds. A bond is a contractual debt obligation to repay a stated amount (called the principal or par value, typically $1,000) on a specified date (termed the maturity) and periodic interest, or coupon, payments. The stated interest or coupon payments are determined by the specified interest rate or coupon rate at the time the bond was issued. If the contractually obligated payments are not made, then the bond is in default, and the bondholders may have to call on the assets of the company as compensation.

For most bonds, the coupon rate is fixed for the life of the bond. Because of large fluctuations in interest rates in recent years, some bonds have been issued with variable, or floating, interest rates. For variable rate bonds, the interest rate is restated at specified intervals based on a specified reference to a market index of interest rates; for instance, LIBOR (the London interbank offering rate).

For fixed coupon bonds, changes in interest rates subsequent to the date of issue affect the bond price in the secondary market. If general market interest rates go up (or down), the price of the bond will go down (or up) in order to continue to provide a fair interest rate in subsequent interest rate environments. These adjustments occur so that the bond's yield to maturity (interest plus principal repayment) will approximate the current market rate of interest for bonds of similar maturity and quality. The price that an investor is willing to pay for a bond is a function of the par value of the bond, the coupon rate, the maturity, and the prevailing interest rates. The formula for determining the proper secondary price shown below is similar to the present value calculations discussed in Chapter 4.

$$P = \sum_{j=1}^{m} \frac{CP_1}{(1 + i)^1} + \frac{CP_2}{(1 + i)^2} + \ldots . \frac{CP_m}{(1 + i)^m} + \frac{PAR}{(1 + i)^m}$$

where

P = Market price of the bond
CP = Periodic coupon payment
i = Current market interest rate
PAR = Par value of the bond
m = Maturity period of the bond

If, for instance, a company like Consumer, our example firm in Chapter 4, had issued $2 million bonds at 12% and the rate of interest on bonds of a similar maturity and quality rose from 12% to 15.7%, the market price of Consumer's bonds with two years remaining until maturity would drop from $2 million to $1.8 million in order to provide a 15.7% yield to new purchasers. Conversely, if market rates dropped, the bond price would rise. The present value (the price) of bonds with long maturities is more affected by interest rate charges.

If the market price of a bond is known but the effective interest rate (the yield to maturity) is not, it is possible, using the same formula, to calculate the yield to maturity (i).

For conventional bonds, the amount the company borrows is the same as the principal or par value of the bond, net of issue costs, of course. Recently a number of zero-coupon bonds have been issued. These bonds do not require any periodic coupon payments. Instead, the par value of the bond is much larger than the amount that is originally borrowed (the cost of the bond to the investor): essentially, the interest is accrued and paid in the par value—final repayment.

Determining the return on these bonds is a simplification of the yield-to-maturity calculation since there are no coupon payments. The following simplified formula would be used:

$$\text{Price} = \frac{PAR}{(1 + i)^m}$$

Using this formula, if a firm issued a zero-coupon bond today at a price of $275 per bond returning $1,000 in 10 years, the effective yield, or yield to maturity, would be 13.8%. Not all bonds retire the entire principal amount at the specified maturity date of the bond. Many bonds require periodic principal reductions called sinking funds. The purpose of these sinking funds is to reduce the risk that the borrower will not be able to repay the par amount. Sinking funds may be placed in a trust account to be held until the maturity date. For publicly traded bonds it is more common for the company to simply purchase some of the existing bonds in the market. This reduces the total amount of bonds outstanding and has the effect of reducing the total principal amount.

In addition to reducing the amount of bonds outstanding through sinking-fund requirements, companies may choose to retire the bonds before the specified maturity. This process is termed refunding or calling the bonds. Companies are especially interested in doing this if interest rates fall. They can call the existing bonds and then refinance with lower cost debt. To protect against this, many bonds have call protection. This means the bonds cannot be called for a specified period of time or may be called only if a stated premium is paid to the bondholders.

As a further protection for the bondholders, the bond contract or indenture may limit the company in other ways. Frequently the company will be required to maintain certain levels of assets or to limit the total amount of debt. Often these restrictions or covenants are specified in the form of ratios—the kind we discussed in Chapter 1. If any of the bond covenants are violated, the bond is deemed to be in technical default and is immediately due for payment.

The general risk to the borrower is reflected in the bond rating. Bond ratings are important because bonds with higher potential for default (lower ratings) must pay a higher coupon interest rate to compensate investors for the risk. Several organizations publish bond ratings—Moody's and Standard & Poor's (S&P) are the two most widely known. Based on these independent organizations' assessments of the general credit risk of the borrower, bonds are assigned a rating with Aaa (Moody's) or AAA (S&P), indicating the most creditworthy bonds—those with the lowest risk of default. The ratings decrease through Aa/AA and so on with high-risk bonds rated at Caa/CCC or below. These high-risk bonds are called high-yield or junk bonds.

2. Equity Markets

There are two types of equity investments, common stock and preferred. Both of these equity instruments differ from debt in that there is no contractual obligation to provide any return to the investors. Dividends may be paid to the equity investors, but only after all obligations have been paid to the bondholders.

Preferred stockholders do have a preferential position over common shareholders, hence the name preferred stock. The dividend that is to be paid on the preferred stock is a stated amount. This dividend must be paid before any dividend can be paid to the common shareholders. If the company has insufficient funds to pay this dividend, it may be omitted without causing a default. Usually, any previously omitted preferred dividends must be paid before dividends can be paid to common shareholders. Preferred stock with this provision is termed cumulative preferred. However, preferred shareholders only receive the stated dividend. Because the dividend is stated, like an interest payment, preferred stock is similar to debt, yet it is also similar to equity.

Once the required preferred dividend has been paid, the common shareholders may receive any dividend that management deems appropriate. In addition to owning the residual income of the company, common shareholders elect the board of directors, which is usually responsible for approving the corporate dividend policy.

For most common stock the dividend income is the smaller part of the potential return. Most investors invest in common stock with the expectation that the price of the stock will increase. The change in the market price of the stock is termed capital appreciation if the change is positive.

Whereas changes in the prices of bonds are primarily related to interest rate changes, the determinants of changes in stock prices are not quite so easy to isolate. Factors that affect the general economy, such as interest rates and the rate of economic growth, affect all stock prices. In addition, the market price may be affected by the industry outlook as well as by the prospects for the specific company. Whereas bond prices tend to move in unison based on interest rate movements, at any given time some stock prices will be rising and some will be falling.

The combination of dividend income and capital appreciation determines the return earned by the equity investors. Since future return is uncertain at the time an equity investment is purchased, there are several methods investors use to forecast what the return will be. These methods will be discussed later in the chapter.

A continuing controversy surrounds the issue of whether analysts can forecast market price movements. The argument rests on whether the markets are efficient. In an efficient market, all available information is known to all participants in the market and is reflected in the current market prices. Many managers and investors believe that the market may not always be efficient and that an astute analyst can find information that has not been adequately evaluated by the market. This could allow stocks to be overvalued or undervalued. While academic evidence shows that the markets are relatively efficient, several recent studies have suggested that there may be some inefficiencies that astute investors can exploit.

The important objective for managers is to manage a company in a way that leads to increases in the market price of its common stock. This can be accomplished through investing in assets and projects that yield a return greater than the cost of the funds invested. To do this, managers have to obtain capital at the lowest possible cost. It is essential for managers to understand what the cost of capital is so they can invest in projects with higher returns. This will create value for the company's investors.

While investors look at returns, timing, and risk, the firm's managers have one goal in mind as they finance the firm: to obtain capital at the lowest possible cost using the two basic sources of capital, debt and equity. The proportion of debt that the firm employs as part of its total capital is called *leverage*. Managers want to leverage the firm in such a way as to minimize the weighted average cost of capital.[1]

Why is there an optimal capital structure—a proportion of debt that will minimize the company's cost of capital, thereby maximizing its value? There are only two reasons. First, someone, such as the U.S. Internal Revenue Service, allows the company an unusual benefit that reduces the cost of capital: interest is a tax-deductible expense, thus reducing the cost of debt. Second, some investors (lenders or shareholders) do not really understand what they are doing and allow the company to have money at a rate lower than reasonable for the risk they are taking.

Lenders do appear to charge rates lower than do providers of equity capital, but they also take less risk than do shareholders—their claims supersede those of either common or preferred shareholders in case of bankruptcy. That is why debt precedes equity on the balance sheet and why lenders are willing to charge a somewhat lower rate than the implicit rate required for equity.[2] However, as lenders' claims take precedence over shareholders' claims, shareholders are put in a riskier position—and thus should charge more. The lower cost of debt should thus be balanced in the firm's overall capital cost by the higher cost of equity; the weighted average cost of capital should not change unless either the lenders or shareholders misprice their risk (charge too low a rate).

To calculate the weighted average cost of capital, analysts need three basic pieces of information:[3]

1. The after-tax cost of debt.
2. The cost of equity.
3. The proportions of debt and equity in the firm's capital structure.

This chapter will discuss the means of calculating each of these three factors. Every step requires the analyst's judgment as well as her or his mathematical skill.

II. DETERMINING THE COST OF DEBT

Most firms use debt to finance a portion of their assets. As shown in Exhibit 5–1, over the past 18 years, the proportion of debt used by U.S. firms has ri-

---

[1]While there are conflicting theories about the impact of leverage on the cost of capital, here we assume that moderate amounts of debt are desirable and will lower the average cost of capital. It is only with high debt levels that shareholders begin to require added return for the risk of increased leverage.

[2]In fact, lenders may establish their own priorities. For instance, the claims on the company by holders of debentures (a form of debt) take precedence over the claims by holders of subordinated debentures.

[3]In making investment decisions, we are investing new or marginal funds into projects. These new funds may come from the shareholders, in the form of retained profits or new issues of common stock, or from newly placed debt.

EXHIBIT 5-1 Annual Growth of Capital Structure and Its Composition (all nonfinancial business corporations)

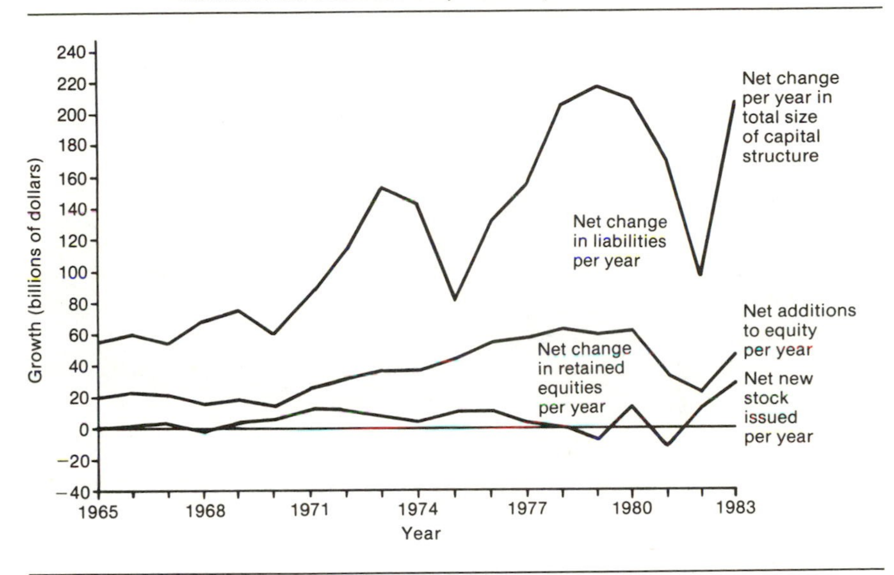

SOURCE: Federal Reserve Board of Governors, "Flow of Funds."

sen dramatically. When a firm borrows money, it promises to return that money, called the *principal,* and while the firm has use of that principal, it promises to pay a charge, *interest,* for its use.

The interest rate charged is designed to compensate the lender for the time that the funds will be in the borrower's possession and for the risk that either the principal will not be returned and/or the interest will not be promptly paid. The more uncertain the lender is about the stability and reliability (the *quality*) of the borrower, the higher the interest rate charged. Exhibit 5–2 shows the market rates of interest during the past decade on publicly traded debt of varying qualities. Aaa-rated debt is the highest quality corporate debt security. The interest rate on the best quality corporate debt is higher than that on government debt of the same maturity.

Just as the reliability of the borrower affects the interest rate, so does the length of time that the borrower wishes to use the principal. The longer the debt's *maturity* (the length of the loan), the higher the interest rate in most circumstances. Exhibit 5–3 shows the market rate of interest on debt of the same quality but different maturities at several points in time. The normal line is upward-sloping like that on 6/1/80. An upward slope is normal since lenders who provide capital for longer times require, quite logically, more return. At some points in time, this upward-sloping curve, the *yield curve,* does not exist. For instance, during the 1970s, the relationship between the market rate of interest and debt of different maturities has sometimes been perverse. This has been particularly true in periods of high inflation. Exhibit 5–3 shows two typical and two inverse (3/1/81 and 12/1/81) yield curves. How-

EXHIBIT 5-2 Interest Rates for Debt of Different Qualities

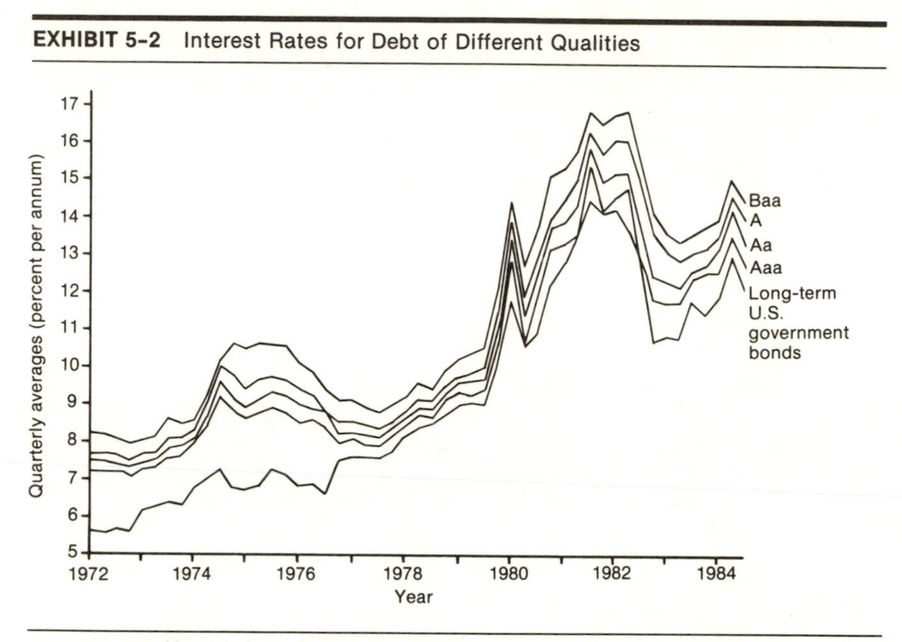

SOURCES: Moody's Bond Record, August 1981, for corporate yields; Federal Reserve Bulletin, 1976–1980, for U.S. government yields.

ever, the typical relationship is the upward-sloping yield curves shown for 6/1/80 and 9/1/80.

In addition to interest payments, a number of special features may be required by the lender. For instance, specific assets may be pledged to support the loan, the lender may require seniority over other's claims in the case of bankruptcy, or the loan may be convertible into common or preferred stock under certain conditions. Each feature offers the lender different levels of protection from risk and thus carries a somewhat different cost, which is reflected in the interest rate.

The pre-tax cost of debt is the ratio of the interest rate to the principal amount of the debt. Since interest payments are tax deductible, we calculate all capital costs on an after-tax basis. To determine the after-tax cost of debt, this ratio is multiplied by one minus the corporate tax rate. In other words,

$$R_d = \frac{I}{P}(1 - t) \tag{1}$$

where

R_d = After-tax cost of debt
I = Interest payment
P = Principal received by the company
t = Corporate tax rate

For example, if Consumer, Inc., wanted to borrow $2 million, would be expected to pay interest of $240,000 per year, and had a corporate tax rate of 40%, the after-tax cost of this debt would be calculated as follows:

$$R_d = \frac{\$240{,}000}{\$2{,}000{,}000}(1 - .40)$$
$$= .12\,(1 - .40)$$
$$= .072 \text{ or } 7.2\%$$

For purposes of doing investment analyses, the after-tax cost of debt should not be based on the debt the firm has already borrowed. That debt

EXHIBIT 5-3 Interest Rates for Debt of Different Maturities

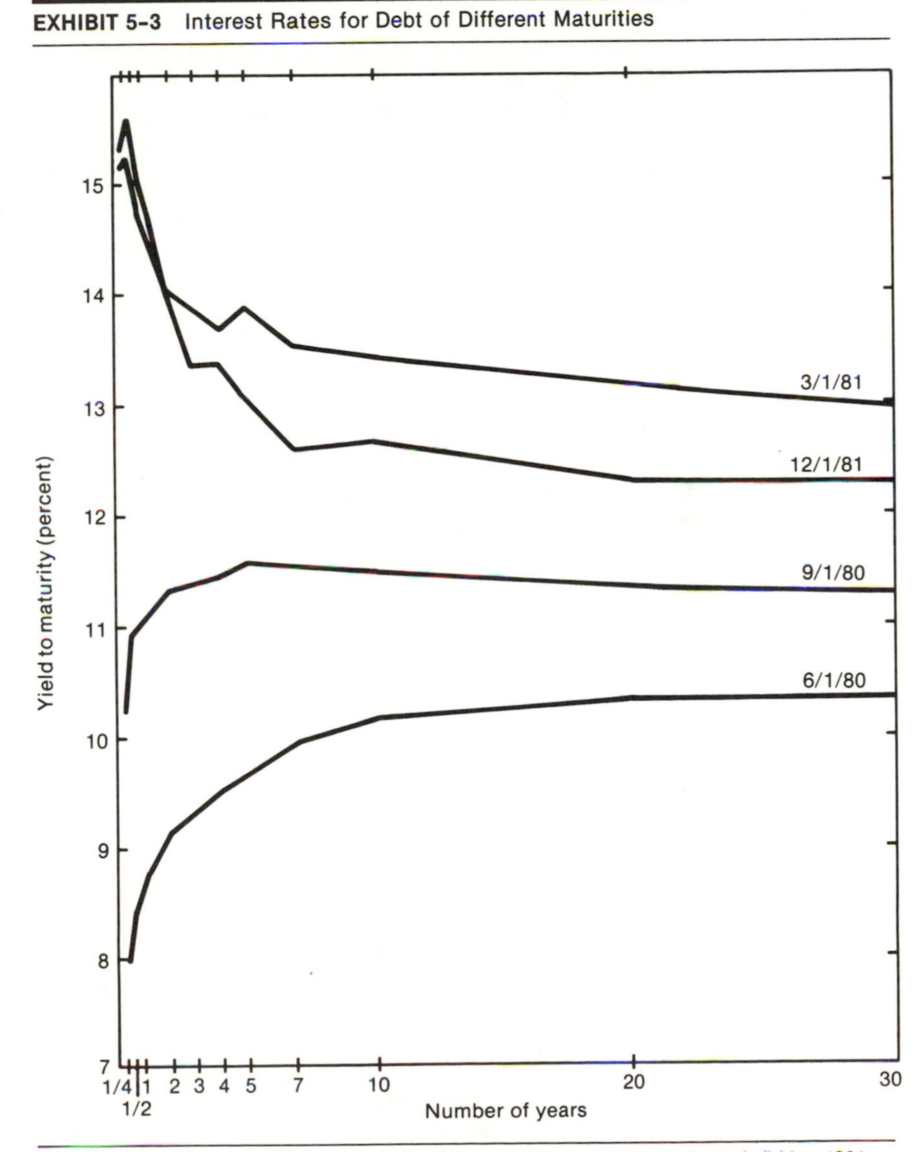

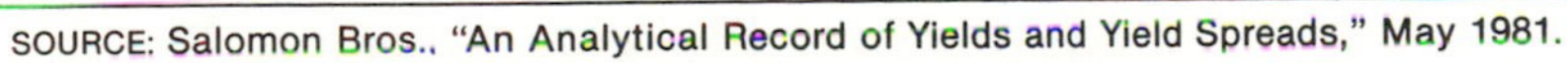
SOURCE: Salomon Bros., "An Analytical Record of Yields and Yield Spreads," May 1981.

has already been used by the firm to finance assets currently in use. The interest payments Consumer, Inc., is currently making are not relevant to future investment decisions. Only costs of the new funds are relevant. Thus, we want to calculate the marginal cost of debt, the cost of new debt required to finance new assets.

Calculating the marginal cost of debt is simple enough if the firm is currently negotiating a loan. How does the analyst estimate the marginal cost of debt if the firm is not negotiating with lenders for debt funds?

There are several ways in which the analyst can obtain the needed estimates. First, by looking at rates charged other firms of the same risk or quality, the analyst can determine the current rate of interest for comparable firms. For a company like Consumer, Inc., the analyst might look at the yield on the publicly traded debt issued by such fast-food firms as Wendy's, Inc., or McDonald's.

A second approach is to examine the cost of a company's publicly traded debt, its bonds. Bonds traded in the public markets are often sold at a price that is different from the price at which they were originally sold by the issuing firm. The current yield to maturity, described earlier in this chapter, can then be used to estimate the cost of issuing new debt.

In estimating the marginal cost of debt for the firm, the analyst may be using the costs of debt with different features. Different features usually result in different interest rates. The marginal debt cost will be an average of the costs of several kinds of debt used by the company. Most analysts exclude short-term (current) debt from the calculation of the marginal cost of debt, primarily because it will be repaid within one year. Recently, however, analysts have reconsidered the exclusion of short-term debt. Short-term financing has become an important source of funds for many firms, either because borrowers are waiting for long-term rates to drop or because lenders prefer frequent rate revisions. The best rule for an analyst to follow is to exclude short-term debt if it is being used to supply temporary needs (such as seasonal inventory) but to include the cost of short-term funds that represent permanent financing for the firm's assets.

III. DETERMINING THE COST OF EQUITY

Shareholders, like other lenders, expect to earn a return on the funds they provide—a return that compensates them for both the time that the funds are made available to the firm as well as for the risk that the firm will not provide the expected return. The returns for common stock, however, come from quite a different source than the returns from debt. Returns from common stock come from the dividends the common shareholder will receive over the term of his or her investment in the firm and/or the gains to be realized by the investor on the sale of the stock resulting from increases in the market price of the stock above the price originally paid.

How do analysts estimate the returns that shareholders will require? If the firm were owned by a single shareholder or a small group of shareholders, the analyst could simply ask them, "What return do you expect this firm to earn on your behalf?" If the shareholder replied, "Fifteen percent would satisfy me; I would not want to buy a larger share of the firm, nor would I want to sell the ownership position I already have," the analyst would know that the shareholder's required return—the cost of equity—was 15%. However, few firms whose stock is bought and sold on the stock exchanges have such limited ownership. As a result, we must find a way to estimate the return required by a large number of dispersed shareholders.

There are two groups of methods for estimating the cost of equity. The first group of methods place a value on the firm's earnings. Since the value of a shareholder's stock in the firm is created by reinvested earnings (known as *retained earnings*), analysts often estimate the cost of equity by evaluating the earnings of the firm. The second group of approaches could be called capital-market estimations. Since investors require higher returns for riskier securities, these capital-market methods categorize all securities by risk and then estimate the cost of equity according to the stock's risk.

1. Earnings Valuation: The Dividend Discount Method

A simple means of estimating the cost of equity (R_e) is to calculate the ratio of projected earnings per share (EPS) to the current market price per share (P_o):

$$R_e = \frac{EPS}{P_o} \tag{2}$$

or

$$R_e = \frac{1}{PE}$$

We will use this approach to estimate the cost of equity for Consumer, Inc. Consumer's recent stock price was $15 per share, and the earnings estimated for the next 12 months were $1.80 per share. The cost of equity would be calculated as follows:

$$R_e = \frac{\$1.80}{\$15.00}$$

$$= .12 \text{ or } 12\%$$

By itself, however, this equation is actually only a rough measure of the cost of equity. The equation assumes that the firm pays 100% of its earnings to shareholders—or that if it does reinvest any funds, these do not create any value for the shareholders. In other words, the equation assumes that the net present value of all reinvestments is zero. Suppose that these assumptions are valid in this case. Consumer, Inc., will either pay out all of its earnings or reinvest them without creating value. Under either of these circumstances, we could rephrase equation (2) by substituting the next year's dividends for the next year's earnings per share. In other words,

$$R_e = \frac{EPS}{P_o} = \frac{D_1}{P_o} \tag{3}$$

where

$$D_1 = \text{Dividends for the next year}$$

But these assumptions are too simple. It is more likely that a portion of the earnings will be reinvested in the firm and that these investments will create value—that the firm will grow over time. Equations (2) and (3), as they are now expressed, ignore the investor's expectation that the firm will grow.

To include this growth we could use the following formula.

$$P_o = \frac{D_1}{(1 + R_e)} + \frac{D_1(1 + g)^2}{(1 + R_e)^2} + \frac{D_1(1 + g)^3}{(1 + R_e)^3} + \ldots + \frac{D_1(1 + g)^n}{(1 + R_e)^n} \tag{4}$$

Note that we have rearranged the formula, setting the growing dividends equal to the price. This is simply to make it easier. The growth rate (g) is the rate at which the dividends are expected to grow each year. If the firm is growing at a constant rate, often the case with slower growth, mature firms, we can account more simply for this expected growth from reinvestment (denoted as g). We may rewrite equation (4) in the following way:

$$R_e = \frac{D_1}{P_o} + g \tag{5}$$

This formula is known as the *dividend discount* or *dividend growth model,* a widely used and accepted method of valuing a firm's shares.

Let's apply this model to Consumer, Inc. The expected dividend for the next year (D_1) is \$.40, the market price is \$15 per share, and the firm is paying out 30% of its earnings in dividends.

$$R_e = \frac{\$.40}{\$15.00} + g$$

$$R_e = 2.7\% + g$$

The problem for the analyst now is to determine g—that is, to determine the growth that shareholders expect from the 78% of earnings that Consumer is retaining.

There are several ways to estimate expected growth. One is to use the firm's average historic rate of growth. Another method is to forecast the expected growth. Yet another method requires the analyst to forecast the return on equity and use this estimate to calculate expected growth:

$$g = (1 - PO)\,ROE \tag{6}$$

where

ROE = Expected return on equity
PO = Percentage of earnings expected to be paid out as dividends

This is the growth rate that a firm can sustain without a change in its capital structure. While there are other ways to estimate future growth, this method forces the analyst to evaluate the effects of new investments in the firm. If Consumer, Inc., continued to pay out 30% of its earnings as dividends and expected its return on equity to maintain a historic 20% rate, we could calculate shareholders' expected growth as follows:

$$g = (1 - .30) \times (.20)$$
$$= .14 \text{ or } 14\%$$

Consumers' cost of equity would be calculated thus:

$$R_e = \frac{\$.40}{\$15.00} + .14$$
$$= .167 \text{ or } 16.7\%$$

We do not adjust for taxes because common stock dividends are not tax deductible and are therefore already the after-tax cost.

There are a number of problems with the simple dividend discount model as shown in equations (5) and (7). It cannot be used in the following circumstances:

1. The firm pays no dividends.
2. The growth rate is higher than the discount rate.
3. The growth rate is not constant.

Many firms do not pay dividends and do not have constant growth rates. For such firms, other methods of calculating the cost of equity are available. Many of these methods draw upon rearranged and expanded versions of the dividend discount model, as shown below.

$$R_e = \frac{D_1}{P_o} + g \tag{5}$$

$$P_o = \frac{D_1}{R_e - g} \tag{7}$$

$$P_o = \frac{D_1}{(1 + R_e)^1} + \frac{D_2}{(1 + R_e)^2} + \ldots \frac{D_n}{(1 + R_e)^n} \tag{8}$$

$$P_o = \frac{D_1}{(1 + R_e)^1} + \frac{D_2}{(1 + R_e)^2} + \ldots \frac{D_n}{(R_e - g)} \tag{9}$$

$$P_o = \frac{D_1}{(1 + R_e)^1} + \frac{D_2}{(1 + R_e)^2} + \ldots \frac{P_n}{(1 + R_e)^n} \tag{10}$$

These models are all versions of equation (4) and can be very useful in different circumstances. Equation (8), for instance, allows the analyst to

---

[4]We could use yet another version of the dividend discount method. Instead of using dividends we would use free cash flow—cash not retained and reinvested in the business: Free cash flow = Revenues − Costs − Investment + Noncash Charges (e.g., depreciation). Simply replace the estimated dividends with free cash flow. This is especially useful in evaluating firms that pay out dividends in excess of revenues—dividends that are not really funds available to shareholders but a return of capital.

forecast the dividend the firm is expected to pay each year in the future.[4] For firms that are not growing at a constant rate, this version of the model allows the analyst to avoid the use of a constant rate of growth—a rate needed when equation (5) is used. It is, however, quite difficult to forecast dividends into the distant future.

Equation (9) affords the analyst the best features of equations (7) and (8). To use equation (9), the analyst explicitly forecasts dividends for a short time into the future, perhaps until the firm has matured and can be expected to grow at a more normal and constant rate. The analyst then uses the constant growth formula (7) to account for all dividends beyond that point. This method is often used by investment analysts to value the common stocks they follow. Typically, their year-by-year forecast of dividends is for 5 to 10 years.

Finally, equation (10) can be used by assuming the stock is held for a period of time and then sold. The analyst forecasts year-by-year dividends for several years and the anticipated price for which the stock will be sold in the future. That price, of course, will reflect the value the new buyer places on dividends he or she will receive once the transfer is made. However, many analysts find it easier to forecast a price for which the stock can be sold at a later date than to forecast constant growth rates or dividends year-by-year over a long period.

The many versions of equation (4) were presented not to confuse the reader but to give the financial analyst, confronted with different situations and various kinds of data, a variety of useful tools. One method will not work in every circumstance.

2. Capital-Market Estimations: Risk-Premium Methods

The dividend discount model, as we have seen, evaluates earnings or dividends in order to calculate the cost of equity for the firm. At times, however, estimating earnings or dividends may be difficult. In those circumstances, analysts can estimate the cost of equity according to the security's risk. This approach, called *capital-market estimation,* relies on the concept that investors require additional return to compensate them for risk. This extra return is known as the *risk premium.* The concept can be expressed mathematically thus:

$$R = R_f + R_p \tag{11}$$

where

R = The total return that investors require
R_f = The return on a hypothetical risk-free security
R_p = The risk premium

Several different ways of using this simple concept to estimate the cost of equity have been developed. We will discuss two methods: the stock-bond yield-spread method, and the capital asset pricing model.

The stock-bond yield-spread method. This method calculates cost of equity by means of two key variables: (1) the firm's pre-tax cost of debt and (2) the firm's historic difference between its costs of debt and of equity. Expressed mathematically,

$$R_e = R_d + (\dot{R}_e - \dot{R}_d) \tag{12}$$

where

R_e = The cost of equity
R_d = The current pre-tax cost of debt (the yield to maturity on the firm's bonds)
• = To indicate historic data

Let us use this formula to calculate Consumer's cost of equity. If the historic equity/debt cost difference (the spread) has been 5% and the current pre-tax cost of debt is 12%, we would calculate Consumer's cost of equity in this way:

$$\begin{aligned} R_e &= R_d + (\dot{R}_e - \dot{R}_d) \\ &= 12\% + 5\% \\ &= 17\% \end{aligned}$$

The 17% is close to the cost of equity that we calculated with the dividend discount model. The two methods usually do not yield the same results, however. If they do not, the difference in results may be due to the fact that the difference between the yields of stocks and bonds is not always constant. Exhibit 5–4 shows annual returns on the Standard & Poor's 500 Index and on a high-grade corporate bond index. This exhibit shows that the differences between stock and bond returns are not as constant as the stock-bond yield-spread method would imply. Thus, while this approach provides a quick estimate, it should not be used unless its results are to be verified by another method.

The capital asset pricing model. The simple risk-premium model described by equation (11) could be rewritten to include a term denoting the difference between the average risk of all securities in the market and the risk of one firm's security. We would write the new equation thus:

$$R_{ej} = R_f + x_j (R_m - R_f) \tag{13}$$

where

j = A particular firm
x = A measure of the risk for the particular company's stock
R_m = The return on an asset of average risk
R_f = The return on a hypothetical risk-free security

This formula could also be called the *relative risk premium model,* since it contains a factor, x, to indicate the relative risk of the particular security. All the other factors remain constant from company to company.

EXHIBIT 5-4 Returns on Common Stocks and Bonds

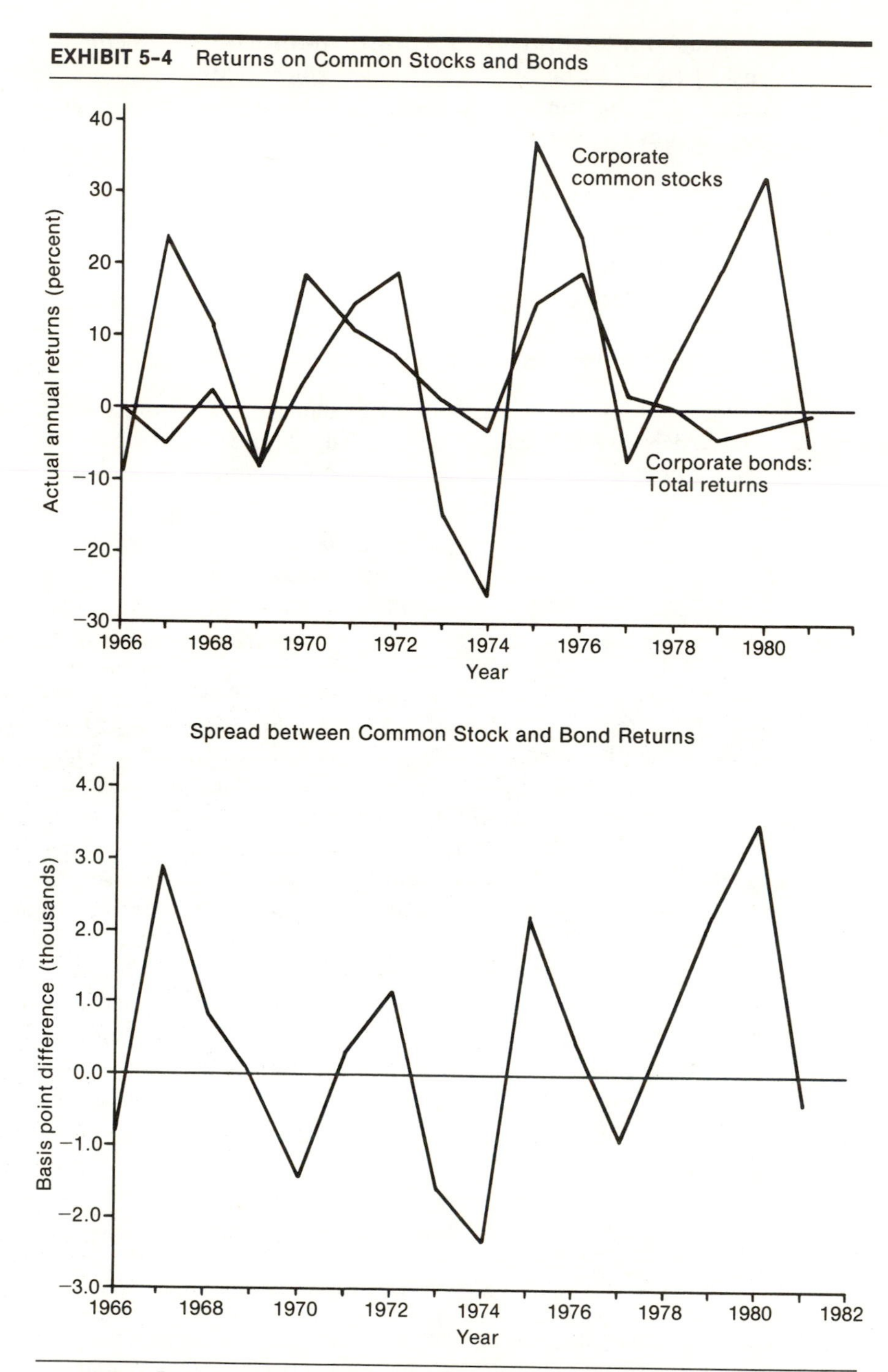

SOURCE: Roger G. Ibbotson and Rex A. Sinquefield, *Stocks, Bonds, Bills, and Inflation,* (Charlottesville, Va.: Financial Analysts Research Foundation, 1982).

EXHIBIT 5–5 Risk/Return Trade-Off

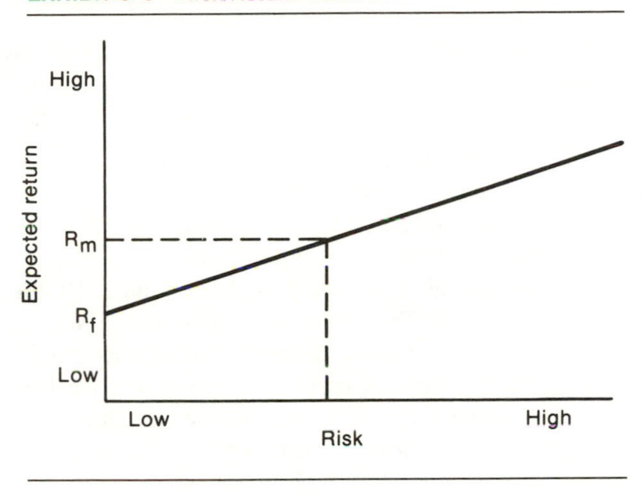

This is a very intriguing adaptation. The model suggests there is a relationship between risk and return; in fact, the higher the risk, the higher the expected return. Exhibit 5–5 depicts this relationship. Since investors require a return for illiquidity, the line starts at R_f, the return required from a riskless security. The solid line represents the return required at each level of risk. This risk/return concept seems quite realistic: investors do expect greater rewards for taking greater risks. However, in order to use this method we must define and measure risk.

The capital asset pricing model (CAPM) is an attempt to make the relative risk premium model usable. In the CAPM, risk is defined as the covariance of a stock's returns with those of an asset of average risk. This definition is a bit different from the usual definition of risk as total variability. Covariance rests on a simple idea: it is not the total variability of the returns of each security that is important to the investor. Instead, it is how each security contributes to the total variability of the investor's portfolio. We could, for instance, place a security with cyclical returns (such as an automobile company's common stock) with a security whose returns are countercyclical (such as an automobile replacement parts manufacturer's common stock). When the auto manufacturer was doing well, the replacement parts manufacturer would be experiencing a slump. The converse would also be true. The resulting returns from the portfolio would be quite stable: that is, they would not be very risky, according to the CAPM's definition of risk.

The only difference between the relative risk premium formula (13) and the CAPM is that the CAPM defines risk as the covariability of stock returns. According to the CAPM,

$$R_{ej} = R_f + \beta_j (R_m - R_f) \quad (14)$$

where

β_j = Beta, a measure of the covariance between the returns (dividends plus capital gains) of a security of average risk and those of the company's stock. All other factors as previously defined.

To estimate Consumer's cost of equity based on this approach, we must estimate the risk-free rate of return, the expected return on the average asset, and the covariability of the returns on Consumer's stock with those on the average asset.[5] To use the CAPM, we need forecasts for R_p, R_m, and β. To demonstrate how the analyst might use the model, we will use 10.2%, which was the return on a 10-year U.S. Treasury note as of June 1, 1985, for R_f; we will use 14.5%, a forecast of the return for the Standard & Poor's 500 Index as estimated by a group of financial analysts, for R_m; and for the covariability, or risk, of Consumer's returns, β_j, we will use 1.5, an estimate based on the historical relationship of the covariability of Consumer's returns with those of the Standard & Poor's 500 Index.[6] Using these estimates, we can calculate Consumer's cost of equity thus:

$$\begin{aligned} R_{ej} &= R_f + \beta_j (R_m - R_f) \\ &= 10.2 + 1.5 (14.5 - 10.2) \\ &= 16.7\% \end{aligned}$$

While in this case the CAPM provides a result that is quite close to those of other methods, this is not always true. The analyst is wise to use several approaches to corroborate any cost-of-equity estimate.

Each of these models requires considerable judgment on the part of the analyst. If the results are approximately the same, the analyst can have more confidence in the estimate. However, if each method results in very different costs of equity, the analyst must think carefully about the source of the variations. The analyst's choice of data could be inconsistent from model to

---

[5]Considerable controversy surrounds the theory and use of the CAPM. The reader should become familiar with the problems before becoming a frequent user. Since these problems are lengthy and complex, they are beyond the scope of this book. See for instance Harrington (1986) for a description of the uses and problems with the CAPM.

[6]The typical method of estimating a beta is to use a version of the simple linear regression ($y = a + bx$) and the monthly total rates of return for the stock and for an index like the S&P 500:

$$R_j - R_f = \alpha_j + \beta_j(R_m - R_f) + \epsilon_j$$

where

α = The intercept of the linear regression
β = The slope of the line
ϵ = The errors that occur because of a nonperfect fit of the line to the data
j = To designate the stock or portfolio

As any financial analyst knows, using history as a predictor for the future is filled with danger. The danger is no less here.

model; the forecasts could be optimistic or pessimistic; or the shareholder's concept of future returns could be quite different from that of the analyst. After careful execution of the model, the analyst must corroborate the forecasts, remembering that the purpose of all forecasts and calculations is to capture the shareholder's expectations of future returns, not management's hopes and beliefs.

3. Other Concerns in Determining Equity Costs

New equity issues. When a firm issues new equity, it incurs additional expenses that we have not yet discussed. The firm issuing new equity must register the issue with the Securities and Exchange Commission, and the firm must rely on the advice of lawyers, accountants, and underwriters to do so. In addition to registering the stock, the underwriter usually buys the issue from the firm, thus guaranteeing its sale. The underwriter then resells the stock to the public—for a fee.[7] The average cost of these services can range from 4% to 15% of the equity issue, depending on the size of the company, the amount of stock to be issued, and the underwriter's confidence that the firm's stock will sell quickly.

Using the dividend discount method (5), we can calculate the cost of newly issued equity by using the following equation. For Consumer, Inc., a small regional company, a new issue would be more expensive than the average stock issue. Let us assume that new issue costs (N) would be 8% for Consumer. We can then calculate the cost of newly issued equity as follows:

$$R_j = \frac{D_1}{P_0(1 - N)} + g \tag{15}$$

$$= \frac{.40}{15.00(1 - .08)} + 14.0\%$$

$$= \frac{.40}{13.80} + 14.0\%$$

$$= 2.9\% + 14.0\%$$

$$= 16.9\%$$

To maintain the value of Consumer, Inc., the newly issued equity funds would have to be invested at a slightly higher return than would retained earnings because newly issued common stock has the additional cost of issuance to be covered.

Cost of retained earnings. Each year a firm can generate net income after taxes and dividends (retained earnings). Managers may use these

[7]For a smaller fee the underwriter may make a best effort to sell the stocks or bonds. In a "best-efforts" sale, the underwriter does not guarantee the sale of the securities.

funds to increase the firm's assets or to reduce its debt, or the funds may be held temporarily in cash or marketable securities. Some managers consider retained earnings to be "free" funds, but that is certainly not true from the stockholders' point of view. If managers had returned the funds to the stockholders, the stockholders could have invested the funds themselves. Thus, retained earnings have a cost—the cost of the opportunity that the shareholders lose when funds are retained by the firm.

In exchange for this opportunity cost, stockholders expect retained earnings to create value for them. Thus, the cost of retaining earnings is the cost of equity.

Preferred stock. Preferred stock also causes additional problems because preferred stock is a cross between debt and equity. Like debt, preferred stock offers a fixed payment—fixed dividends. In bankruptcy, preferred shareholders take precedence over common shareholders. However, if the preferred dividends are not paid, the firm cannot be forced into bankruptcy as it may be if it fails to pay the interest on debt. For investors, owning preferred equity is somewhat less risky than holding common stock and more risky than being a lender. Preferred stock is also unlike debt in that the firm does not have to repay the principal amount.

We can calculate the cost of preferred stock as follows:

$$R_p = \frac{PD}{PP_o} \tag{16}$$

where

PD = Preferred dividend
PP_o = Preferred stock price
R_p = The cost or return required on preferred stock

Consumer, Inc., had a very small amount of preferred stock that had been issued when it was founded. It has subsequently been repurchased by the firm. At the time of the repurchase, the dividend was \$1.30 per share per year, and the market price was \$9.25 per share. The cost of preferred at the time it was retired can be calculated thus:

$$R_p = \frac{\$1.30}{9.25}$$

$$= .140 \text{ or } 14\%$$

Once again, there would be no tax adjustment because preferred dividends are not a tax-deductible expense.

IV. CALCULATING THE WEIGHTED AVERAGE COST OF CAPITAL

Our intention in this chapter was to calculate the weighted average cost of new or marginal capital. This weighted average can be calculated by multiplying the cost of debt and the cost of equity by the respective portions of debt and equity to be raised by the firm. In other words,

$$R_a = R_d \frac{D}{V} + R_e \frac{E}{V} \tag{17}$$

where

R_a = Weighted average cost of capital
D = Amount of debt in the firm's capital structure
E = Amount of equity in the firm's capital structure
$V = D + E$
R_d = After-tax cost of debt
R_e = Cost of equity

Thus far, we have calculated R_d (7.2%) and estimated R_e (approximately 16.7%) for Consumer, Inc., but we have not yet estimated the proportion of debt, D/V, or equity, E/V, used by the firm.

While calculating the amounts of debt and equity used to finance the firm might appear to be quite simple, it is, like most of the analyst's jobs, not completely straightforward. The capital structure that we want to use in calculating the weighted average cost of capital is the marginal or "target" capital structure—that capital structure wherein sufficient capital is raised to finance all value-creating investments. For some firms, this target capital structure is one where the cost of capital is at its minimum. For other firms, the target capital structure reflects the managers' decision to keep the proportion of debt to equity within a certain range.

For simplicity, let's assume for a moment that Consumer, Inc.'s current book-value capital structure is the same as its market-value and target capital structures. The book-value capital structure is the percentage of debt and equity currently financing the assets of the firm. It can be calculated directly from the balance sheet. The market-value capital structure is calculated by taking the current market values of the company's debt and equity and recalculating the same percentages. In Consumer's book-value capital structure, 65% of the capital is equity and 35% is debt. We will also assume that the managers expect to have $250,000 in new retained earnings for the year. Since 65% of the capital structure is equity, the maximum funds available for investment are $384,000 ($250,000/.65 = $384,000) unless new equity is issued. If the Consumer management plans capital expenditures of no more than $384,000, then the cost of capital will be 14.4%, as shown in Exhibit 5–6.

If Consumer needs more than $384,000 to finance its capital budget and to keep the capital structure at the targeted proportion of 65% equity, it will have to resort to newly issued stock to finance an increasing portion of the needs. Thus, if the budget is $1 million, because of the costs of issuing new equity, the cost of capital will be slightly higher, as shown in Exhibit 5–7. Similar changes would have to be made whenever Consumer, Inc., had fully exploited any source of debt or equity and had to resort to the next available, but more expensive, source.

We made this example especially easy by assuming that the book value (the balance sheet value), the market value (the balance sheet value recalculated using the market values of securities), and management's target capital

EXHIBIT 5-6 Weighted Average Cost of Capital (up to $384,000)

(1) Component	*(2) Proportion*	*(3) Cost*	*(4) (2) × (3)*
Debt (taxes = 40%)	35%	7.2%	2.5%
Equity:			
Retained earnings	65	16.7	10.9
New common equity	0	16.9	0
Weighted average cost of capital			13.4%

EXHIBIT 5-7 Weighted Average Cost of New Capital ($1 million budget)

(1) Component	*(2) Proportion*	*(3) Cost*	*(4) (2) × (3)*
Debt (taxes = 40%)	35%	7.2%	2.5%
Equity:			
Retained earnings ($250,000)	25	16.7	4.2
New common equity	40	16.9	6.8
Weighted average cost of capital			13.5%

structure were all the same. If they were not, we would use the market value of the new capital being raised to calculate the proportions of debt and equity.[8] It is not appropriate to use either book value or market value if they differ from the target for the funds being raised.

Once again, we have a deceptively simple calculation. A firm in need of capital usually does not simultaneously issue debt and equity securities just to fit its target capital structure. Rather, the firm would issue first one and then the other depending on prices and availability in the capital markets. Over time, however, the firm would issue sufficient debt and equity to meet its targeted capital structure. Thus, while the actual capital raised in a single year might be all equity and its cost higher than the average, we would use the weighted average cost of capital as the return required for any project that is of the same risk as the firm. For investments where the risk is not equal to that of the firm, adjustments such as those described in Chapter 4 would be necessary.

V. SUMMARY

In estimating the weighted average cost of marginal capital, the analyst's judgment is required again and again. The cost of equity is elusive: we are

[8]While many firms use their book-value structure as the target, as analysts we are concerned with the market value of the marginal capital raised. If the target is the same as the book-value capital structure, the market value of the capital raised will be in the same proportions as the book value, regardless of the market value of the capital already in use by the firm.

trying to estimate what investors expect from owning a share of our firm. While we have several approaches that will help the analyst make the estimate, each must be used thoughtfully. Furthermore, as the conditions in the world and domestic economy change, the capital markets react, and investors' expectations change—sometimes quite rapidly. When these changes occur, the firm itself may change—new projects are announced, old projects succeed or fail. Once again investors' expectations change, and so will their required return on equity. The analyst must not only estimate an elusive figure but do so at the same time as that figure is changing. Skill and judgment take the financial analyst's job beyond the mechanical and the routine, making it a continual challenge.

SELECTED REFERENCES

For general information about the stock and bond markets, see:

Fogler, H. Russell. *Analyzing the Stock Market.* Columbus, Ohio: Grid, 1978.

Sharpe, William F. *Investments.* 3d ed. Englewood Cliffs, N.J.: Prentice-Hall, 1985.

For further explanations of the process and problems in calculating the costs of debt and equity, see:

Brealey, Richard, and Stewart Myers. *Principles of Corporate Finance.* 2d ed. New York: McGraw-Hill, 1984, chap. 9.

Solomon, Ezra, and John J. Pringle. *An Introduction to Financial Management.* 2d ed. Santa Monica, Calif.: Goodyear Publishing, 1980.

Weston, J. F., and E. F. Brigham. *Managerial Finance.* 7th ed. Hinsdale, Ill.: Dryden Press, 1981.

For those with a further interest in the capital asset pricing model and discounted cash-flow methods of equity valuation, see:

Brealey, Richard, and Stewart Myers. *Principles of Corporate Finance.* 2d ed. New York: McGraw-Hill, 1984, chaps. 4 and 8.

Harrington, Diana R. *Modern Portfolio Theory, The Capital Asset Pricing Model and Arbitrage Pricing Theory: A Users Guide.* 2d ed. Englewood Cliffs, N.J.: Prentice-Hall, 1986.

For historic data from the stock and bond markets and information about comparable firms, see:

Dun & Bradstreet, *Key Business Ratios.*

Ibbotson, Roger G., and Rex A. Sinquefield. *Stocks, Bonds, Bills and Inflation.* Charlottesville, Va.: Financial Analysts Research Foundation, 1982.

Robert Morris Associates, *Annual Statement Studies.*

Arnold Bernhard & Co., Inc., *Value Line Investment Survey.*

STUDY QUESTION

1. The Kauph Company was in the process of developing a discount rate to evaluate the capital projects which had been proposed for the following year. The com-

pany, with net income of $504,000 in 1984, had been growing steadily, with both sales and earnings increasing at about 10% per year. The firm's return on equity had also been fairly constant at about 12% per year. Absent any change in the company's strategy, these trends were expected to continue into the future. At the end of 1984, the Kauph Company had an A bond rating. Debt on the balance sheet had been issued at an average rate of 10%. Long-term A-rated bonds were currently being sold at 11.75%. Kauph's stock was selling for $18.50; 300,000 shares were outstanding; and the company consistently paid out 24% of earnings in dividends. Because of its steady growth and performance, Kauph's returns were estimated to have a Beta of 0.98.

Based on the data given below compute the company's marginal weighted average cost of capital using:

a. The dividend discount model, where g = (1 – Payout)(ROE).
b. The stock-bond yield-spread method.
c. The capital asset pricing model (six-month Treasury bills were selling for around 8.5% and the expected market return was 16%).

	1983	*1984*	*1985 (projected)*
Profit after tax (42% tax rate)	$ 458,182	$ 504,000	$ 554,400
Earnings per share	$1.52	$1.68	$1.85
End-of-year market price/share	$15.20	$18.50	$18.50
Current assets	$2,255,665	$2,383,661	$2,729,354
Net long-term assets	4,793,289	5,305,569	5,799,876
Total assets	$7,048,954	$7,689,230	$8,529,230
Current liabilities	$1,174,826	$1,227,692	$1,421,538
Long-term debt	2,055,945	2,261,538	2,487,692
Common stock ($5 par value)	1,500,000	1,500,000	1,500,000
Retained earnings	2,318,185	2,700,000	3,120,000
Total long-term debt and equity	$5,874,128	$6,461,538	$7,107,692
Total liabilities and equity	$7,048,954	$7,689,230	$8,529,230

Financing Capital Requirements

A frequently stated and probably universally accepted goal of a company's management is to maximize the value of the company to its investors. Value, in this case, is the total market value of the company's securities. Typically, the securities are grouped into the two categories discussed in Chapter 5: equity, which consists of common and preferred stock, and debt. The total market value is the sum of the value of all the securities owned by investors in the company.

It has been satisfactorily demonstrated that the value of the securities is related to the earnings and cash flow of the company. Thus, investors are essentially purchasing a claim on the earnings or cash flow stream of a company when they invest in it. The debt holders have a senior claim on a company's assets and are paid a fixed return through interest charges. The residual earnings, or cash flows, accrue to the equity owners, with the preferred stock owners having a senior or preferred position.

Because of this earnings/cash flow/value relationship, managers trying to create or increase the value of a company have focused primarily on the earnings and cash flow stream. The assumption is that, through alterations in the cash flows and earnings of the company, the value of the company can be increased. This concept has been discussed in the chapters on working-capital management and capital budgeting.

This focus on the earnings/cash flow stream was emphasized by a series of studies that commenced in the late 1950s with a study by Modigliani and Miller. These studies suggested that the value of a company was related only to its earnings/cash flow stream and was independent of the nature of the securities used to provide the financing. The total market value of the company was hypothesized to be determined by the expected return on assets (earnings before interest) and the riskiness of the earnings stream.

These hypotheses countered the traditional approach to capital structure which held that the total market value of the company was affected by the capital structure. The traditionalists maintained that the stream of earnings/cash flows could be sold to investors in several different packages and that the alternatives chosen could result in different market valuations and costs of capital for the company.

The theoretical work by Modigliani and Miller did propose that the capital structure could affect the market valuation of the company because of the tax environment. Since interest costs in the United States are currently tax-deductible, the after-tax cost of debt is significantly lower than the after-tax cost of equity. Because of the difference in tax treatment between interest and equity costs, Modigliani and Miller contended that it is advantageous for companies to substitute debt for equity, thereby increasing the leverage. They hypothesized that companies could maximize their market value by maximizing the use of debt financing.

The extreme of this position would be a company with 100% debt financing. Modigliani and Miller and others realized that this would not be feasible. As companies increase their debt financing, they also increase the risk of bankruptcy. Thus, the interest costs charged as well as the expected return by equity investors would increase: these higher bankruptcy costs begin to offset the tax benefits of higher leverage at some point.

The issue is to determine the point where the costs of increased leverage begin to reduce the benefits of substituting the lower cost debt for higher cost equity. Despite three decades of research, academicians and practitioners have not been able to satisfactorily demonstrate how to assess this optimal point. The view that the capital structure does influence the market value of the company is still generally held, however. Thus, the financial manager has the task of attempting to find the optimal capital structure—one that maximizes the value of the company and, thereby, minimizes the cost of capital.

I. DEBT CAPACITY AND DEBT POLICY

In assessing what the optimal debt level should be, managers must recognize that the use of any debt brings some risks. Because debt entails contractual obligations to make cash payments for interest and principal, the company incurs the risk that there will be insufficient cash available. Obviously, the greater the leverage, the higher this financial risk will be. While this high leverage might lower the cost of capital for the company, it also places the company in risk of bankruptcy or insolvency.

To ensure that the company can remain solvent, the cash availability should be evaluated. The company should determine what cash is available to service the debt obligations. This cash availability then provides a limit on the amount that a company should borrow. A company that takes on financial obligations in excess of its ability to service them is courting disaster.

During good times with a steady predictable cash flow, companies are not likely to encounter financial difficulties. It is during the "down" times when the cash flow is reduced that problems are encountered. Thus, the cash flow determinant of debt serviceability should be developed based on scenarios of cash shortage.

The factors that might lead to a cash shortage will be different for each firm. For some companies, an unusual demand for its products and the resulting need for cash to finance growth might be the downside scenario. For other companies, an economic recession with a decline in sales might cause cash problems. Whatever the case, the company should examine the cash flows under the maximum likely cash shortfall to determine its ability to meet the debt payments and remain solvent.

There may be actions that a company can take to free up cash during these difficult periods. For example, during a recession a company might postpone capital investments. If the problem is caused by too rapid growth, the company might decide to reduce its credit terms and decrease accounts receivable. After evaluating the impact of all of these alternatives, the company can then determine how much cash would be available to pay the debt obligations. The amount of debt that this cash could service should establish a company's debt limit or debt capacity.

Companies may decide to borrow less than their capacity. Capital structures based on absolute debt capacity might minimize insolvency risks, but they may not maximize the value of the company. The actual leverage the company decides to obtain is termed the debt policy. Whereas the debt capacity is determined by the ability of the company to service the debt, the debt policy is determined by the market reaction. The objective of debt policy is to maximize the market value of the company by minimizing the cost of capital.

The manager must consider all of the risks and returns in determining the appropriate mix of debt and equity. In some ways, this is a marketing problem in that the manager is faced with several different products, the company's financial securities, and several different markets, the potential investors in the company. The financial manager must match the securities with the investors in a way that creates the greatest value for the company. He or she does so by analyzing the potential results of the various financing alternatives on the total market value of the company.

II. FRICTO ANALYSIS

A convenient framework for analyzing the many different factors that affect the capital-structure decision is provided by the acronym FRICTO. The initials represent major factors that the manager should consider.

F—Flexibility
R—Risk
I—Income
C—Control
T—Timing
O—Other

These factors are not listed in order of priority or importance. For each firm, and in different economic environments, the relative importance of the various factors will differ. However, the manager should ensure that they have all been analyzed.

The analytical process is an art rather than a science. The manager must interpret and judge the results. It is not a strictly mechanical process in which computational abilities can be substituted for analytical skill.

For this reason, the analytical process can be best explained through a specific example. We will describe the HTI Company's decision about whether to finance a $60 million production-capacity expansion through a public equity offering or through a privately placed debt issue.

HTI Company designed and manufactured precision testing and measurement instruments. The company had been a leader for many years in the field of precision, high technology, and instruments and had experienced recent rapid growth in sales. This increase was caused by two primary factors.

First, the entire testing and measurement instrument industry was experiencing increased sales growth as a result of the recent development of new digital, microprocessor-controlled instruments. These new instruments were easier to use, more accurate, more reliable, and more adaptable than previous instruments. This new generation of instruments was leading to a demand to replace older equipment and also to an expansion of the primary market for the newer instruments.

Second, HTI Company had developed a line of new process-control instruments based on their testing and measurement instruments. This new line of equipment was gaining rapid market acceptance because of its innovative, patented design that provided more accurate control than competitive equipment.

The company had been operating with some excess production capacity; however, the sales increases were now beginning to tax the ability of the company to meet the growing demand. HTI Company projected an annual increase of sales of at least 20% for the coming five years. On the basis of these projections, senior managers believed that $60 million of financing would be required for working capital and production-capacity expansion.

In early March 1985, the 2.4 million shares of common stock outstanding were trading at about $79.00 per share. The company's investment bankers stated that HTI Company would not have any difficulty selling the required new equity. They believed that the company would be able to sell 800,000 new shares at a net price of about $75 per share.

HTI Company's other alternative was a private placement of 15-year senior debentures with a group of insurance companies. It was expected that the interest rate on the debt would be about 14.75%. The debentures would not be callable, although there would be a sinking-fund requirement, beginning in the fifth year, which would amortize the $60 million principal by the last year of the loan.

The historic income statements and balance sheets for the HTI Company are shown in Exhibits 6–1 and 6–2. Exhibit 6–3 compares the perfor-

EXHIBIT 6-1

HTI COMPANY
Income Statements
(in millions)

	1980	*1981*	*1982*	*1983*	*1984*
Sales	$175.8	$181.1	$193.2	$246.0	$297.1
Other income	1.0	1.0	1.2	1.2	1.4
Total revenue	176.8	182.1	194.4	247.2	298.5
Expenses:					
Manufacturing costs	134.4	139.8	150.6	190.0	221.1
Depreciation	4.2	4.2	4.3	4.3	5.8
Sales and administrative expenses	16.2	17.2	18.0	23.6	29.1
Earnings before interest and taxes	22.0	20.9	21.5	29.3	42.5
Interest	1.2	2.1	2.2	2.2	3.9
Income taxes	10.4	9.4	9.5	13.0	18.1
Net profit	$ 10.4	$ 9.4	$ 9.8	$ 14.1	$ 20.5

EXHIBIT 6-2

HTI COMPANY
Balance Sheets
(in millions)

	1980	*1981*	*1982*	*1983*	*1984*
Assets					
Cash	$ 5.3	$ 4.9	$ 5.0	$ 5.3	$ 5.1
Accounts receivable	16.5	16.0	18.6	21.3	25.4
Inventories	53.2	57.2	61.0	73.8	107.6
Prepaid expenses	.4	.4	.6	.4	.4
Total current assets	75.4	78.5	85.2	100.8	138.5
Investment	11.9	12.3	10.8	9.7	10.8
Property, plant, and equipment	60.7	60.4	64.2	69.5	80.3
Less: Accumulated depreciation	35.8	40.0	44.3	48.6	54.4
Net fixed assets	24.9	20.4	19.9	20.9	25.9
Total assets	$112.2	$111.2	$115.9	$131.4	$175.2
Liabilities and Equity					
Accounts payable	$ 7.8	$ 6.2	$ 8.6	$ 10.6	$ 15.6
Notes payable	8.5	10.0	—	1.0	23.3
Current portion, long-term debt	1.0	1.0	.8	.8	.8
Taxes and other liabilities	11.4	6.5	.7	6.2	6.7
Total current liabilities	28.7	23.7	10.1	18.6	46.4
Long-term debt	8.6	7.0	19.4	17.9	21.6
Equity	74.9	80.5	86.4	94.9	107.2
Total liabilities and equity	$112.2	$111.2	$115.9	$131.4	$175.2

EXHIBIT 6-3 HTI Company, Common Stock Data

Year	Average Stock Price	Earnings per Share	Dividends per Share	Price-Earnings Ratio	Composite S&P 500 Index*
1980	$34.94	$4.33	$1.75	8.1	118.8
1981	35.55	3.92	1.55	9.1	128.1
1982	32.15	4.09	1.60	7.9	119.7
1983	42.93	5.88	2.35	7.3	160.4
1984	67.88	8.54	3.40	8.0	160.4
Period ending:					
January 1985	72.63	8.54	3.40	8.5	179.6
February 1985	78.50	8.54	3.40	9.2	181.2

Note: 2 million shares outstanding on February 28, 1985.
*Standard & Poor's Composite Index of 500 Common Stocks, 1941-43 = 10.

mance of the common stock for HTI Company with overall market prices. Using the FRICTO framework, let's analyze the alternatives.

1. Flexibility

Every company wants to be able to raise capital quickly to fund unforeseen needs—to be flexible. These unforeseen needs could arise from several different events—competitors' actions, changes in economic activity, fire or other casualty losses, disruption in supply of raw materials, governmental regulations, and many others. The problem with these situations is that the company is not able to forecast the timing or the magnitude of such catastrophic occurrences. Thus, the financial manager must prepare in advance to deal with these situations, usually by maintaining a financing reserve.

This financing reserve is much like an insurance policy. The company estimates the magnitude of the potential events and their impact on the company and then decides on the appropriate amount of insurance or financial reserve. For a company that sees itself as exposed to very few or relatively minor external uncertainties, a small reserve may be sufficient. On the other hand, companies that face great uncertainty may want to ensure that sufficient financing is available to fund the company in times of great need.

Each company is unique in its exposure to external uncertainties, and each must determine individually its appropriate level of financial flexibility. The process of estimating the amount of required flexibility is not an easy task for managers. They are expected to determine the impact of events that may not have previously occurred.

One approach to ascertaining the needed flexibility is to ask the question, "What is the worst sequence of events that could happen?" Then, using this disaster scenario as a basis, managers can assess the likelihood of its occurrence and its impact on the company's need for funds. Managers can then consider a series of scenarios that are less disastrous but more likely to occur. After assessing the external financing requirements for each scenario, the managers can then determine how much risk, the probability of exhausting available funds, they are willing to assume. They can then determine how much financial reserve to maintain.

HTI managers initially projected a combination of events as their disaster scenario: a worldwide depression limiting overall demand for their products, a severe shortage of the semiconductor components for their products, and the introduction of a new technology by their competitors.

The first two problems were probably mutually exclusive: because of shrinking demand, a worldwide depression would probably lead to an oversupply of semiconductors. Additionally, the lead time for technological changes was large enough so that they would not have to respond immediately. Thus, HTI's managers concluded that a more likely scenario was one where competitors reduced prices to maintain or increase their market share. HTI's management concluded that a significant amount of additional outside capital would be required from external sources if this occurred—about $40 million. In fact, the probability of price cutting was small enough that a $40 million reserve was unwarranted; $20 million would be sufficient. Since these funds might be needed quickly, the reserve should be in more rapidly available debt.

If they raised the full $60 million they needed by issuing equity now, they would retain their flexibility: with additional equity in the company, the $20 million in debt would be more readily available. By borrowing the $60 million, the company might find it difficult to borrow the $20 million later. Thus, an immediate equity issue retained HTI's flexibility.

2. Risk

Risk is similar to flexibility in making a capital-structure decision. The primary difference is one of definition. Risk is defined as those events that management can foresee, the events that management can predict and perhaps has already experienced. Flexibility deals with the unknowns.

The most common source of risk is the impact of business cycles. Cyclical expansions and contractions strain the ability of the company to service product demand, to maintain proper inventories, and to control its resources adequately. These strains are best demonstrated in the effect on the cash flow of the company. As economic conditions change, the company will be pressed to find adequate cash flow to meet all of its obligations.

In addition to the problems caused by business cycles, companies face other types of risks. For instance, in some industries, strikes occur with almost the same regularity as business cycles. These disruptions cause problems for the companies being struck as well as for their suppliers and customers. There are other foreseeable problems, such as periodic market gluts and shortages of basic raw materials, that can affect particular industries or companies. In each of these situations, the ability of the company to marshal its cash resources is critical. Since the company meets its various obligations with cash, cash becomes the important measure of the company's ability to survive. While earnings may be important, earnings figures are the result of accounting conventions and must be converted into cash to service debt, pay dividends, and meet payrolls and other obligations.

One measure of the company's ability to meet its cash obligations is the *coverage ratios,* which were described in Chapter 1. These ratios focus on the relationship between a company's fixed obligations, primarily debt service, and the resources it has available to meet them. Obviously, the higher the coverage, the lower the risk. Let's look at HTI and it's coverage ratios.

In 1984, the HTI Company's coverage ratios were very high. For example, the earnings before interest and taxes (EBIT) were significantly in excess of the interest expense (I).

$$\text{Earnings interest coverage} = \frac{\text{EBIT}}{\text{I}} = \frac{\$42.5}{\$3.9} = 10.9$$

This ratio means that the company was covering its interest obligations with earnings by about 11 times. This afforded the company a considerable safety margin if earnings fell.

Because interest must be paid with cash, cash flow coverage may be a more meaningful ratio. Since for an outside analyst cash flow figures can be difficult to obtain, an approximation of the cash flow-to-interest ratio uses earnings before interest and taxes (EBIT) combined with the depreciation.

$$\text{Cash flow interest coverage} = \frac{\text{EBIT} + \text{Depreciation}}{\text{I}} = \frac{\$42.5 + \$5.8}{\$3.9} = 12.4$$

Using this cash flow approximation, HTI's coverage of the interest expense increases.

However, interest expense is not the only element of debt service. The company must also meet any sinking-fund requirements. Since the sinking fund is paid from after-tax funds, the payment must be adjusted to a before-tax basis. Because HTI Company paid an effective tax rate of about 47%, each \$1.00 of sinking funds required earnings before taxes of \$1.89, or \$1.00/(1.0 − Tax rate).

$$\text{Cash flow debt service coverage} = \frac{\text{EBIT} + \text{Depreciation}}{\text{Interest} + [\text{Sinking fund}/(1 - \text{Tax rate})]} = \frac{\$42.5 + \$5.8}{\$3.9 + (\$.8/.53)} = 8.9$$

Even including the sinking-fund requirements, the company still had a healthy debt service coverage.

HTI Company had consistently maintained a dividend payment, and management believed that the dividend payment was important to shareholders and should not be altered except under dire circumstances. Since the dividend on common stock is paid after taxes, the dividend payment must also be adjusted to a before-tax basis.

$$\text{Cash flow contractual payment coverage} = \frac{\text{EBIT} + \text{Depreciation}}{\text{I} + [(\text{SF} + \text{DIV})/(1 - \text{Tax rate})]}$$

$$= \frac{\$42.5 + \$5.8}{\$3.9 + [(\$.8 + \$8.2)/.53]}$$

$$= 2.3$$

If HTI had other major contractual payments, for instance lease payments, they could also be included in calculating this ratio. Including the dividend payment significantly reduces the coverage ratio. The dividend payment, however, is a discretionary item and could be omitted in times of financial stress.

Although this analysis suggests that HTI Company has had sufficient coverage against past risks, the critical question is, how will the two financing alternatives change the future risk? To compare HTI's two financing alternatives, let us assume that the EBIT would increase as projected at 20% per year to $51 million in 1985 and that depreciation expense over the same period would increase by 20% to $7 million.

Common stock alternative. If HTI Company maintains the $3.40 dividend per share and if the interest expense and sinking-fund payments remain the same as they were in 1984, their projected coverage for 1985 would be:

$$\begin{array}{c}\text{Forecasted cash flow}\\ \text{contractual payment coverage}\end{array} = \frac{\text{EBIT} + \text{Depreciation}}{\text{I} + [(\text{SF} + \text{DIV})/(1 - \text{Tax rate})]}$$

$$= \frac{\$51 + \$7}{\$3.9 + [(\$.8 + \$10.9)/.53]}$$

$$= 2.2$$

Debt alternative. Assuming that dividends remain at $3.40 per share and that the interest on the $60 million of debt is 14.75% and the debt is outstanding for the entire year, the coverage for 1985 would be:

$$\begin{array}{c}\text{Forecasted cash flow}\\ \text{contractual payment coverage}\end{array} = \frac{\text{EBIT} + \text{Depreciation}}{\text{Old I} + \text{New I} + [(\text{SF} + \text{Div})/(1 - \text{Tax rate})]}$$

$$= \frac{\$51 + \$7}{\$3.9 + \$8.9 + [(\$.8 + \$8.2)/.53]}$$

$$= 1.9$$

Regardless of the alternative chosen, the HTI Company will be somewhat more risky in 1985 than it was in 1984. Common stock financing provides slightly better coverage for 1985, and since the interest charges and sinking-fund payments for the debt alternative will change in future years, additional coverage ratios for future years should be calculated as well. However, if the assumption of a constant dividend is maintained, the equity alternative will continue to provide slightly better coverage.

It is also important to note that these calculations provide only an approximation of the cash available to service obligations during an adverse cycle. The company may be able to generate additional cash internally through astute management of inventories, accounts payable, accounts receivable, and capital expenditures. Thus, cash could increase during periods of declining sales and decline during periods of increasing sales. This, in fact, is what most companies have discovered. The critical factor for the management of a company is to identify the economic situation and to respond quickly to minimize any adverse impact that the situation may have on the cash position of the company.

In calculating the coverage of the sinking-fund requirements, we assumed implicitly that the debt in the company would not be replaced or refinanced. An argument can be made that debt is, and should be, a permanent part of the capital structure of the company. In this case, sinking funds would be continually refunded rather than retired. If this is the strategy, then sinking-fund requirements would not be included in the coverage calculations.

3. Income

One of the obvious impacts on shareholder value is income and changes in income. If a particular form of financing increases the riskiness of the firm, this risk should be offset by increased income. New funds are generally invested in productive assets, with the benefits from the investments accruing to the investors. Since the debtholders have a fixed, although senior, claim, the residual benefits belong to the common shareholders. That is why management should analyze the income or value from the shareholders' point of view. Such an analysis is also consistent with the concept that management should maximize the value for the shareholders.

In determining the impact that the financing decision will have on the income of the shareholders, two general costs need to be considered: first, the explicit cost of the financing, the impact on the earnings per share; and second, the implicit cost, or the impact on the market price of the stock.

Earnings per share impact. To determine the explicit cost, as reflected in the earnings per share of the HTI Company, managers estimate the effects that each of the financing alternatives would have on the company's earnings per share. This analysis is similar to the coverage analysis that was undertaken to estimate the impact of risk on the company. The analysis starts with the assumption that the earnings before interest and taxes will be the same, regardless of the method used to finance the company, and that earnings are a good proxy for the value the investor will obtain.

Comparing the impact of the two alternatives indicates that the common stock alternative would result in a lower earnings per share figure for the forecast 1985 period. Although the total earnings for HTI have increased to $25 million from $20.2 million, the additional shares have diluted the impact of increased earnings on individual shares. Each owner now holds a smaller piece of the pie, although the total size of the pie has increased. The reduced earnings per share is a common occurrence since the additional common stock dilutes the benefits of stock ownership. (See Exhibit 6-4.)

The comparison between the effects of the financing is often shown graphically. Exhibit 6-5 shows this comparison, known as an *EBIT chart,* for the HTI Company. Each line shows the earnings per share for a financing alternative given different EBIT levels. Since the relationships are linear, it is only necessary to determine two points to plot each of the lines. Typically, analysts determine the breakeven point—that is, the EBIT level where the earnings per share figures are equivalent for the financing alternatives—in addition to one other point. For HTI, at any EBIT level above $39.5 million, the debt alternative will provide greater earnings per share. The earnings per share (EPS) at the breakeven point are $5.91.

$$\frac{(EBIT - I_n - I_o)(1 - t) - P}{CS_d} = \frac{(EBIT - I_n - I_o)(1 - t) - P}{CS_e}$$

where

- $EBIT$ = Breakeven EBIT level
- I_o = Interest payments on old debt
- I_n = Interest payments on new debt
- t = Tax rate
- P = Preferred dividends applicable to the alternative under consideration
- CS_d = The number of common shares outstanding with the debt alternative
- CS_e = The number of common shares outstanding with the equity alternative

Assuming that the preferred dividends are the same under either alternative and that no additional interest costs are incurred with the equity alternative, the breakeven formula can be solved for the EBIT level as follows:

$$EBIT = \frac{(CS_d \times I_o) - (CS_e \times I_o) - (CS_e \times I_n)}{CS_d - CS_e} + \frac{P}{(1 - t)}$$

Although it would appear that the debt financing is preferable, it is important to consider that HTI surpassed the breakeven EBIT and EPS levels only in the last year, 1984. Although debt financing does provide higher EPS for the projected growth range of the company, HTI Company has recently passed the point at which debt financing would have resulted in lower earnings per share.

EXHIBIT 6-4 HTI Company, Impact of Financing on Earnings per Share ($ millions except per share data)

Common stock alternative:	
Estimated 1985 EBIT	$51.0
Less current interest costs	3.9
Estimated 1985 profit before taxes	47.1
Less taxes @ 47%	22.1
Estimated 1985 net profit	$25.0
Number of original shares	2.4
Plus number of new shares issued	.8
Total number of outstanding shares	3.2
Estimated 1985 earnings/stock financing	$7.81/per share
Debt alternative:	
Estimated 1985 EBIT	$51.0
Less current interest costs	3.9
Less new interest costs (assume full year)	8.9
Estimated 1985 profit before taxes	38.2
Less taxes @ 47%	18.0
Estimated 1985 net profit	$20.2
Number of outstanding shares	2.4
Estimated 1985 earnings/debt financing	$8.42/per share

The EBIT chart demonstrates the results of leverage. As can be seen, the slope of the debt-financing line is greater than the slope of the common-stock-financing line. This means that, for the same growth in EBIT, the growth in earnings per share under debt financing exceeds the growth in earnings per share with stock financing. This increased rate of change is the primary advantage of utilizing leverage, or increased debt, in financing the firm. The greater the difference in the slopes of the two lines, the greater the relative change and the greater the effect of the leverage.

Although our focus has been on the benefits of leverage, it is important to note that, below the breakeven point, leverage works against the shareholders. When the EBIT falls below this point, the impact of the leverage will be reversed, and the shareholders will suffer.

Dilution also affects the dividends per share. On the basis of a dividend payout of 40% of earnings, HTI Company would expect to pay the following 1985 dividends:

	Common Stock Alternative	*Debt Alternative*
Estimated 1985 EBIT	$51.0 million	$51.0 million
Estimated 1985 net profit	$25.0	$20.2
Estimated 1985 dividends @ 40% of profit	$10.0	$ 8.1
Number of shares outstanding	3.2	2.4
Estimated 1985 dividends per share	$ 3.13	$ 3.37

EXHIBIT 6–5 EPS-EBIT Chart, HTI Company

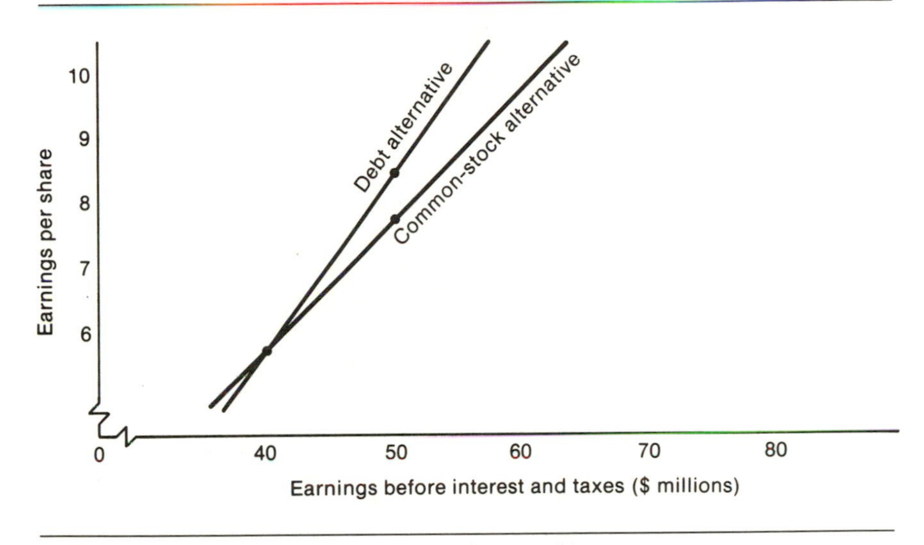

Just as it affected earnings per share, the dilution caused by the added shares reduces the estimated dividends per share. For both of the financing alternatives, the EBIT is expected to increase by 20%, yet the estimated dividends per share (DPS) would be lower than the actual 1984 dividends. This decrease is caused by the interest cost associated with the debt financing or by the dilution associated with the common-stock financing. This relationship between the dividends per share (DPS) for the common-stock financing and those under debt financing is graphed in Exhibit 6–6. The result is similar to the EPS-EBIT chart we drew for HTI.

Under normal circumstances, the cost of the debt alternative is lower than the cost of the common-stock alternative because of dilution. However, with the debt financing, there may be some implicit or hidden costs that make debt more expensive and reduce its value to the shareholders.

Market value impact. Since the value to the shareholders consists of dividends and changes in the market value or stock price, the impact that new financing has on the market price should be considered. However, for most companies, the dividend income is a relatively small percentage of the changes in the total value, and price changes are of greater importance.

Stock analysts commonly relate the market price to the earnings per share through the price-earnings ratio or earnings multiple. The PE ratio is believed to capture the investor's expectations about growth and risk. If the PE ratio remains constant, then the change in the market price of the stock would be a direct result of the change in earnings per share. With a constant PE ratio, the financing alternative that causes the least dilution (in other words, that requires the fewest number of shares outstanding) will generate

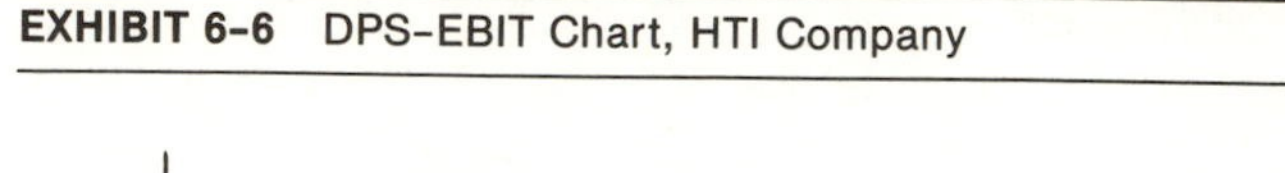

EXHIBIT 6-6 DPS-EBIT Chart, HTI Company

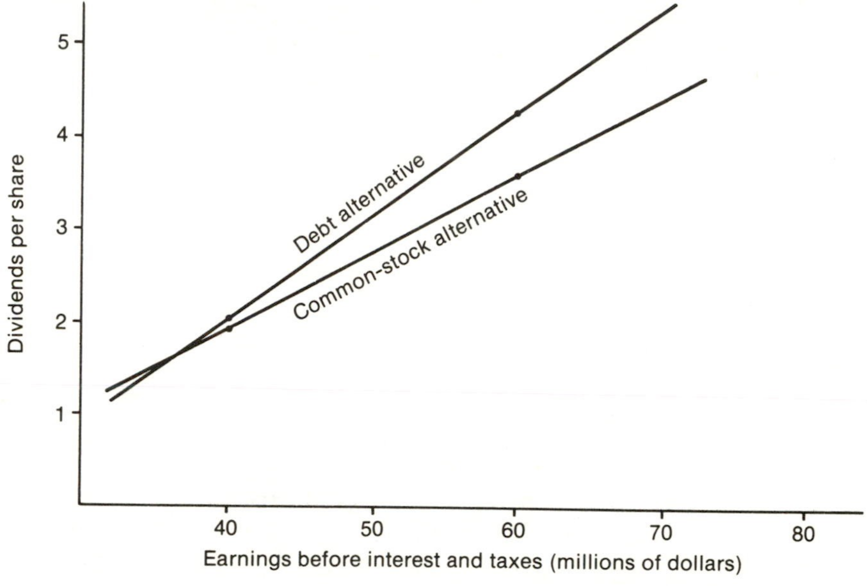

the most favorable impact on the market price of the stock and will yield the greatest improvement in the shareholder's value.

The assumption that the PE ratio will remain constant is critical. If the ratio changes because of the financing decision, then the market value of the stock may be affected, which in turn would affect the value of the company to the shareholders. Under normal circumstances, financing with debt will lead to higher earnings per share, but the higher leverage brings with it some risks. If shareholders became sufficiently worried about the additional risks of the higher leverage, the PE ratio could decline. This decline could offset the increased earnings per share, leaving the market price of the stock unchanged or perhaps even lower. Let's examine the market value problem using HTI's circumstances as an example.

HTI's PE ratio in early March 1985 was about 9. This was a slight increase over the PE at the end of 1984. The market prices for the common stock at the end of 1985 assuming a constant PE, would be higher if debt were used for financing.

	Common-Stock Alternative	*Debt Alternative*
Estimated 1985 EPS	$ 7.81	$ 8.42
PE ratio	9	9
Estimated 1985 stock price	$70.29	$75.78

If the shareholders view a debt-financed HTI Company as being more risky because of the lower coverage ratios and decreased flexibility, the PE would drop to reflect the perceptions of increased risk. The question is: How far would the PE ratio need to fall before the shareholders lose the advantages of increased leverage? In other words, at what PE ratio will the stock price remain constant? Using the $70.29 equity alternative stock price, we can see that the debt alternative PE must drop to 8.4. Since this was the PE level at the end of the 1984, such a decrease would not be unrealistic.

	Common-Stock Alternative	*Debt Alternative*
Estimated 1985 EPS	$ 7.81	$ 8.42
PE ratio	9.0	8.39
Estimated 1985 stock price	$70.29	$70.29

Since this is an analysis requiring judgment, it is often useful to compare the company with others in the industry. If the company's new financial structure appears similar to other companies, then it is less likely that the PE would change as a result of the financing decision. It might change for other reasons, for instance, if there were a change in the general level of market PEs, but not as a direct result of the change in capital structure.

HTI Company as compared to others in the same industry is shown below.

	Industry Average	*Estimated 1985 HTI with Common-Stock Alternative*	*Estimated 1985 HTI with Debt Alternative*
Interest as a percent of sales	1.1%	1.1%	3.6%
Long-term debt as a percent of equity	27.0	11.4	67.7
Net profit as a percent of equity	12.3	13.7	16.9

If HTI Company were to finance through debt, its financial structure would be more highly leveraged than the average among other companies in the industry. Looking behind the simple averages, we could see that the industry is very fragmented, and capital structures vary widely among the various companies. Thus, the common shareholders may be more tolerant of the higher debt than would shareholders in another industry.

Note that with more debt, the return on equity, a measure frequently used in investment analysis, improves from 13.7% to 16.9%. However, even with the dilutive effects of equity financing, the estimated return for 1985 for HTI Company exceeds the 1984 industry average of 12.3%.

The impact of these factors on the market price is called the implicit or *hidden cost,* because the results of changes in the PE multiple and the stock price are not reported on the company's financial statements. These changes are reflected in the value of the shareholders' investments in the company, and the implicit nature of such effects does not minimize their importance in the analysis of financing structure alternatives. Since the managers' objective is to maximize the value of the company to the shareholders, managers must be cognizant of the impact their financing decision will have on the market price of the company's common stock.

4. Control

Another aspect of dilution is the potential loss of ownership control. An issue of new common stock can expand the existing ownership and dilute voting control of the company. Whether this dilution is important depends on the distribution of ownership of the company. For companies with a significant proportion of the ownership in the hands of an individual or small group of shareholders, the ownership dilution issue may be critical. If the existing owners wish to maintain their dominant voting position without buying the new stock, then an equity issue may not be appropriate. Typically, the dilution issue is critical at three levels of control: when the ownership block will be reduced below 100%, below 50%, and below 25%.

The problems of introducing outside owners for the first time is usually more of a psychological problem than a managerial one. If the original owners still maintain an ownership position greater than 50%, they are in a position to continue to control the affairs of the company. The primary change will be that outside owners now have an interest in the operations of the company and may require additional accounting, reporting, and legal efforts.

There may be some compelling reasons for issuing outside equity. Not the least of these reasons is the need to develop a market for the equity to provide for liquidity in the owner's holdings. Another factor that may force a company to admit outside owners is rapid growth that has exceeded the company's debt capacity. For these or other reasons, the owner or ownership bloc may believe that selling equity to outsiders is necessary.

This is typically not an easy decision for the owners to make, however. Once outside owners are involved, the original owners can maintain operating control so long as they own 50% of the voting common stock. Thus, the 50% hurdle is a difficult one for many owners to pass. Usually the need for outside equity must be severe before the controlling owners will relinquish their 50% equity control.

For publicly held companies with a widely distributed ownership position, it is usually possible to effectively control the company with an ownership bloc of 20% to 25%. Through solicitation of proxy votes, an insider group with a significant minority position can usually dominate the managerial decisions and control the operations of the company. Dilution of this bloc through the issuance of additional shares could eliminate this effective control: therefore, this barrier is another critical point in evaluating the equity-control issue.

Other than at these critical points, the dilution of control is not usually a significant issue. Obviously, for a company with a widely dispersed ownership and no significant ownership blocs, the control issue is typically moot.

Recently, there have been instances of companies using equity dilution as a means of thwarting unwanted takeover bids. Through issuing new stock, the company dilutes the ownership that an unfriendly suitor may have gained, thereby making the takeover more difficult.

Although the equity control issue is more easily assessed, debt financing may also impose some control issues. Frequently, lenders impose restrictions on the operations of the company in the form of debt covenants. These covenants may specify certain actions that the company may or may not undertake and/or limit other actions. For example, the loan covenants may require the company to maintain specific levels of working capital, to limit additional borrowings, to limit the amounts of dividends, and to comply with other restrictions. The purpose of these covenants is to protect the lender's investment in the company, but their effect may be to restrict the ability of managers to operate the company as they believe necessary.

In the HTI Company's situation, the control issues were not critical. The ownership was distributed over a large group, with no bloc exercising effective control. The proposed loan agreement did include some restrictive covenants; however, the limitations were within the ranges that managers believed appropriate. It was therefore concluded that the debt covenants would not cause any control problems.

5. Timing

In considering timing, management has two primary concerns—(1) the use of long-term versus short-term financing and (2) the sequencing of financing issues.

Since the external capital is typically used for some productive purpose within the company, the earnings and market price of the common equity are expected to increase. The company is often tempted to postpone a permanent change in the capital structure by using short-term financing. Then the company will be able to refinance (roll over) the short-term, temporary financing into either long-term debt or common stock when the company's profits have improved. At that time, the company may finance its long-term capital at more favorable rates and thereby minimize its cost of capital.

Although this argument is tempting, management must consider the potential consequences of the delay. By delaying, managers are implicitly forecasting that rates will be more favorable in the future. Although any forecast of interest rates and market prices is difficult, the consequences of missing the forecast are especially severe in planning capital structure. If forced to raise capital in unfavorable markets, the company will bear the impact of that decision for several years. Exhibit 6–7 shows the rapidity with which short-term rates change. In the 1970s, this strategy was especially dangerous.

EXHIBIT 6-7 Quarterly Short-Term Interest Rates, 1930–1984 (quarterly averages)

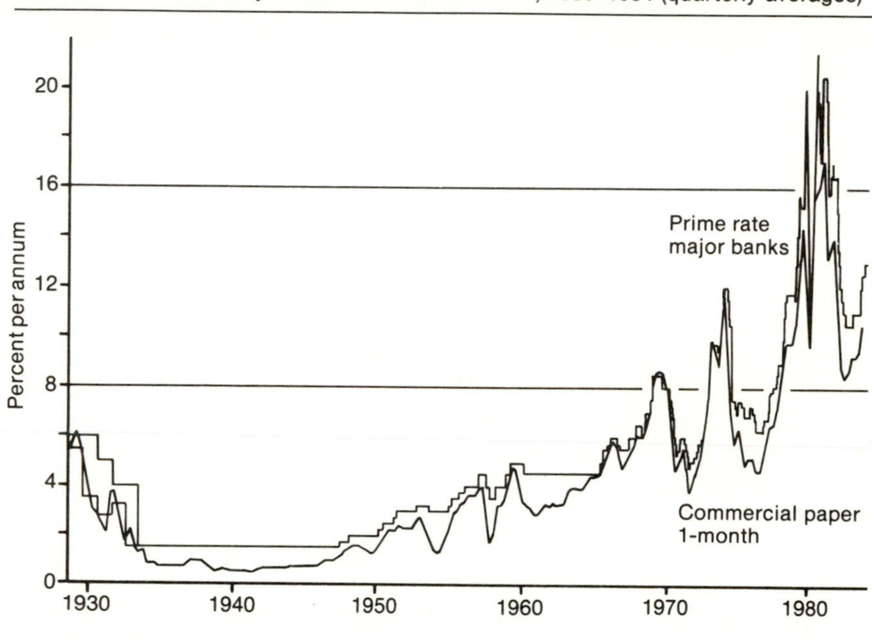

SOURCE: Board of Governors of the Federal Reserve System, *1984 Historical Chart Book,* p. 99.

For the HTI Company, this use of short-term debt was not considered. While the short-term financing would cost HTI only 10½% in March 1984, the company believed that the risks of the short-term, interim financing were too high to be considered. While there was the possibility that the long-term financing costs might drop if the company could wait until the earnings position of the company improved, management believed that because of the interest rate uncertainty the risk was too great.

For most growing companies, the problem is not whether to issue debt or equity, but when to do so. Growth brings with it the continuous need for funds, and most companies find that they are unable to finance their growth through internal sources only. Recognizing that the use of external capital is inevitable, companies should seek the most opportune time to enter the markets.

Typically, managers are tempted to delay issuing new equity as long as possible. This delay is due to the belief that, in a growing company, the earnings will steadily increase; therefore, the stock issue should be delayed to take advantage of the impact of increased profitability on the stock price.

For HTI Company, this argument was especially pertinent. The stock price had recently been increasing and was at an all-time high. By delaying the issue, could the stock be issued at a higher price, thus reducing the number of shares and the adverse impact of dilution?

There were risks offsetting the advantage of waiting. By using the $60 million of debt financing, HTI Company would almost exhaust its debt capacity and would be limiting its future financing alternatives. For any future external financing they might be forced to the equity market. If, in general, the stock market was depressed, HTI's stock price might be depressed as well, despite the improved earnings of the company. Thus, the company might be forced into an unfavorable market, thereby losing the expected advantage of delaying the equity issue.

The sequencing issues force management to evaluate whether the potential gains from delaying the equity offering are worth the risks of reduced flexibility and possibly unfavorable markets. Obviously, the managers' decision will be influenced by their confidence in forecasting future economic events.

6. Other

The "other" category of the capital structure decision includes those factors that may be relevant to a particular firm but were not included in the flexibility, risk, income, control, or timing categories. Since each decision is unique, there will be specific factors that should be included in the analysis for some decisions but not for others. Questions which might be considered include: (*a*) how quickly the funds are needed; (*b*) whether the market for common stock should be broadened; (*c*) what impact the decision will have on existing warrants, options, convertible debentures, and other financing instruments; and (*d*) whether the markets are currently stable or fluctuating.

7. HTI Company's Financing Decision

HTI Company decided to finance its requirements through an equity offering. Even though the additional shares would dilute the earnings and dividends per share, management believed that the common stock financing had significant advantages in providing additional flexibility and in avoiding the riskiness of a major increase of debt. Management expected the company to continue to grow and believed that additional financing would be required in the future. The equity financing was thought to provide the most flexibility for future financings as well as to provide a borrowing reserve for unforeseen future circumstances. Management also decided to take advantage of the prevailing high stock price and not to risk waiting and the potential of a price decline.

III. SUMMARY

Although HTI Company's financing decision involved only two alternatives, the FRICTO framework of analysis could be used to evaluate alternative methods of financing as well. It is simply an analytical framework for examining the capital-structure decision.

The task of the financial manager is to assess different factors and scenarios and determine the capital structure that will yield the optimum value for the company. Unfortunately, there is no simple formula that can be used to determine the optimal decision. For the time being, capital-structure analysis as all financial analysis will remain a managerial art.

SELECTED REFERENCES

For a more detailed examination of value creation through capital structure, see:

Fruhan, William E., Jr. *Financial Strategy.* Homewood, Ill.: Richard D. Irwin, 1979.

For additional information on assessing debt capacity, see:

Donaldson, Gordon. "Strategy for Financial Emergencies." *Harvard Business Review,* November–December 1969, pp. 67–79.

Donaldson, Gordon. "New Framework for Corporate Debt Policy." *Harvard Business Review,* September–October 1978, pp. 149–64.

For other discussions of capital structure, see:

Brealey, Richard, and Stewart Myers. *Principles of Corporate Finance.* 2d ed. New York: McGraw-Hill, 1984, chaps. 13–15, 17–18.

Pringle, John J., and Robert S. Harris. *Essentials of Managerial Finance.* Glenview, Ill.: Scott, Foresman, 1984, chaps. 13–14.

Ray, Marvin E., and David L. Scott. *Finance.* Cambridge, Mass.: Winthrop Publishers, 1979.

VanHorne, James C. *Financial Management and Policy.* 6th ed. Englewood Cliffs, N.J.: Prentice-Hall, 1983, chaps. 9–10.

The seminal articles on the irrelevance of capital structure are:

Modigliani, Franco, and Merton H. Miller. "The Cost of Capital, Corporation Finance, and the Theory of Investment." *American Economic Review,* June 1958, pp. 261–97.

Modigliani, Franco, and Merton H. Miller. "Corporate Income Taxes and The Cost of Capital: A Correction." *American Economic Review,* June 1963, pp. 433–43.

STUDY QUESTIONS

1. The Traie Company was planning a $15 million expansion to their product line which was expected to increase sales by 20% to $150 million. Management expected to be able to continue to earn a 13% return on sales before interest and taxes. Traie's balance sheet showed the following capital structure: (*a*) long-term debt of $25 million at 7% with annual sinking-fund requirements of $2.5 million/year; (*b*) $15 million worth of 8% preferred stock; and (*c*) two million shares of common stock with a par value of $2/share. Traie's management was considering two financing alternatives:

   a. A debt issue of $15 million at 10% with an annual sinking fund of $1.5 over the loan's 10-year life:

b. An equity issue of 1 million shares of common stock netting $15/share.

Prepare an EBIT chart to analyze the alternatives using the existing and projected sales and EBIT levels for points of reference. What are the earnings per share at the equivalency point? How do you interpret this?

2. Traie management currently had a policy of paying 25% of available earnings out in dividends. Analyze and compare the present dividend payment to those likely under both financing alternatives at the projected level of sales.

3. Compute the implicit and explicit costs of the two alternatives using the following data. How do you interpret your findings relative to the implicit costs of the equity issue?

	Earnings per Share	Dividends per Share	Average Stock Price	Price-Earnings Ratio
1981	1.96	—	$ 5.88	3
1982	2.20	—	$ 7.70	3.5
1983	2.40	$0.75	$10.80	4.5
1984	2.63	$0.81	$15.78	6.0
1985	3.03	$0.91	$18.18	6.0

(2 million shares outstanding (1981–85)

4. Traie's balance sheet is shown below, along with some industry ratios. Analyze the effects of both financing alternatives on the company's riskiness as well as its return characteristics. (For purposes of simplicity, consider the preferred stock part of long-term debt.) Current depreciation is $4 million/year; proposed depreciation is $4.75 million/year.

Assets (in millions)	
Current assets	$ 54
Long-term assets	80
Total assets	$134
Liabilities and Equity (in millions)	
Current liabilities	$ 40
Long-term debt	25
Preferred stock	15
Common stock ($2 par)	4
Retained earnings	50
Long-term debt and equity	94
Total liabilities and equity	$134
Industry Characteristics	
Return on assets	10%
Return on equity	12%
LTD/(LTD + OE)	45%
Interest/sales	1.5

5. Based on your answers to Questions 1–4, which alternative would you recommend the Traie Company pursue?

Merger, Acquisition, and Corporate Valuation

Merger activity in the United States by domestic and nondomestic firms has burgeoned, particularly during the late 1960s, the late 1970s, and the early 1980s, as shown in Exhibit 7–1. Managers engaged in this activity have given a number of reasons for making acquisitions:

1. To lower financing costs.
2. To diversify and thus reduce risk.
3. To increase the earnings per share of the acquiring firm.
4. To use excess funds.
5. To provide needed funds.
6. To purchase an undervalued stock.
7. To take advantage of economies of scale.

These are seven quite different reasons for an acquisition or merger. However, all these reasons can be reduced to only one—to create value for the firm's shareholders. This creation of value comes only as the result of synergy between the merging firms.

Creating value is a familiar goal, one that was used in discussing capital investment decisions in Chapter 4 and financing decisions in Chapter 6. The goal is the same here because an acquisition or merger is essentially an investment. Although an acquisition is usually larger than the typical capital investment, the acquired firm must still generate an adequate return for shareholders. If an acquisition is just like any other corporate investment, why then do we devote another chapter to its discussion?

There are four reasons. First, since acquisitions usually require large investments, firms frequently have separate staffs of acquisition analysts. Second, these analysts often borrow their analytical tools from stock analysts rather than following capital-investment techniques and criteria. The stock analyst's approach is used because many acquisitions are made by purchas-

EXHIBIT 7-1 Merger and Acquisition Activity

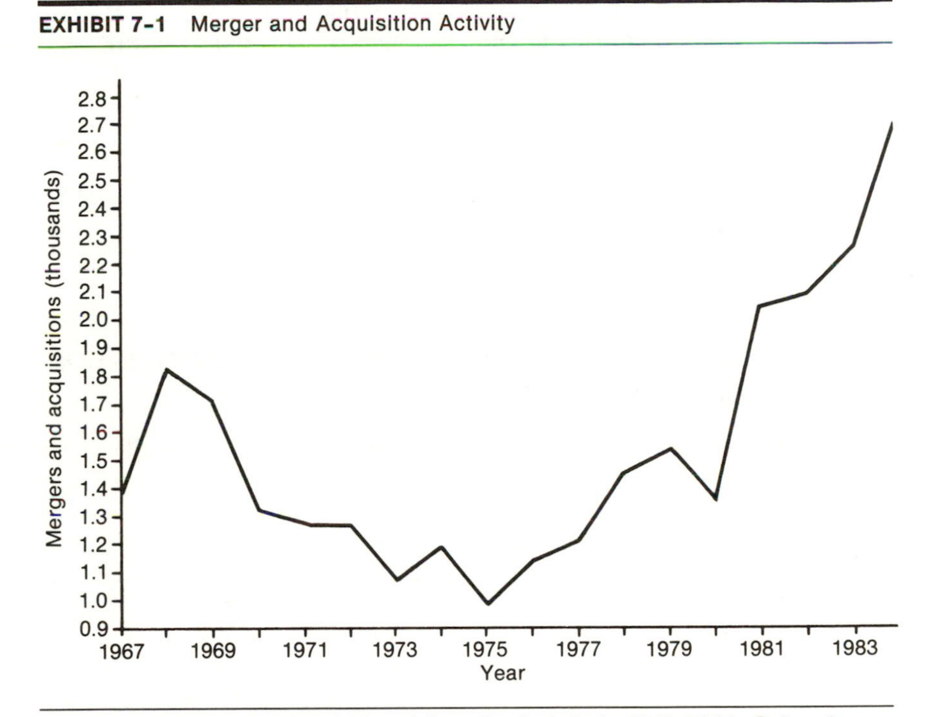

SOURCE: *Mergers and Acquisitions,* Information for Industry (Philadelphia, Pa.), various issues.

ing the stock of the acquired firm with the cash or securities of the acquiring firm. Since stock is used or exchanged in the transaction, stock analysis techniques appear appropriate. Third, acquisitions are a separate topic because the real benefits of a merger can be difficult to identify and awkward to evaluate due to the fact that their costs and benefits are unusually influenced by tax and accounting issues. Fourth, the acquisition decision is an excellent example of how a manager can create value for the company.

Despite these difficulties, an acquisition is essentially a complex capital investment. Thus, the capital investment framework can be adapted and used to determine whether or not a potential acquisition will create value for the acquiring firm's shareholders. In this chapter, we will recommend and describe present value analysis of cash flows as a method to value and price an acquisition. We will then discuss some of the other valuation techniques currently used by acquisition analysts, focusing particularly on earnings analysis.

I. PRESENT VALUE ANALYSIS OF CASH FLOWS

There are three steps the analyst must follow in valuing an acquisition:

1. To identify the present value of the company to be acquired (NPV_Z).

2. To identify the present value of the acquiring firm (NPV_X).
3. To identify the present value of the joined firms, post merger (NPV_{XZ}).

The marginal value of the acquisition (ΔNPV_{XZ}) depends upon the relationship of the three variables:

$$\Delta NPV_{XZ} = NPV_{XZ} - (NPV_X + NPV_Z) \quad (1)$$

Let's use an example to demonstrate the analysis of an acquisition based on this concept and the problems an analyst will face.

1. Calculating the Marginal Value of an Acquisition without Synergy

Consider two mature firms, both growing just enough to offset the effects of inflation: in real terms, neither is growing. One firm, Kitchen Craft (KC) Industries, manufactures kitchen cabinets; the other firm, Zeus, Inc., prints, binds, and distributes religious pamphlets and books. For the present, let's suppose that the current net cash flow for each firm is a good estimate of the annual cash flows over the foreseeable future. Zeus is slightly less risky than KC, and, although its net cash flows are lower, its weighted average cost of capital is also lower. To calculate the marginal value of the acquisition, we first need to measure the net present value of each of the two firms—in other words, what is the value of each firm to its shareholders? So that the calculations can be simplified, we will assume that each firm's net cash flow will remain the same every year in perpetuity. By making such an assumption we can use the yearly net cash flow (NCF) to calculate net present value thusly,

$$NPV_A = \frac{NCF_A}{R_A} \quad (2)$$

where

R_A = Weighted average cost of capital for company A
NCF_A = Yearly net cash flow for company A
NPV_A = Net present value of the cash flows for company A

As you saw in Chapter 5, this method of calculating net present value is appropriate only for a firm that is not growing.[1]

[1]In Chapter 5, we wrote a similar formula from the perspective of the capital markets. We wrote the no-growth valuation as

$$P_0 = \frac{EPS}{R}$$

or

$$P_0 = \frac{D_1}{R}$$

Those valuation formulas are essentially equivalent to formula (2) above in which we used the notation commonly used in evaluating capital investments from the corporate perspective.

EXHIBIT 7-2 Net Present Value—Two Nongrowing Firms

	Kitchen Craft Industries	*Zeus, Inc.*	*KC-Zeus*
Net cash flow per year (NCF)	\$500,000	\$200,000	\$700,000
Weighted average cost of capital (R)	10%	8%	9.3%
Net present value (NPV)	\$5.0 million	\$2.5 million	\$7.5 million

The net present values for KC and Zeus are shown in Exhibit 7–2. We have assumed that the combined firm, KC-Zeus, is a simple combination of the two preacquisition firms; there are no synergies thus the risk would be the weighted average for the two firms, and the net present value would be the sum of the net present values of KC and Zeus, as shown in Exhibit 7–2. Using this information the marginal value of the acquisition (ΔNPV_{KCZ}) can now be calculated using formula (1):

$$\begin{aligned}\Delta NPV_{KCZ} &= NPV_{KCZ} - (NPV_{KC} + NPV_{Z}) \\ &= \$7.5 - (\$5.0 + \$2.5) \\ &= \$0.0\end{aligned}$$

Why, you may wonder would two firms merge if there was no change in value; if there are no added benefits, or synergies, such as reduced risk or increased returns? These are good questions. The answer is that value from an acquisition also depends on the price paid for the acquisition. If a fair price is paid for Zeus by KC, then there is no benefit or loss to the shareholders of either firm. A fair price paid by KC for Zeus would be one that neither creates nor destroys value—one that would exactly equal the present value of the benefits from Zeus, \$2.5 million. The present value of benefits of \$2.5 million gained in the acquisition of Zeus are exactly offset by the \$2.5 million cost. If, by skillful negotiation, KC management can acquire Zeus for less than \$2.5 million, KC's shareholders would gain value, while those investors holding Zeus stock would lose value. A simple formula can be used to show the importance of pricing to value:

$$NRC_{Z} = Q_{Z} - NPV_{Z} \tag{3}$$

where

NRC_{Z} = Net real cost to acquire
Q_{Z} = Price to acquire
NPV_{Z} = Present value of the target firm with no synergistic benefits

If KC pays \$2.5 million for Zeus, the value created for their shareholders would be:

$$\begin{aligned}NRC_{Z} &= \$2.5 - \$2.5 \\ &= \$0.0\end{aligned}$$

If KC paid more than \$2.5 million, its shareholders would lose value. For instance, if the price were \$3.0 million, the loss would be \$500,000 as shown below.

$$NRC_Z = \$3.0 - \$2.5$$
$$= \$0.5$$

And if they negotiated skillfully and paid \$2.0 million for the \$2.5 million in benefits, \$500,000 in value would be transferred to KC's shareholders. Thus, in the most simple case, the manager faces two problems. First, he or she must place a value on both firms, and second, a price must be determined. The two are not the same.

2. Calculating Marginal Benefit of an Acquisition with Synergy

Our calculations thus far have assumed that the acquisition offers no new benefits. What if the combined companies have cash flows in excess of what the two firms would have alone? The increased cash flows could come from a variety of synergies. For example, Zeus may be operating at full capacity with a large backlog of orders for its products, while Kitchen Craft may have an empty manufacturing facility that could be used, with little change, to produce the religious tracts for Zeus's customers. KC's unused capacity, combined with Zeus' need for capacity, would increase cash flows without offsetting costs: more pamphlets could be printed and sold without adding to the combined firm's plant capacity. Thus, the combined firm would have a larger net present value than the simple sum of the two firms' values. In Exhibit 7–3 we can show these increased cash flows.

Using formula (1), the marginal value of the merger would be calculated thus:

$$\Delta NPV_{KCZ} = NPV_{KCZ} - (NPV_{KC} + NPV_Z)$$
$$= \$8.0 - (\$5.0 + \$2.5)$$
$$= \$8.0 - \$7.5$$
$$= \$0.5$$

As a result of combining the two firms, we have an additional \$500,000 in present value benefits. There is value created through merger. Of course, the price paid for Zeus by KC will determine which firm's stockholders benefit from the acquisition.

Let us calculate the value to KC's stockholders if KC were to pay \$2.5 million for the acquisition. Remember, this acquisition creates new benefits as a result of synergies. Thus, formula (3) cannot be used without adjustments. The value to KC's stockholders (V_{KC}) equals the marginal value of the acquisition minus the net real cost (the price paid to acquire):

$$V_{KC} = \Delta NPV_{XZ} - NRC_Z \qquad (4)$$

EXHIBIT 7-3 Net Present Value of Combined Firms: Synergistic Benefits

	Kitchen Craft Industries	*Zeus, Inc.*	*KC-Zeus*
Net cash flow per year	$500,000	$200,000	$745,000
Weighted average cost of capital	10.0%	8.0%	9.3%
Present value	$5.0 million	$2.5 million	$8.0 million

Using formulas (1) and (3) we can rewrite this equation so we can determine the value KC's shareholders will receive:

$$\begin{aligned} V_{KC} &= \Delta NPV_{KCZ} - NRC_Z \\ &= [NPV_{KCZ} - (NPV_{KC} + NPV_Z)] - [Q_Z - NPV_Z] \qquad (5) \\ &= [\$8.0 - (\$5.0 + \$2.5)] - [\$2.5 - \$2.5] \\ &= \$0.5 \end{aligned}$$

Since the change in value as a result of the acquisition is $500,000 and the change in value for KC's shareholders is also $500,000, Kitchen Craft stockholders receive the $500,000 of new value created by the acquisition.

If V_{KC} were less than $500,000, the gain from the acquisition (and the increase in value) would be shared by the shareholders of both firms. For instance, if KC paid $2.8 million, the value gained by KC's stockholders calculated using formula (5) would be:

$$\begin{aligned} V_{KC} &= [\$8.0 - (\$5.0 + \$2.5)] - [\$2.8 - \$2.5] \\ &= \$0.5 - \$0.3 \\ &= \$0.2 \end{aligned}$$

And Zeus's shareholders would receive the remainder:

$$\begin{aligned} V_Z &= NPV_{KCZ} - V_{KC} \\ &= \$0.5 - \$0.2 \\ &= \$0.3 \end{aligned}$$

Only at a price of $2.75 million would the two groups of shareholders share equally in the increased value.

These formulas are simply a means of examining the price and value of benefits. However, we made the analysis deceptively straightforward by assuming that the benefits and the resulting present values had already been determined. The practicing analyst must estimate these benefits. Projecting the costs and benefits of the combined firm is subject to even greater forecasting error than is forecasting the cash flows for the original entities. For example, we said that Zeus expects to benefit by using KC's excess capacity. However, the benefits of using that space may depend on such factors as the availability of local labor, the suitability of the space, and unpredictable conversion costs. The benefits may be quite different than originally forecast. Further-

EXHIBIT 7–4 Kitchen Craft Industries Free Cash Flow Forecasts—5% Real Growth (in thousands of dollars)

	1985	*1986*	*1987*	*1988*	*1989*
Sales	$11,250	$11,813	$12,403	$13,023	$13,674
Operating expenses	10,350	10,868	11,411	11,981	12,580
Net income before tax	900	945	992	1,042	1,094
Tax (50%)	(450)	(472)	(496)	(521)	(546)
Net income after tax	450	473	496	521	547
Depreciation	50	50	50	50	50
Increase in working capital	(70)	(73)	(77)	(81)	(85)
Increase in property, plant, and equipment	(161)	(168)	(177)	(186)	(195)
Net free cash flow	269	282	292	304	317
Terminal value	0	0	0	0	5,470*
Total cash flow	$ 269	$ 282	$ 292	$ 304	$ 5,787

*1989 earnings/cost of capital ($547/.10). This terminal value presumes that KC does not grow in real terms after 1989 and depreciation is reinvested to keep assets viable.

more, this example of synergy is simple and relatively easy to quantify. Most acquisitions provide far greater forecasting ambiguity. If the acquired firm does not change the acquiring firm, analysts often use a short-cut—only the cash flows for the acquired firm, with and without synergy, are forecast and valued.

Risk and the impact of an acquisition on risk are also difficult to estimate. In the KC-Zeus example, we made the analyst's life simple by assuming that the business risk of the new firm was simply the average of the two firms' risks prior to acquisition. This simplifying assumption rarely holds true in practice. For example, joining a cyclical to a countercyclical firm will greatly reduce the risk of the combined firm, all other factors being equal. Joining two firms with the same cyclicality would have the opposite effect.

Our Zeus-KC example is a simple demonstration of the basic capital investment approach to acquisition analysis.

Rarely will the analyst find two firms merging where neither is growing in real terms. To value growing firms the analyst must forecast the net annual cash flow for each firm. Since companies must invest in assets to grow, the analyst must include estimates for the increase in assets in the forecasts. As an example, if KC were to introduce a new product that would spur growth in real terms of 5% for the next five years, it would need increases in net working capital (current assets minus current liabilities) and property, plant, and equipment. Exhibit 7–4 provides the forecast for KC. After five years, KC is expected to stop growing. At that point, we can estimate the value of KC just as we did in Exhibit 7–3. Each of the cash flows, including the terminal value, is discounted at KC's cost of capital (10%) for a present value of $4.5 million. This is value greater than we found for KC without real growth. The analyst's job is to consider the effect one business will have on the other—to anticipate the magnitude, timing, and uncertainty of the merged firm's flows.

II. EARNINGS VALUATION METHOD

To avoid elaborate projections of cash flows, benefits, and risks, some analysts use the relationship of a firm's projected earnings to its stock price to calculate a price for the acquisition. To use this approach, the analyst first estimates the earnings of the firm to be acquired (or uses historical earnings as an estimate of future earnings). The second step is to estimate the relationship between these earnings and the stock price, the price-earnings ratio (*PE*). From this, the analyst calculates the estimated price per share of the acquired firm as follows,

$$\text{Price per share} = \text{EPS} \times \text{PE} \tag{6}$$

where

$$\begin{aligned} \text{EPS} &= \text{Earnings per share in the last 12 months} \\ \text{PE} &= \text{Estimated price earnings ratio for the firm after acquisition} \end{aligned}$$

Suppose that Zeus's earnings over the past 12 months have been \$170,000, and 100,000 shares of stock are outstanding. Earnings per share would be \$1.70 (\$170,000/100,000). If the analyst estimated a price-earnings ratio of 9 for Zeus, the analyst could calculate the price per Zeus share as follows:

$$\begin{aligned} \text{Price per share} &= \text{EPS} \times \text{PE} \\ &= \$1.70 \times 9 \\ &= \$15.30 \end{aligned}$$

At a price per share of \$15.30, the total price for Zeus would be \$1.53 million (\$15.30 × 100,000 shares). This price is less than the net present value calculated for Zeus by the cash flow projection method.

Is this new price reasonable? As a method of valuation, several factors make us question the validity of the price-earnings ratio method. First, in using this approach we assume that recent earnings represent the real earning power of the firm. In the past several years, the reported earnings of U.S. corporations have become less and less representative of the firms' *economic* earnings. The effects of inflation and the accounting treatment of those effects, combined with changes in accounting methods for such items as unrealized foreign exchange losses and gains, have made the reported earnings of U.S corporations resemble only vaguely their real earning power.

Second, this method also assumes that the price-earnings ratio is a reliable indicator of value. While the current PE of a publicly traded firm reflects its shareholders' present estimates of its future as an independent company, it does not reflect the potential synergies that might result from a merger. To estimate the value of the synergies using the earnings valuation approach, the analyst must forecast the new earnings post-merger and what the PE ratio would be if the merger were known to investors. Thus, the ana-

EXHIBIT 7-5 Furniture/Home Furnishings Manufacturers (price-earnings data)

Company	*1983*	*1984*
Armstrong World	10.8	7.2
Bassett Furniture	11.2	9.7
Flexsteel Industries	6.0	9.2
Henredon Furniture	13.4	11.0
Lane Company	9.8	7.8
La-Z-Boy Chair	7.8	7.3
Leggett & Platt	9.6	8.5
Miller (Herman)	10.8	13.4
Mohasco Corporation	10.6	8.4
Thomas Industries	10.6	8.0

SOURCE: *Value Line Investment Survey,* May 3, 1985.

lyst faces a real problem in determining the appropriate PE. The current PE reflects prospects without merger, and a PE reflecting the potential for merger is difficult to estimate. The firm's current PE is only a starting point for this estimation. If the acquisition is expected to create value, the analyst is justified in using a higher estimate for the earnings of the PE. But the problem is that there is no simple method for estimating this revised PE. As an example, Exhibit 7–5 provides the price-earnings ratios for a similar industry—the home furnishings industry.

Nonpublicly traded firms present the analyst with even more problems. Since the stock has no market price, there is no current price-earnings ratio to use as a starting point. Analysts often use the average PE for a group of similar but publicly traded firms as the proxy for this unobtainable PE. To use this proxy method, the analyst must assume that firms in the same industry or with similar earnings records are equally risky and that the market will pay a standard multiple of earnings for stocks of equivalent risk. However, these assumptions are not always valid. The price-earnings multiples of comparable stocks in comparable industries can be very different.

In addition to these problems, this method assumes that the earnings stream will remain constant over time and that short-term earnings and market prices are good indicators of value. The net present value method, on the other hand, assumes that any acquisition with a positive marginal value will increase the value of the firm and that the increased value will eventually be reflected in the market price of the firm's stock. The logic behind the net present value method is clear and powerful.

While we would dismiss the earnings-multiple method as the sole approach to valuing an acquisition, it can be put to good use by the analyst. It can be used to put the present value analysis into a capital-market perspective. We can compare the PE that is implied by a present value analysis to a PE estimated using the earnings analysis. For Zeus we had the following information:

Cash flow per year	$200,000
Earnings per year	$170,000
Discount rate	8%
Net present value	$2.5 million
Number of shares	100,000

The implied price-earnings ratio would be equal to the present value per share, divided by the earnings per share:

$$\text{Implied PE} = \frac{\text{PV/Share}}{\text{Earnings/Share}} \tag{7}$$

$$= \frac{\$2{,}500{,}000/100{,}000}{\$170{,}000/100{,}000}$$

$$= \frac{\$25}{\$1.70}$$

$$= 14.7$$

This implied PE is greater than the PE we used in the earnings analysis of Zeus. The difference in price-earnings ratios indicates that our present value estimate is higher than the value that the market would set on the common stock. There are two possible reasons for the discrepancy: (1) our predicted cash flows may be greater than those the market is forecasting or (2) our predicted risk (incorporated in the cost-of-capital estimate) could be lower than the market's prediction.

To acquire Zeus, KC would probably have to pay more than the current market price for the stock. To do so, the KC managers must be convinced that the acquisition will create added value for their shareholders. Otherwise, the shareholders would be far better off if they were to buy Zeus's stock for themselves in the public market at the current market price rather than to have KC acquire it for them.

This use of the earnings-valuation method, then, can provide a double check on the present value analysis of cash flows.

III. OTHER VALUATION TECHNIQUES

A number of other valuation techniques are used by acquisitions analysts. These should only be used as supplements to the present value analysis, not as substitutes for it.

1. Book Value

This valuation technique is quite simple and lacks any but the most simplistic of reasons for its use. Book value (net assets minus liabilities), calculated by using the balance sheet figures, can mistake value considerably, for several reasons:

1. Book value depends upon the accounting practices of a firm. Thus, book value is usually only a vague approximation of the real economic value of a firm.
2. Book value ignores intangible assets. Intangibles—copyrights, trademarks, patents, franchise licenses, and contracts—protect the right of a company to market its goods and services and thus have value. If the book value of the assets is less than the present value of the cash flows of the firm, intangible assets could account for the discrepancy.
3. Book value ignores the price appreciation of real assets. Since assets are valued on the balance sheet at their depreciated costs, some assets (for instance, land, precious metals, and gems) may be valued far below even their liquidation value.

2. Liquidation Value

Liquidation value is the cash value that the acquirer would receive if the assets of the acquired firm were sold. This method of valuation is useful if the acquirer intends to sell the assets of the acquired firm. The method may also be used to aid in determining the fair book value of under- or overvalued assets. Analysts sometimes use liquidation value as a floor price for the acquisition. If liquidation value exceeds the present value, this indicates the company is worth more if sold.

3. Replacement Cost

Replacement cost is a measure of the cost of replacing the assets of the potential acquisition. While some analysts use it to set a ceiling price on the acquisition, replacement costs are often difficult to estimate.

4. Market Value

Often a good starting point in estimating the acquisition's price is the market value of the firm's stock. If stock is publicly traded, the market value is simply the market price per share times the number of shares. The reason that market value is only a starting point should be clear from the present value analysis we performed for Zeus and Kitchen Craft Industries. If the acquisition is expected to increase value for the shareholders of one or both firms, this increase in value is unlikely to be reflected in the public price of the common stock of either firm. (Of course, the expectation of increased value may be reflected in the price once the merger becomes public knowledge.) Thus, if there are synergies and value will be created, the current market prices underestimate the present value of the merged firms. Still, the market price of the stock is a benchmark from which the analyst can begin.

Under a certain set of circumstances, all these values should be the same. Liquidation value should reflect what a buyer is willing to pay for the earning power of the assets. Thus, a liquidation value, if it could be obtained, should be close to the value estimated using the present value analysis. Likewise book value, if it truly reflected the economic value (the earning power of the assets), would also be similar. Only because of estimation errors and accounting conventions are the values different and thus not equivalent.

IV. SUMMARY

There is only one purpose in making an acquisition—to create value for the shareholder. Value can be created through increased returns or reduced risk, changes that the shareholders could not make by themselves. In general, this increase in value comes from increased capacity being matched with a need for that resource—a matching that could not occur unless the two firms merged. The analyst's task is to estimate the effect of a merger on a firm's return and risk characteristics. Since earnings are, at best, only a vague indication of real value, the analyst should project the cash flows prior to and after the merger. Other valuation techniques, such as earnings analysis, should be used merely to corroborate the present value analysis based on projected cash flows.

SELECTED REFERENCES

For methods of analyzing a merger, see:

Myers, Stewart C. "A Framework for Evaluating Mergers." In *Modern Developments in Financial Management*. New York: F. A. Praeger, 1976.

Salter, Malcolm S., and Wolf A. Weinhold. *Diversification Through Acquisition*. New York: Free Press, 1979, part II.

For two studies on the relative values of mergers, see:

Mueller, D. C. "The Effects of Conglomerate Mergers: A Survey of the Empirical Evidence." *Journal of Banking and Finance,* December 1977, pp. 315–48.

Rumult, Richard. *Strategy, Structure and Economic Performance,* Boston: Division of Research, Harvard Business School, 1974.

For a discussion of the merger phenomena, see:

Business Week, June 3, 1985, pp. 88–100. "Do Mergers Really Work?"

STUDY QUESTIONS

1. The Ray Company, a growth-oriented enterprise, was considering making an acquisition in the spring of 1981. It had two prospects they designated as X Com-

pany and Y Company for confidentiality reasons. Based only on the data given below, which company would you recommend they pursue?

	X		*Y*	
	Shares of Common Stock	*Cash Flow per Share*	*Shares of Common Stock*	*Cash Flow per Share*
1976	400,000	$1.75	300,000	$1.67
1977	400,000	$1.89	305,000	$1.84
1978	400,000	$2.04	500,000	$1.25
1979	400,000	$2.20	505,000	$1.39
1980	400,000	$2.38	507,000	$1.55

2. Compute the maximum price the management (and shareholders) of the Kupp Corporation should be willing to pay to acquire the Klick Company, and the minimum price Klick's management should accept. Both companies operate in the same industry, and although neither one is experiencing any rapid growth, both provide a steady stream of earnings. Kupp's management was encouraging the acquisition due to the excess plant capacity available at Klick, which it hoped to use. The Klick Company had 50,000 shares of common stock outstanding, which were selling at about $6 per share.

	Kupp Corporation	*Klick Company*	*Combined Entity*
Profit after tax	$48,000	$30,000	$ 92,000
Net cash flow/year	$60,000	$40,000	$120,000
Weighted average cost of capital	12.5%	11.25%	12%

KLICK COMPANY
Balance Sheet

Assets		**Liabilities and Owners' Equity**	
Current assets	$273,000	Current liabilities	$137,000
Net PP&E	215,000	Long-term liabilities	111,000
Other	55,000	Owners' equity	295,000
Total assets	$543,000	Total liabilities and owners' equity	$543,000

3. Smyth Instrument Company wishes to acquire Robinson Research Lab through a merger. Smyth Instrument expects to gain operating efficiency from the merger through distribution economies, advertising, manufacturing, and purchasing.

The weighted average cost of capital for Smyth and Robinson are 12.2% and 10.5%, respectively. Neither company has any long-term debt outstanding. The effective cost of capital after the merger is estimated to be at 11%. The projected growth rate for both of the firms is 4% per year. The current net cash flow per year is $6.45 million for Smyth and $2.2 million for Robinson. Based on an analysis of the synergism for the combined company, the combined net cash flow would have been $9.45 million if the two had been combined for the past year.

Calculate the price Smyth Instrument should offer to acquire Robinson Research and the price above which Robinson should accept the merger offer.

CHAPTER 8

Financial Strategy

In previous chapters, we have examined individual segments of financial management. Taking each in isolation, we have reviewed the basic framework to be used by financial managers in assessing the relevant factors that contribute to the value of the company.

While this fragmented approach is useful for learning how to deal with the various financial decisions, it is important for the manager to understand that each decision is not an isolated event. Each decision impacts the financial characteristics and strategy of the company, and the astute financial manager recognizes all relevant factors and how they are affected by any financial decision.

For example, in Chapter 4 we discussed how to analyze the investment of funds in a new project. What you may not have considered at that time was the effect on the company that a major capital investment can have; for instance, major projects require funds. Often those funds are raised in the capital markets. In the process of investing in the project, the capital structure and costs of capital for the company can also be changed.

While many firms isolate their investment decisions from the financing decisions, taken together all the financial decisions constitute a financial strategy for the firm; and the manager must understand the impact of each on the firm. Explicitly ignoring these relationships can result in a strategy no manager would design. The financial strategy should not be the unplanned sum of isolated decisions. Rather, each decision should constitute a part of a well-devised and understood strategy.

I. FINANCIAL POLICY

Financial decisions can be grouped into two general categories—investment decisions and financing decisions. The first group deals with the issue of what financial resources will be needed. The second deals with how to provide the required financial resources.

The investment decisions, as we have discussed, are concerned with what assets are required by the company to pursue its expected business strategy. These needed assets include investments in working capital as well as such things as plant and equipment. The magnitude of the funds required for these investments will depend on the availability of investment opportunities and the value each is expected to provide the company.

Having decided what investments are acceptable, the company can then estimate the magnitude of its funding requirements. We believe that some companies approach these decisions in the reverse order. If no viable investments are available, then the company need not secure any additional financing and may pay out its earnings in dividends. Thus, the decisions should be: (1) What are the acceptable projects? and (2) What funds are needed to finance these projects?

Having estimated the amount of funds needed, the next step is to estimate the funds that are available from the firm's own operations—retained earnings. These are the shareholders' funds and should be managed as such. Internally available funds, in excess of those required for value-creating investments, should be returned to the shareholders in the form of dividends. If outside funds are required, the sources are limited to various types of debt and equity.

In financing new investments, the financial manager must decide what percentage of the requirements should be financed with debt versus equity. Since all debt must be raised outside the company, the managers can only deal with the specific features of the debt, for instance, with the maturity of the debt or with its private or public placement. On the equity side, however, the financial manager must decide whether new equity should be issued or to use only retained profits. This decision is naturally affected by the level of expected profits and the amount to be paid in dividends to the shareholders. The interrelationships of these various decisions are illustrated on Exhibit 8–1.

The exhibit highlights the decisions that must be made by the manager in creating a financial strategy. The interrelationships of the decision are obvious and can be expressed as follows:

$$\Delta A = \Delta D + NI - D + NE$$

where

$$\begin{aligned} \Delta A &= \text{Change in assets} \\ \Delta D &= \text{Change in debt} \\ NI &= \text{Net income} \\ D &= \text{Dividends paid} \\ NE &= \text{New equity} \end{aligned}$$

As with any equation, if we specify all but one of the variables, then we can solve for the value of the remaining factor. For example, if the debt-equity ratio and the dividend payout are set by corporate policy, then for any level of investments and associated profits, the requirement for new equity will be established by default.

EXHIBIT 8-1 Interrelationships of Financial Decisions

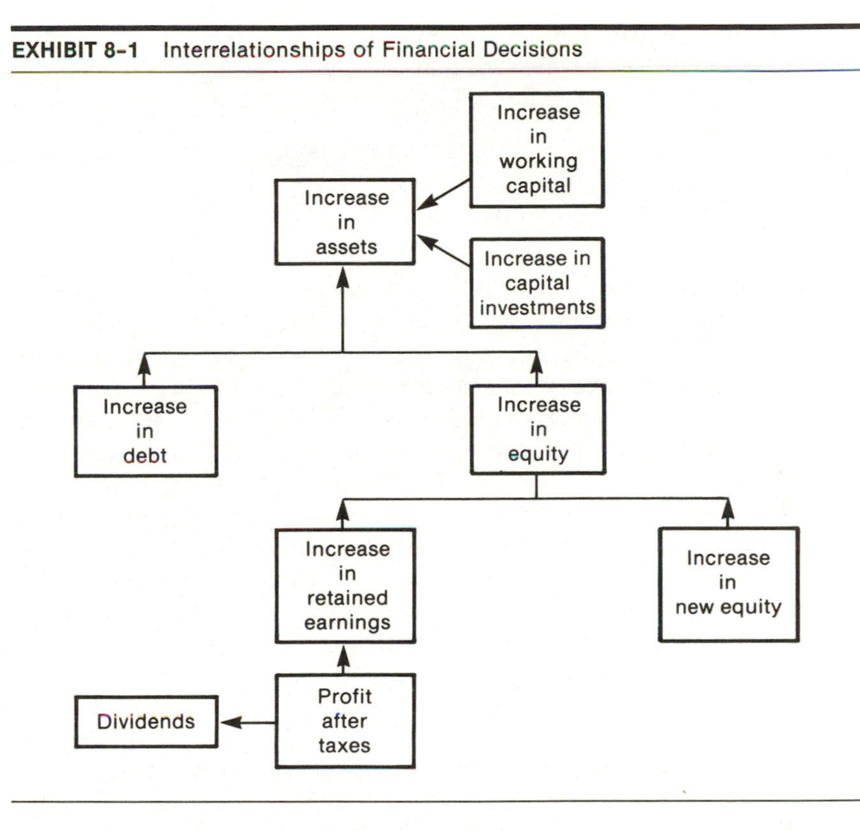

The recognition of these interrelationships has allowed the development of the mathematic models to assess the financial strategy of a company. By using these computer-assisted models to undertake the calculations, managers are able to define the relationships and analyze the results of various courses of action—various scenarios.[1] Generally these models examine the interrelationships of only two variables at a time.

II. RETURN ON EQUITY

The desired result of the financial policies is to increase the investor's return. Since the debt investors have a fixed return, the primary beneficiaries of a successful financial policy will be the equity investors. The return on equity is a useful ratio for examining the impact of the financial policies on the shareholders. There are several factors that affect the return on equity—the tax environment, leverage, and the profitability of the company.

In the early 1900s, the Du Pont Company introduced a method of financial analysis that has become widely used. The concept of this method is to

[1]See Appendix A for further explanation of financial modeling.

break a ratio into several component parts. The impact of each of these subratios can then be analyzed individually. To examine the factors that affect the return on equity, a modification of the Du Pont approach provides the following:

$$\frac{\text{Net income}}{\text{Equity}} = \frac{\dfrac{\text{Net income}^{2}}{\text{Sales}} \times \dfrac{\text{Sales}}{\text{Assets}}}{1 - \dfrac{\text{Debt}}{\text{Assets}}}$$

This system of evaluation indicates that a company can increase its return on equity through increasing the profitability of its operations, through increasing the asset utilization, and/or through increasing the leverage. For example, a company with lower profitability could earn a return on equity comparable to a less leveraged firm by increasing the debt level in its capital structure. Of course, a company could change a combination of these factors.

The advantage of using this modified Du Pont approach is that it facilitates coordinating financial planning. By varying one factor and holding the others constant, the analyst can determine what the impact on return on equity would be.

III. SUSTAINABLE GROWTH

Another concept of financial strategy that is frequently analyzed using a Du Pont approach is sustainable growth. Although growth in sales and assets is the objective of most companies, it can be a mixed blessing. Sales growth may increase gross profits, but at the same time, it generates a continuous demand for funds to finance that growth. As we described in Chapter 3, to increase sales, the typical company must increase its inventories and accounts receivable as well as its investment in other assets to manufacture the products. Financial theory suggests that as long as the expected return provided by selling additional products exceeds the costs of production—including the financing costs—the company will operate profitably and will be able to finance its growth. The financing will be available through both internal and external sources.

In some situations, companies prefer not to resort to the external capital markets to finance their growth. In particular, many prefer to avoid issuing new equity. The owners of companies that are privately owned often prefer to limit the equity investments in the company. In publicly held corporations when the common stock position is controlled by a single owner or a small

---

[2]The profit margin can be further decomposed into:

$$\frac{\text{Net income}}{\text{Sales}} = \frac{(1 - t) \times (\text{EBIT} - \text{I})}{\text{EBIT}} \times \frac{\text{EBIT}}{\text{Sales}}$$

which shows the impact of the tax rate (t) and the interest expense (I) on the profit margin.

group of shareholders, these owners also may prefer not to issue new stock. The concerns about issuing new equity are not limited to closely held companies, however. During some economic cycles, managers may perceive the costs of issuing new equity stock to be extremely high. In fact, during some periods, there have been almost no issues of new equity in the markets.

In these situations, managers are concerned about how rapidly their firms can grow without needing additional outside equity capital. Although managers may decide to limit all new capital, they more frequently decide to forgo the equity markets. Instead, the companies will continue to borrow and leverage the equity built up through retained earnings.

The problem, then, is to forecast how rapidly sales can increase while the company finances the required new assets through retained earnings and new debt alone. This level of growth is called *sustainable growth*. Although it can be determined through a trial-and-error process by calculating pro forma statements using different growth rates and examining the results, a more straightforward method can be used to calculate the sustainable growth rate.

Assuming that the dividend payout, after-tax profit margin on sales, total-debt-to-equity ratio, sales-to-assets ratio, and assets-to-debt ratio remain constant over the forecast period, the rate of sustainable growth (G) can be expressed mathematically as follows:

$$G = \frac{\text{Sales}}{\text{Assets}} \times \frac{\text{Net income}}{\text{Sales}} \times \frac{\text{Assets}}{\text{Debt}} \times \frac{\text{Debt}}{\text{Equity}} \times \frac{\text{Earnings retained}}{\text{Net income}}$$

This model will provide an indication of how much growth a company can accomplish using only debt and internally available equity. One would expect the highest sustainable growth rate from companies with high profit margins, high leverage, low dividend-payout ratios, and high asset utilization.

These expectations are borne out by the industry average sustainable growth rates shown on Exhibit 8–2. Based on industry averages, the industries with the highest sustainable growth rates are those with high debt-to-equity ratios, low dividend payout ratios, and low assets-to-sales ratios. It is important to note that these are growth rates sustainable without using external equity. For some industries, the actual growth rate may be lower than the sustainable rate, which would mean an ability to pay increased dividends. On the other hand, for growth in excesss of the sustainable rate, external equity would be required.

When applied to a specific company, the manager can similarly compare the expected growth rate to the sustainable rate. If the managers find the sustainable rate too low, they will then be in a position to undertake actions to improve the company's ability to finance more rapid growth. This could be done by planning to issue external equity, reducing the dividend, increasing the debt-to-equity ratio, improving the profitability of the investments, or increasing the asset utilization. Using this simple model, the manager can determine which variables might have the greatest impact on the growth rate and will then be able to focus attention on those factors.

EXHIBIT 8–2 Sustainable Growth Rates for Selected Industries

	Industry Average					
	Sustainable Growth	*Sales/ Assets*	*NI/ Sales*	*Assets/ Debt*	*Debt/ Equity*	*RE/ NI*
Advertising agencies	23%	3.1	0.04	1.14	1.9	0.84
Radio and TV broadcasting	20%	1.0	0.09	3.13	1.0	0.71
Electronic components	16%	1.8	0.05	2.07	1.1	0.79
Trucking	11%	2.4	0.03	1.54	1.3	0.79
Air transportation	10%	1.3	0.02	2.51	1.9	0.81
Soaps and toilet goods	8%	2.3	0.05	2.98	0.7	0.35
Coal mining	7%	1.3	0.05	1.70	1.2	0.53
Paper products	7%	2.1	0.03	2.04	1.0	0.51
Soft drinks	5%	2.2	0.04	2.34	0.7	0.37
Computers and office equipment	5%	1.4	0.05	1.69	1.0	0.42
Motor vehicles	5%	2.0	0.02	1.14	1.9	0.56
Pharmaceuticals	4%	1.7	0.05	3.11	0.7	0.23
Department stores	4%	2.2	0.02	1.11	1.5	0.49
Petroleum refining	2%	2.3	0.01	2.78	1.0	0.36
Ferrous metals	(2)%	1.6	(0.01)	2.16	1.1	0.59

SOURCES: Robert Morris Associates, 1984 Annual Statement Studies; Dun & Bradstreet, 1983–84 Industry Norms and Key Business Ratios

IV. SUMMARY

The return on equity and sustainable growth concepts are only two illustrations of the value of financial planning and modeling. With the results of various financial policies and decisions available for analysis, the manager is in a position to be able to determine the courses of action that can lead to an increase in the value of the company. This increased value can be achieved through investment decisions, financing decisions, and/or a combination of both. The best financial strategy is the one that will result in an increased return for the owners without an increase in risk.

Can the financial manager create this value? To this, we answer yes. It is certainly not a simple task; yet it is one that we believe astute managers can achieve. We hope that this book will provide assistance in the accomplishment of that goal.

SELECTED REFERENCES

For discussions of the value and impact of financial planning, see:

Brealey, Richard, and Stewart Myers, *Principles of Corporate Finance*. 2d ed. New York: McGraw-Hill, 1984, chap. 26.

Fruhan, William E., Jr. *Financial Strategy*. Homewood, Ill.: Richard D. Irwin, 1979.

Porter, Michael E. *Competitive Strategy*. New York: Free Press, 1980.

Steiner, George A. *Strategic Planning*. New York: Free Press, 1979.

For a further discussion of sustainable growth, see:

Higgins, Robert C. "How Much Growth Can a Firm Afford?" *Financial Management,* Fall 1977, pp. 7–16.

For a review of modeling concepts, see:

Bryant, James W. *Financial Modeling in Corporate Mangement*. New York: John Wiley & Sons, 1982.

The interrelationships of financial decisions are detailed in:

Francis, Jack Clark, and Dexter R. Rowell. "A Simultaneous Equation Model of the Firm for Financial Analysis and Planning." *Financial Management*, Spring 1978, pp. 29–44.

Sihler, William W. "Framework for Financial Decisions." *Harvard Business Review*, March–April 1971, pp. 123–35.

Financial Modeling

It has long been recognized that forecasting performance—whether it is estimating the effect of marketing plans, predicting the cost savings from introducing new production methods, or forecasting future cash needs—is an art rather than a science. Although sophisticated statistical and mathematical techniques have been developed to aid in forecasting, these procedures have only *assisted* managers in dealing with the uncertainty; they have not *eliminated* it.

An additional technique that has been developed to help managers in coping with uncertainty is financial modeling. Modeling consists of determining the variables that affect the results in a situation and defining the relationships between these variables in mathematical terms. Because the results of such models are typically stated in financial terms, the technique has come to be known as financial modeling. If properly used, the modeling process will provide insights that will assist managers in making better-informed decisions.

I. INTRODUCTION TO MODELING

One reason for the usefulness of models is that the technique provides a means for managers to examine the effects of the uncertainty of forecasts through sensitivity or "what if" analysis. Using this approach, managers develop forecasts and then change the values of the variables used in estimating the future results. Managers can then determine what the results would be if the values for the variables were to differ from those originally projected. By evaluating the sensitivity of the results to these changes, managers are able to examine the riskiness or uncertainty of the projections. In addition, managers are able to determine which variables have the greatest impact on the results and therefore warrant the greatest scrutiny if the plans are implemented.

Despite the managerial value of this approach, it has typically been used to evaluate only plans or projects that would have a significant impact on the company. The primary reason for restricting its use has been the cost of developing the projections and the recalculations needed for the sensitivity analysis. Before the development of computers, the necessity of hand calculations obviously limited the practicality of sensitivity analysis. Even using computers, it was usually necessary to develop a specific computer program for each model. This meant that the manager needed to explain the project to a systems analyst or programmer, wait for the program to be written, and then—working with the programmer or analyst—evaluate the results.

Using the computer to perform the calculations for sensitivity analysis has been greatly facilitated in recent years with the development of "modeling languages." These computer languages are specialized computer programs designed to simplify the creation of models or forecasted relationships. Once the manager has specified the relationships between the variables in a model, the computer then goes through the laborious process of performing the calculations. Because the languages are "user friendly," managers can use them without the assistance of computer programmers. Modeling languages allow the manager to do what he or she does best—THINK—and the computer to do what it does best—CALCULATE.

Originally, these languages were developed to run on large mainframe systems. Now, many modeling programs have been created for use on micro-computers. The most well-known of these programs are generically called electronic spreadsheets because of their similarity to the spreadsheets used in manual projections. Appendix B provides an introduction to one of the most popular spreadsheet programs, Lotus 1-2-3. In addition, the mainframe modeling languages have been adapted to the micro-computer environment. The combination of these spreadsheet and modeling programs has made computer-based modeling available for all levels of management.

II. THE MODELING PROCESS

Regardless of the type of modeling approach used, either a spreadsheet or modeling language, the general process of developing a model is similar. The procedure for creating a model can be summarized in the following six steps.

1. Determine the Objectives

Before starting to create the model, it is important to understand what information the model is expected to provide. In other words, what is the purpose of the model? The answer to this question will provide the manager with the objectives for the model and the required detail that the model should include.

If the manager does not have a good idea of what the model should accomplish before the development process commences, there is obviously no way of knowing whether the model is doing what it is supposed to do. If the manager doesn't know where he is going, he won't know what direction to go, nor will he know if he has arrived.

Although this step seems obvious, many modeling projects start with the manager deciding to "build a model." Such general approaches are unlikely to provide useful results. Unless the manager has a specific use in mind and constructs the model to fit that use, the model will not be a useful managerial tool.

2. Specify the Variables

After deciding what the model is supposed to do, the manager can then determine which variables or factors are important to include in the model. The number of different variables and detail of the data depend on the nature and objectives of the model. For example, if the objective of the model is to provide information about required inventory levels, the model will require detailed forecasts about expected orders, delivery times, production capacities, throughput times, etc. On the other hand, a pro forma financial statement model might require only a few general income, expense, and balance sheet accounts.

The time horizon for the model will also affect the level of detail required for the model. Monthly cash account projections for the next year would require more detail for the relevant variables than would an annual cash account projection for a five-year model.

The general approach is to match the detail of the input with the required detail of the output. If the objectives of the model are to provide detailed results, then the model should include all variables stated as specifically and in as much detail as possible. If the model objectives are broad and general, then the variables needed for the model can be accordingly more general and less detailed.

3. Define the Relationships

After determining the relevant variables to include in the model, the next step is to define the relationships between the variables. These relationships are stated in mathematical terms. For example, if maintenance expense for a particular machine is expected to be $100 for each 500 hours of operation, the relationship could be expressed as:

$$\text{Maintenance expense} = \$100 \times (\text{Operating Hours}/500)$$ [1]

In determining what the relationships are, most managers start with historical relationships. If the cost of goods sold for a company has historically

---

[1]The procedures for naming the variables and the mathematical operations used to specify the relationships vary between different modeling systems.

been 85% of sales revenue, this would be a good starting relationship for the model. There may, however, be relationships that are expected to differ from historical patterns, or the model may contain relationships with which the company has not had previous experience. In these cases, the manager must rely on expectations for the model specifications. In any case, the relationships could, and should, be altered and the results examined using sensitivity analysis.

4. Construct the Model

Having defined the relationships among the relevant variables, these relationships are then combined to form the model. The specific procedures for combining these mathematical statements will depend on the modeling system being used. (See Appendix B for instructions on entering model statements using Lotus 1-2-3.) Different systems require the model to be constructed in different ways. Some systems are almost "free form" with no particular order required. Other systems are more procedural in nature and require that the statements be placed in a specific order. The instruction manual for the particular system being used must obviously be referenced for the proper procedures to be used in constructing the model.

Too often managers undertake the model construction step as the first stage rather than the fourth stage in the modeling process. As a result, the model requires extra time to develop or may never provide meaningful results. As in any other type of construction project, having a plan and assembling the materials (the variable relationships) facilitates the final construction.

5. Validate the Model

Having constructed the model, it is critical to test it to ensure that it is working correctly. Mistakes do occur. There is no failure in making the mistakes; the failure comes in neglecting to find and correct them. Too often managers accept the results of the model without verifying the accuracy of the output. This can lead to disastrous results.[2]

In examining the model, unusual results are an immediate clue that a mistake may have been made. Other than this obvious method, the only reliable way to ensure that the model is providing reliable results is to manually work through each step in the model to verify its accuracy.

This manual verification is naturally much easier with simple models. Therefore, it is a good procedure when developing complicated models to separate the model into simpler pieces and validate each piece. The model

---

[2]See "How Personal Computers Can Trip Up Executives," *Business Week*, September 24, 1984, pp. 94–102.

can then be expanded by including each piece after it has been tested. This approach simplifies the building and testing of the model.

6. Document the Model

Unfortunately most modelers stop once the model has been constructed and tested. The problem with ending at this stage is that few, if any models, are self-explanatory. The explanation of what the model is doing and of the nature of the relationships used in the model is not critical when the manager uses the model immediately. The problem occurs when others use it or when the manager returns to it after a lapse in time. There may be subsequent questions about how the model was constructed or what it does. For this reason, it is important to provide documentation for the model explaining the variables and relationships used, critical assumptions, and other relevant factors. This documentation becomes an invaluable reference for understanding the model and greatly facilitates its use.

The documentation process begins with the construction of the model itself. The interpretation of the model can be increased by using variable names whenever possible. SALES IN YEAR 1 or SALES1 is more understandable than B3. Most spreadsheet programs allow the assigning of names to ranges or blocks of variables. Most modeling systems allow the inclusion of comments. The use of these features provides a type of self-documentation for the model.

The usefulness of the model is greatly increased if other managers can understand and use it. If the model is only to be used occasionally, a well-documented model will save the manager time each time it is used.

III. SENSITIVITY ANALYSIS

The process of planning, constructing, and testing a model is a labor-intensive and often time-consuming task. If the manager has no intention of evaluating any of the relationships included in the model, then the use of a computer-based modeling system may not be required. However, since the relationships between variables are rarely known with certainty, the ability to change the relationships and observe the results is an important managerial tool. This process of sensitivity analysis is where computer-based modeling excels.

Sensitivity analysis is often called "what if" analysis because it allows the manager to ask the question, "What if the value of the relationships or variables were changed?" Since the computer can quickly recompute the model following changes in any of the variables, it is a simple task for the manager to vary any of the relationships. Obviously, if the recalculations of the model were to be done manually, every change would require a significant amount of time. The use of the computer reduces the recalculation time to seconds.

This ease of recalculating the model with changed assumptions has its dangers, however. Because it is so easy to make changes in the variables, it is possible to become overwhelmed with numbers. When the calculations were done by hand, managers only made the changes in the relationships that were believed to be realistic and possible. Although computer modeling systems have removed the time constraint, they should not be used to replace managerial deliberation. Changing variables over unrealistic ranges may result in more data than the manager can assimilate and use. Instead of providing too much data, which leads to "analysis paralysis," the modeling approach should lead to better managerial analysis and decision making.

The crucial skill is to determine which variables to analyze. The manger should be seeking insights and understanding of the problem, not simply a vast array of numbers. Although these critical variables will differ from model to model, there are a few general comments that can be made.

Most models are based on a few key assumptions, such as a sales forecast or a cost level. Sensitivity analysis should be performed on these "keystone" variables to determine how sensitive the results are to changes in these key assumptions.

If variable relationships were based on changes from historical results or were forecast for areas where the company had no previous experience, the manager should examine the effects of changes in these relationships. An efficient means to do this is through an iterative approach. The manager makes several runs or iterations of the model, changing the value for one or more of the variables for each iteration. The more uncertainty surrounding any relationship, the greater the need for sensitivity analysis on the relationship.

In addition to this "what if" sensitivity analysis accomplished by changing the value of one or more relationships, the manager may also wish to determine what the relationship between certain variables would need to be to achieve a certain specific or optimum value for another variable. For example, the manager could alter the sales expense values to achieve a certain net profit margin level. If the sales expense figure was reasonable, the manager could then use this as a planning or performance objective. This process is called optimization or goal seeking.

Some modeling systems are designed to allow the manager to easily perform this optimization or goal-seeking analysis. On any system, it is possible to do the analysis through a trial-and-error process of changing the value of one variable and observing the results on the goal or target variable. This process would be repeated until the target or optimum results occurred. Although a more laborious process, this approach may provide useful results.

Another approach to sensitivity analysis is to develop various sets of relationships based on different scenarios. The manager determines possible future events or combinations of events and runs the model using the appropriate relationships for each of these scenarios.[3] For example, in modeling a new product introduction, the manager may develop scenarios for possible

[3]See Robert E. Linneman and John D. Kennell, "Shirt-Sleeve Approach to Long-Range Plans," *Harvard Business Review*, March–April, 1977, pp. 141–150.

competitive reactions, different economic environments, and alternative marketing strategies.

Some modeling systems also allow the manager to use probability distributions. Instead of a specific relationship between variables, the manager can include a range of values for the relationship with a probability distribution for the values in the range. The modeling system would then randomly select one value from the range, calculate the results of the model using that value, select another value, calculate the results, and so forth for a specified number of iterations. This approach, known as Monte Carlo simulation, provides the manager with a distribution of outcomes instead of a specific or "point estimate" of the results.[4]

Monte Carlo simulation provides useful information about the range of possible results and therefore the riskiness of the outcomes. Unlike goal seeking, however, if the simulation capabilities are not available on the modeling system, it is difficult to duplicate the process through successive recalculations of the model.

IV. SUMMARY

The purpose of all these analytical techniques is to provide the manager with useful information to aid in decision making. The advantage of using a modeling system is that the manager can directly examine the results of various decisions before having to implement the decisions. The manager can examine the results of various alternatives and test the effects of changing relationships or variable values. This enables the manager to better understand the risks of the alternatives and provides useful information for monitoring critical variables.

The power of the modeling approach is now available to all managers with the development of microcomputers and modeling systems that run on these sytems. The proper use of financial models will provide for better decision making by managers.

---

[4]See David B. Hertz, "Risk Analysis in Capital Investment," *Harvard Business Review*, September-October, 1979, pp. 169–181.

Using Lotus 1-2-3

As discussed in Appendix A, computer-based financial modeling, or Decision Support Systems, as the programs are sometimes called, has revolutionized the use of computers in business applications. There are many different modeling programs available for both large, mainframe computers and microcomputers such as the IBM Personal Computer. The programs vary in price, ease of use, and level of sophistication.

A popular approach to financial modeling on microcomputers has been the development of electronic spreadsheets. These programs simulate the familiar matrix or spreadsheet format used in accounting. Their popularity is due to the ease with which managers can make changes in the spreadsheet. This, along with their flexibility, facilitates their use in sensitivity analysis.

One of the most popular spreadsheet programs is Lotus 1-2-3. The package follows the current trend in software development in that it includes several different capabilities in one integrated package. In addition to a well-developed spreadsheet program, Lotus 1-2-3 also includes a graphics program and data management system. The advantage of this integrated approach is that it allows the user to easily shift from one type of data analysis to another.

This appendix provides an introduction to the spreadsheet and graphics capabilities of 1-2-3. For a description of the other capabilities, refer to the 1-2-3 User's Manual. In addition, Lotus has prepared a very useful Tutorial Diskette, which provides detailed instruction in the use of the program. This appendix is not intended as a replacement for either of these. The best procedure is to work through the tutorial program and refer to the User's Manual for detailed examples and descriptions of the 1-2-3's capabilities. The following segments are designed to provide only the bare essentials necessary to begin using the spreadsheet and graphics facilities.

I. GETTING STARTED

1. Open the door of diskette drive A, the one on the left, by lifting up on it. Slide the 1-2-3 diskette into the drive. Make sure that the label side is up and that the end with the label enters last. Close the door of the diskette drive.

2. Switch on the computer. After a few seconds of internal checking, the diskette drive will whir and make some noises, and the red light on the diskette drive will go on. The computer will ask you to type in the current date and time (in 24-hour format), and then the computer will load the 1-2-3 program.

3. When the program is loaded, the 1-2-3 access menu will appear on the screen, resembling the diagram in Exhibit B–1. The words on the second row of the screen indicate alternate functions of 1-2-3. By selecting from this menu of commands, the user is able to perform various tasks. This multilevel command menu concept is used throughout the 1-2-3 program.

4. The highlighted section of the screen is called the cursor. It is currently over the 1-2-3. You can move the cursor by using the four arrow keys located on the 2, 4, 6, and 8 keys on the numeric keypad section of the keyboard. By pressing the right arrow key, you can scroll through each of the menu alternatives. When the cursor reaches the last function, PC-DOS, if you press the right arrow key again it will return to the first item in the menu, 1-2-3. Notice that as you scroll through the commands, the descriptions on the third line change. The third line shows a description of the particular command that is highlighted by the cursor.

5. 1-2-3 has a built-in Help capability. If at any time you are unsure of what to do, press the F1 key located on the left side of the keyboard. The program will provide some clarifying instructions as well as a menu to access further help messages.

The other function keys have specific uses in 1-2-3. Not all of the functions will be described in this note. Consult the User's Manual for details on the uses of the function keys.

6. To cancel a command, press the Esc key. This will cause 1-2-3 to back up to the previous command menu.

7. To save spreadsheets that you develop with 1-2-3, you need to have a diskette prepared for this purpose. You cannot save spreadsheets on the 1-2-3 program diskette. The process of diskette preparation needs to be done only once. After the diskette has been prepared, it can be used over and over again to store spreadsheets.

To prepare a diskette, move the cursor to the Disk-Manager command and press the ↵ key. (In this note, this will be referred to as the [ENTER] key.) The Disk Manager submenu will appear on the screen. Move the cursor to the Prepare command and press [ENTER]. The program will give you an opportunity to change your mind by asking if you want to proceed with the diskette preparation. Move the cursor to Yes and press [ENTER] or merely

EXHIBIT B–1 1-2-3 Access Command Menu

```
LOTUS Access System (c) 1983 Lotus Development Corp.                MENU
1-2-3   File-Manager   Disk-Manager   Print Graph      Translate    Exit
Enter 1-2-3—LOTUS Spreadsheet/Graphics/Database program
```

press Y, and then follow the computer prompting for preparing the diskette. The reason that the program provides for an opportunity to escape preparing the diskette is that the process of preparation, called formatting, will destroy anything that has already been saved on the diskette.

1. Cautions

A. Handle your diskettes carefully. Do not touch the magnetic surface that is exposed through oval cutouts in the protective plastic cover. Do not place the diskettes on top of your monitor; this can damage the diskettes. When writing on the labels on the diskettes, use only a felt-tip pen.

B. Do not turn off the computer when there is a diskette in the drive and the red light is on. This could damage the diskette.

C. While you are using the 1-2-3 program, do not remove the program diskette from diskette drive A. The system must frequently access data that is stored on the system diskette.

2. Stopping

If you wish to stop using 1-2-3, move the cursor to the Exit command on the 1-2-3 access menu and press [ENTER]. Alternatively, simply turn off the computer. Remember, do not turn off the computer if the red light on a diskette drive is on.

II. ENTERING A MODEL

To enter the spreadsheet program of 1-2-3, move the cursor to 1-2-3 on the access command menu and press [ENTER]. The system will load the spreadsheet program, and the 1-2-3 logo will be displayed on the monitor. Press any key and the logo disappears leaving only a blank worksheet resembling Exhibit B–2.

1-2-3 can be looked at as an electronic worksheet with 256 columns and 2,048 rows. The columns are lettered A, B, C, and so on out to IV. The rows are designated by the numbers 1 through 2048. Each position on the worksheet is identified by the column and row number; e.g., A1, BB45, and so on.

If you have followed the starting steps described above, your worksheet should now show the columns A through H and rows 1 through 20. To see other parts of the worksheet, you must move the cursor.

1. Moving the Cursor

The cursor is the highlighted rectangle at position A1. The cursor is always in position A1 when a new worksheet is started. The position of the cursor determines where entries are made on the worksheet. Note that the position of the cursor is indicated in the upper-left corner of the screen above the worksheet on what is called the cell contents line, as shown on Exhibit B–2.

The cursor can be moved in five ways:

A. Arrow keys. The four arrow keys located on the numeric keypad are probably the most used method of moving the cursor. Pressing on one of the arrow keys moves the cursor one cell in that direction. To increase the speed of movement while using the arrow keys, just depress and hold down the keys.

B. End key and arrow keys. Pressing the End key (the number 1 key on the numeric keypad) followed by one of the arrow keys will move the cursor to the next "break" cell. If the cursor is on a cell with an entry, the cursor will be moved to the cell preceding the next blank cell. If the cursor is on a blank cell, the break cell will be one with an entry.

C. Pg Up, Pg Dn, and ⇥, ⇤ keys. Pressing either the Pg Up or Pg Dn keys will move the worksheet one page, 20 rows, up or down. Pressing the tab keys will move the worksheet one screen width to the right or left. To access the left tab key, you must depress the shift key (↑) while pressing the tab key.

D. F5 (Go To) key. Pressing the F5 key invokes the Go To command. When you press this key, the words "Enter address to go to: A1" appear on the entry line. A1 is the current cursor position. Type in the coordinates of the position where you would like the cursor to be and then press [ENTER]. The cursor will move to the entered position.

E. The Home key. Pressing the Home key (the number 7 key on the numeric keypad) will move the cursor to the upper-left-most position on the worksheet.

If at any time you try to move the cursor to a position outside the limits of the worksheet, you will hear a beep. Don't worry, this does no harm. It is just a signal that you are doing something unacceptable.

2. Entering Words and Numbers

Now that you have familiarized yourself with the movement of the cursor, you can begin to enter words and numbers. As you make an entry, it appears on the screen on the entry line above the worksheet. The column width is nine characters, so entries longer than this will only show the first nine characters when entered on the worksheet. Column size can be increased or decreased as will be explained later.

There are three types of entries:

A. Labels. Labels are a word or some combination of letters, symbols, and numbers. Examples of labels that might be used are SALES, COGS, ASSETS, and MARGIN.

EXHIBIT B-2 The 1-2-3 Worksheet

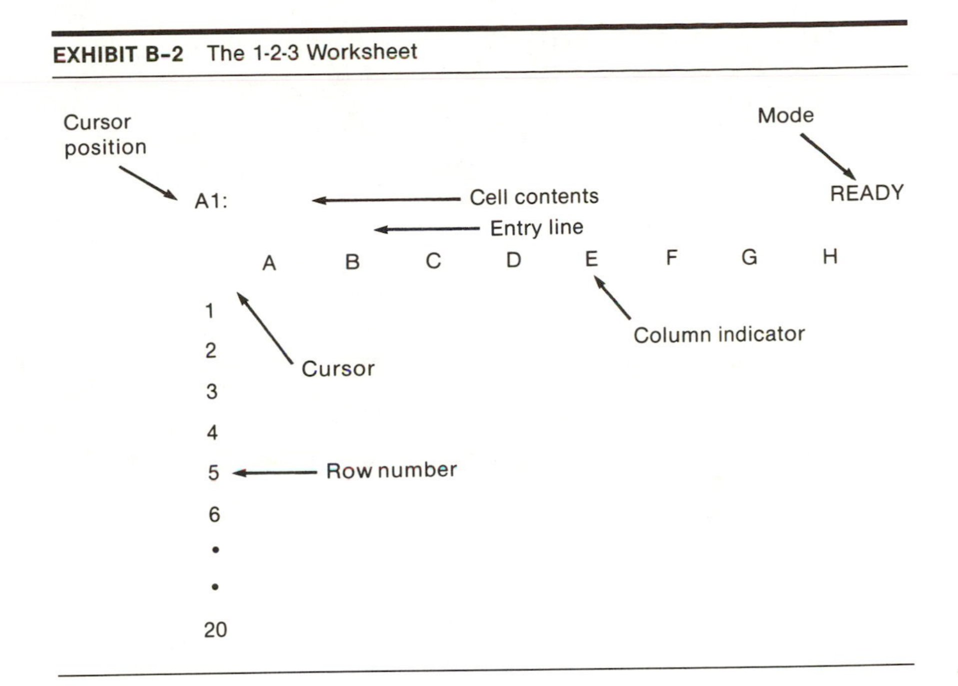

B. Values. Values are numbers that remain fixed or constant. 1-2-3 assumes that all numbers are positive (+) unless indicated. If the number is negative, precede it with a minus sign (−).

C. Relationships. Relationships include all formulas or mathematical expressions. They define the relationship between various cells on the worksheet. In developing relationships, the typical mathematical operators for addition (+), subtraction (−), multiplication (*), and division (/) are used. Other operators described in the User's Manual can also be used. The following are examples of valid relationships:

+B3+B4 (add the contents of positions B3 and B4)
+A40*B20 (multiply the contents of A40 by B20)
+BE10/1.5 (divide the contents of BE10 by 1.5)

3. Things to Remember in Entering Values and Labels

When making an entry, the first character struck tells 1-2-3 whether the entry is a value or label. Once the first character is struck, either VALUE or LABEL will be displayed on the mode indicator in the upper-right-hand corner of the screen. The characters that you have entered will be displayed on the entry line above the worksheet.

Labels usually begin with letters, and values begin with numbers. Ordinarily this shouldn't cause problem except when you want to start a label with (+), (−), or (.), which 1-2-3 assumes are the first characters of a value. To avoid this problem, first type ("); everything after that is assumed to be a label. No quotation marks are needed at the end of the label, just press [ENTER]. Thus, if you wish to make a line on the worksheet, you can type "------ [ENTER].

The (") entry will result in the label being right aligned in the column. If you wish the label to be left aligned, precede the entry with ('). To center the label in the column, use the (^) entry.

Another interpretation problem occurs with position indicators such as A3 and FV256. When the first character is struck, 1-2-3 assumes that you are entering a label. However, you may be attempting to enter a relationship such as A3*FV256. To eliminate this problem, precede the first position indicator with a (+) as in +A3*FV256. The (+) sign indicates to 1-2-3 that you are entering a value or relationship.

Parentheses may be used to change the normal right to left calculation order used by 1-2-3. Suppose the following situation:

Position	*Contains the Value*
A6	10
A7	2
A8	5

If you enter the expression +A6+A7*A8, the result will be 20. 1-2-3 would calculate 2 * 5 = 10 then 10 + 10 = 20. If you want the calculation performed as (+A6+A7)*A8, then you must enter it that way.

It is easier to enter numbers with the keys on the top row of the keyboard. This is because the numeric keypad has alternate functions in 1-2-3. If you want to use the keypad to enter numbers, you must press the Num Lock key. To return the keypad to its alternative uses of moving the cursor, you must press the Num Lock key again.

After you have typed an entry, you must press the enter key [ENTER] or one of the arrow keys to put the entry on the worksheet. Depressing one of these keys indicates that the entry is complete. Once the entry has been included on the worksheet, you will see the entry on the cell contents line.

4. Mistakes and Typographical Errors

Before the [ENTER] is pressed, errors may be corrected using the right and left arrow keys and the ← and Del keys. Pressing the ← key erases the character to the left of the current entry position, the small highlighted underline. The Del key deletes the character at the underline position. Move the highlighted underline using the arrow keys to the appropriate position and then delete the desired character or characters.

After the [ENTER] has been depressed, there are two methods of making changes. You can position the cursor at the cell position you want to change and type a new entry. This will replace the old entry. You can also use the F2 key to enter the edit function and, using the arrow ← and Del keys, make changes as was described above. In the edit mode, you may insert characters by positioning the cursor at the appropriate place and typing the new entries. The insertion occurs automatically without deleting any of the previous characters. In any case, when you are finished, put the entry on the worksheet by pressing [ENTER].

5. A Simple Income Statement

Now that you know how to move the cursor and make entries, let's try to enter a simple income statement.

Assume that for ABC Manufacturing Company:

Sales = $100,000
Cost of goods sold = 65% of Sales
Selling and administrative expense = 15% of Sales
Interest expense = $5,000
Tax rate = 48%

Move the cursor to position A1 and begin to make the entries in the appropriate columns and rows, as shown below. These entries will result in an income statement for ABC Manufacturing that is consistent with the assumptions listed above.

ROWS	COLUMNS A	B
1	SALES	100000
2	COGS	.65*B1 or +B1*.65
3		"-------
4	MARGIN	+B1−B2
5	SG&A	.15*B1 or +B1*.15
6	INTEREST	5000
7		"-------
8	PBT	+B4−B5−B6
9	TAXES	.48*B8 or +B8*.48
10		"-------
11	PAT	+B8−B9

When you are finished your screen should look like this:

```
SALES        100000
COGS          65000
              ------
MARGIN        35000
SG&A          15000
INTEREST       5000
              ------
PBT           15000
TAXES          7200
              ------
PAT            7800
```

As you were typing, there were several things you may have noted.

A. There are no commas in numbers; i.e., 100,000 is typed as 100000. If you enter a comma, the computer will beep and will not accept the entry. If

EXHIBIT B–3 The 1-2-3 Concept

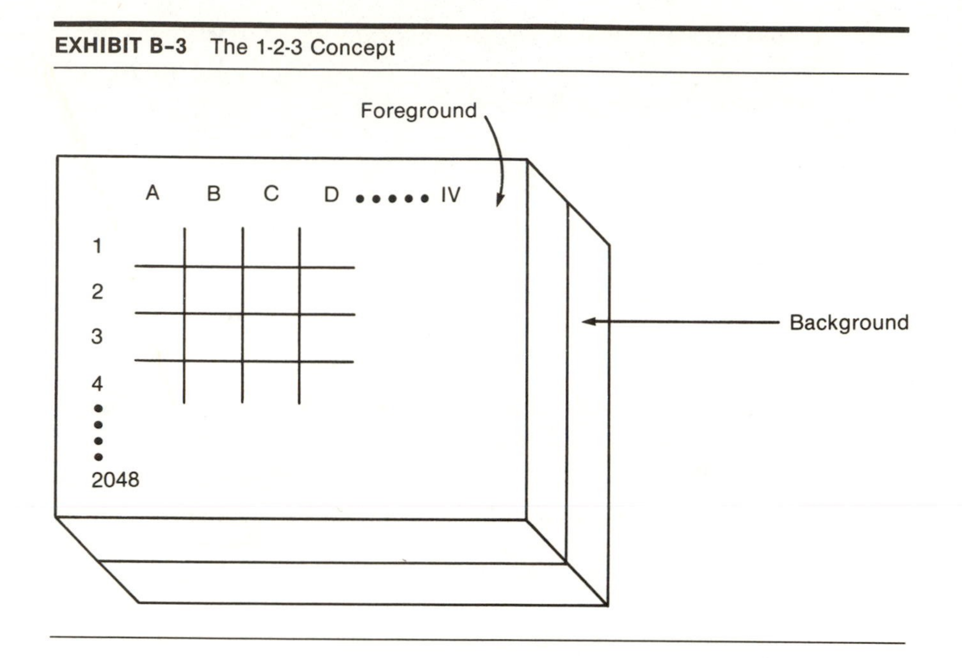

you would like the numbers to be displayed with commas, you can change the numeric formatting as will be described later.

B. Relationships or formulas are not displayed on the worksheet (foreground); however, the formula or relationship is saved in the background. 1-2-3 can thus be thought of as a matrix that is 256 columns wide by 2,048 rows long and 2 deep as shown on Exhibit B–3.

One cannot immediately ascertain by looking at a particular position on the worksheet whether that number is a constant or whether it is the result of a computation involving values in other positions; i.e., that it is related to some other figures on the sheet. The only way to discover how a particular number was derived is to place the cursor at that position. The top line of the 1-2-3 screen above the worksheet, the cell contents line, will then display the cell address together with the entry. In other words, the background for that position will be displayed.

For example, observe the value 65000 in position B2 of your worksheet. If the cursor is placed at B2, the cell contents line (topmost line on the screen) will read as illustrated in Exhibit B–4. This tells you that in position B2 there is a value that is .65 times the entry in position B1.

What happens if there is a change in ABC's income statement? For example, suppose that ABC's cost of sales increases to 68%. To determine the effect of this change on the statement, move the cursor to position B2 and type .68*B1 [ENTER]. You will see that 1-2-3 automatically recalculates the margin, profit before tax, and profit after tax.

EXHIBIT B-4 1-2-3 Screen with Cell Contents Line

B2:	0.65*B1	READY

Changes in other values can be accomplished similarly. This ease of change is what makes 1-2-3 and other modeling programs so useful.

6. Printing the Model

Now that you have completed the income statement, you may wish to print a copy. Most printers used with microcomputers only print 80 columns across a page. This means that if you have a model with a large number of columns, for example 20 columns each nine characters in width, the program will print one part of the model on one page and then continue the model on a second and third page until it is completed. The same continuation procedure is followed for models with more than the 56 rows that can be printed on one page.

1-2-3 is designed to print any contiguous block of the foreground of the worksheet. You simply indicate the upper-left-most position and the lower-right position. The block that is to be printed will be highlighted on the screen.

To print the income statement model, follow these steps:

A. Make sure that the printer is turned on and set for on-line.

B. Position the cursor on the upper-left position of the block, in this case A1.

C. Type /. This is the keystroke that starts all commands. The entry line will read as shown on Exhibit B-5. Each of the words represents different sets of commands or functions that 1-2-3 can perform. You need to select a command from this menu.

D. Move the cursor to the Print command and press [ENTER]. The entry line now shows a subset of commands for printing.

E. Move the cursor to Printer and press [ENTER]. This command tells the system that you want the worksheet printed on the printer. 1-2-3 next provides another submenu of commands for printing on a printer.

F. Move the cursor to Range and press [ENTER]. This command enables you to enter the block or range of positions that you would like printed. Since the cursor was already on position A1, this position is shown followed by the lower right position, B11.

G. You may change the block to be printed by moving the cursor. As you move the cursor, you will notice the range of positions will be highlighted on the screen, and the ending range position on the entry line will change. Press [ENTER] to enter the ending position. The print submenu will again appear on the entry line.

EXHIBIT B-5 1-2-3 Modeling Commands

Worksheet	Range	Copy	Move	File	Print	Graph	Data	Quit

H. Move the cursor to Go and press [ENTER]. The printout should now begin.

I. When the printout is completed, select Quit from the menu to exit from the Print submenu.

7. Saving the Model

Having printed the model, you may now wish to save the model for future use. In order to do this, you need an initialized diskette as described in the section on GETTING STARTED. We will call this the model file diskette. This diskette should be placed in diskette drive B, the right-hand drive, and the door closed. Then take the following steps:

A. Type /. Remember this accesses the modeling commands.

B. Move the cursor to File and press [ENTER]. It is also possible to just type F. Either method displays the File command submenu.

C. Move the cursor to Save and press [ENTER]. The 1–2–3 will ask for the name you wish to give the model.

D. Type A FILE NAME [ENTER]. You may give the model any name that you like. File names can have any combination of eight letters or numbers. No spaces or special characters may be used.

The system will first check the file names already stored on the model file diskette in drive B and will then store the file. The red light on drive B will be on while the program is being stored.

8. Ending a Session

After you have completed a model and printed it for further study, you may want to exit from 1-2-3.

A. Type /.

B. Select Quit from the menu and press [ENTER].

C. Since exiting 1-2-3 will result in losing all worksheet data unless it has previously been saved, the system will ask you to confirm that you want to exit. Press Y to end the session and to return to the Access System menu. You may exit from the Access system using the procedure described previously or simply turn off the computer.

III. MORE COMPLEX MODELS

In the first section, you learned how to enter a simple income statement for one year. The same principles can be applied to writing more complex income statements, balance sheets, cash flow statements, or other financial models. This section will demonstrate how to use 1-2-3 for financial forecasting and planning. In order to do this, let's go back to the ABC Manufacturing Company income statement model you developed in the previous section.

A. Load the 1-2-3 worksheet program as described in the GETTING STARTED section. Put the model file diskette in the B drive.

B. Type /. Move the cursor to File and press [ENTER].

C. Since the cursor is already on the Retrieve subcommand, press [ENTER].

D. The program will display a menu of the file names that have been saved on the model file diskette. Move the cursor to the file you would like to retrieve and press [ENTER].

While the system is loading the file you specified, the mode indicator in the upper right corner of the screen will change from READY to WAIT. When the model is loaded, the READY status will reappear.

1. Clearing a Worksheet

If you have been working on one model and wish to start a different model, you may want to begin with a blank worksheet. To clear a worksheet from the screen, type /W. The W is the first letter of the Worksheet command. Move the cursor in the Worksheet command submenu to Erase and press [ENTER]. The system will ask if you want to erase the worksheet. Enter Y. The confirmation is used because erasing the worksheet will cause all of the data to be lost unless it has previously been saved on a diskette.

2. Copy Command

In order to use 1-2-3 for financial planning, you should use the copy command. The copy command enables you to copy or duplicate relationships, values, or labels across many columns or down many rows. The relationship, value, or label that you wish to copy is called the source position, and the location into which you wish to duplicate or copy the relationship is referred to as the target position.

The source position can be replicated into another position;

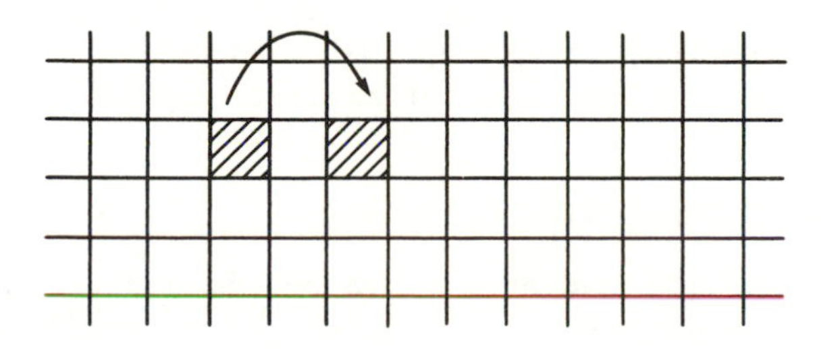

into a range of positions across a row;

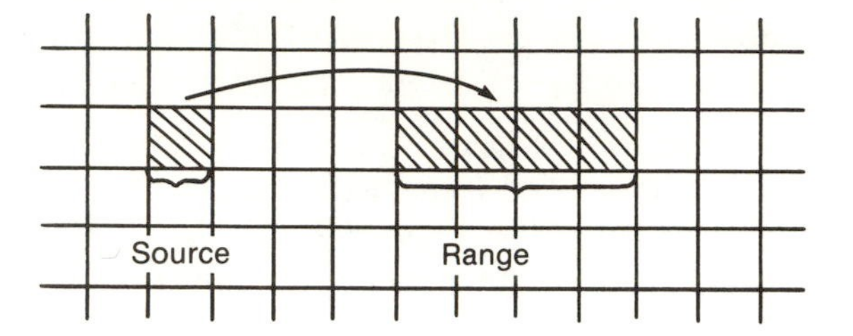

or into a range of positions down a column.

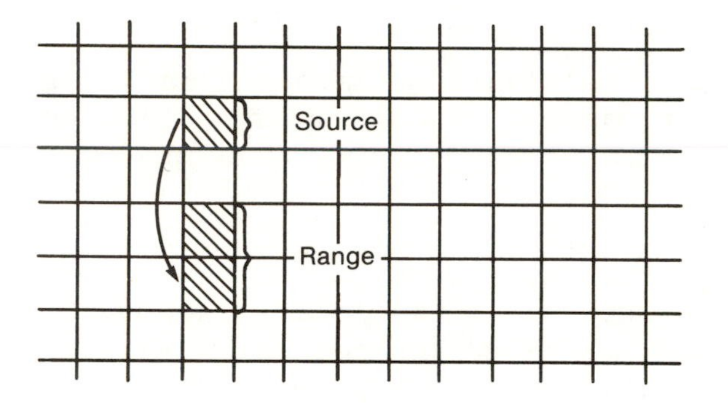

It is also possible to copy a range of source positions into a range of target positions.

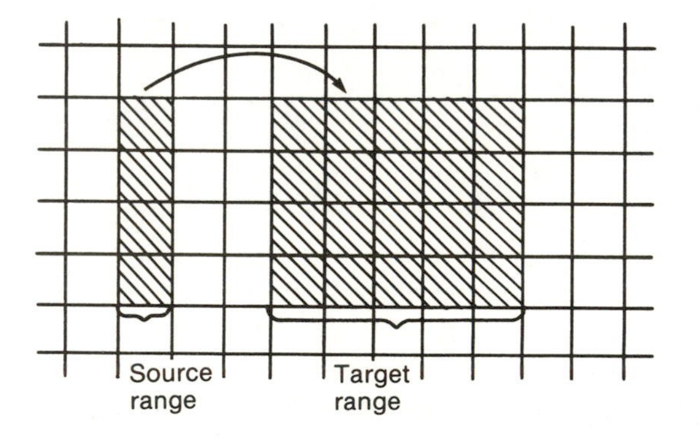

The copy command facilitates quickly expanding a model across a number of time periods once the basic relationships in the source range are established. Obviously, it would be possible to expand the model without using the copy command by laboriously retyping all of the relationships for each time period.

3. Absolute versus Relative Relationships

In defining relationships, cell positions are often used. For example, in the ABC Manufacturing income statement, the entry in position B5 is .15*B1. 1-

2-3 interprets this to mean the value for B5 is calculated by multiplying the value four rows above in the same column by .15. If this relationship were copied into the C column, it would appear as .15*C1. Therefore, in calculating the value for C5, 1-2-3 would look for a value four rows above in the same column, which would now be position C1. This is known as a relative relationship, and this is the nature of most relationships in a model.

Absolute or fixed relations are those where a specific value is accessed regardless of where it may appear in the model. For example, if you wish the model to utilize the specific value in B1, the relationship in B5 would be written as .15*B1. The $ signs indicate an absolute cell address.

When a fixed position is copied, the specified position does not change. For example if .15*B1 were to be copied to C5, the relationship would remain .15*B1.

4. Copying One Position

To copy the label SALES from position A1 into position A15:

A. Move the cursor to position A1.

B. Type /.

C. Move the cursor in the command menu to Copy and press [ENTER].

D. The entry line reads "Enter range to copy FROM: A1..Al," with A1 being the current cursor position. Press [ENTER] to indicate that only the A1 position is to be copied.

E. The entry line will read "Enter range to copy TO: A1" with A1 still the current cursor position. However, we do not want to copy A1 to itself, so move the cursor to the desired position, in this case A15, or type A15 and press [ENTER]. The word sales will now appear in position A15.

5. Copying a Range of Positions

Now that you have copied one label, let's try copying the rest of the labels in one step.

A. Move the cursor to A2. This will be the beginning of the range we wish to copy.

B. Type /C.

C. Type a period (.). The period is necessary to separate the beginning position of the range from the ending position. Although you only typed one period, the entry line will show two periods and now reads "Enter range to copy FROM: A2..A2."

D. Move the cursor to A11, the end of the source range. As you move the cursor, the highlighted positions will increase and the last position indicator in the source range prompt will change to reflect the current cursor location. Press [ENTER].

E. Move the cursor to A16 or type A16. The prompt line will now read "Enter range to copy TO: A16." Press [ENTER]. 1-2-3 will now copy the contents of the source range to the target range beginning in position A16.

6. Copying Relationships

Although copying the labels indicated the usefulness of the Copy command in saving typing, it did not demonstrate the ability of Copy to deal with changing relationships. For example, suppose that sales of ABC Manufacturing are increasing at 10% per year and you want an income statement for the next five years. To accomplish this with 1-2-3, you should:

A. Move the cursor to C1.

B. Type the relationship for a 10% sales growth; e.g., 1.1*B1[ENTER].

C. Type /C.

D. The source range shows C1. Press [ENTER].

E. 1-2-3 is now prompting for the target range. Move the cursor to D1 and press period (.). Then move the cursor to G1 and press [ENTER]. Alternatively, you could type D1. G1[ENTER]. This specifies that C1 should be copied to the target range D1 to G1 to provide the last four years of the forecast.

Since the original expression in C1 was specified as a relative relationship, the formula in D1 will read 1.1*C1. The formula in E1 reads 1.1*D1 and so forth. The sales row on the worksheet should now increase by 10% per year for five years.

It is now possible to copy the rest of the income statement using the same relationships that were used in the orginal model.

A. Move the cursor to B2.

B. Type /C.

C. Type a period (.) and move the cursor to B11. Press [ENTER].

D. Type C2.G2 [ENTER]. This tells 1-2-3 to copy the range from B2 to B11 in the columns C through G.

You should now have an original income statement and five additional years. What happens if you want to change one term and see what the impact is? For example, what happens if COGS changes to 70% of sales? Move the cursor back to B2. Type .7*B1 [ENTER]. Only the profit for that year will change. You must use the Copy command to copy the new relationship in position B2 to the other columns before the income statements for the other years are changed.

IV. CHANGING THE WORKSHEET

In the previous sections, you learned the basics of how to use 1-2-3; however, there are a number of modeling commands that will allow you to alter the display or change the model that you have entered without retyping the model.

1. Changing the Column Width

You may change the column width for the entire model, for a range of columns, or for a single column.

To change the column width for the entire model, key / and then select Worksheet from the command menu. The Worksheet submenu will then appear as follows:

EXHIBIT B-6 Worksheet Command Submenu

Global	Insert	Delete	Column-Width	Erase	Titles	Window	Status

Move the cursor to Global and press [ENTER]. This will display the Global command submenu.

EXHIBIT B-7 Global Command Submenu

Format	Label-Prefix	Column-Width	Recalculation	Protection	Default

Select Column-Width from the menu and press [ENTER]. You can then adjust the column width by specifying a number or by pressing the right and left arrow keys and observing the changing column width on the highlighted cursor on the screen.

To change the column width for a single column, type /W and then select the Column-Width command from the Worksheet submenu. Select Set from the next submenu. You then set the column width either by specifying a number or using the horizontal arrow keys. When the column is at the desired width, press [ENTER].

2. Changing the Numerical Format

The format used for displaying numbers can be changed for the entire worksheet, a range of columns or rows, or for a single position.

To change the display format for the entire worksheet, first press /W to access the Worksheet subcommand menu. Then select the Global subcommand followed by the Format subcommand. The Format subcommand will further display a menu of nine alternative formats for your selection.

Fixed	This format allows you to specify a fixed number of decimal places that will be displayed.
Scientific	This format displays the numbers in scientific notation; e.g., 1.2E5.
Currency	This displays numbers in a dollar and cents format of $x,xxx.xx. You are allowed to specify the number of decimal places to be displayed.
,	This format is the common format for numbers, xxx,xxx. You may specify the number of decimal places to be shown. This format also displays negative numbers in parentheses.
General	This is the default format and allows a floating decimal position to be displayed.

+/–	This is a low-level graphics format that displays the appropriate number of + or – signs for the number in that position.
Percent	Numbers are displayed in a percent format of x.xx%. You may indicate the number of decimal positions to be shown.
Date	The command provides three alternatives for displaying a date.
Text	The text command will display the background formula rather than the calculated value.

To change the format for a specific position or a range of positions, select the Range command from the modeling commands menu. The Range submenu consists of:

EXHIBIT B-8 Range Command Submenu

Format	Label-Prefix	Erase	Name	Justify	Protect	Unprotect	Input

Selecting the Format subcommand provides the same choices as above with the addition of a Reset command. The Reset command changes the format for the specified range to the global format that was specified for the worksheet.

After choosing the format, you will be asked to specify the range of position that should use that format. The range can be a single position, a range of rows, or a range of columns. You specify the range in the same manner used for entering ranges for the Copy command.

3. Inserting or Deleting a Row or Column

Often it is necessary to add a column or row into the middle of a 1-2-3 model. To add a column in the model, place the cursor wherever the new column is needed. The cursor can be placed anywhere in the column. Key /W and then select the Insert subcommand from the menu. Next select Column from the menu. You may insert several columns at once, so the system will prompt for a range to be inserted. You may specify a single column or a range of columns. When you are finished entering the range, press [ENTER] and 1-2-3 will insert the specified blank columns.

Inserting rows is done similarly. Select Row from the Insert subcommand menu and specify the row or range of rows to be inserted.

To delete rows or columns that are no longer needed, use the Delete command. You will be prompted to indicate whether rows or columns are to be deleted and then to specify the range to be deleted. After entering the range, press [ENTER], and the relevant range will be removed from the program. Since the deletions are irretrievable, you should be careful when using this command.

4. Blanking a Position or Range

If you have a position or a range with entries that you would like to change to blanks, this can be done by selecting the Range command followed by the Erase subcommand. You will be asked to specify a range to be erased. When you finish entering the range, press [ENTER]. The range will still be on the worksheet, but it will now be blank. Again, caution in using this command is warranted since the contents are lost once the range is erased.

5. Keeping Titles on Your Monitor

When the cursor is moved to the right beyond the first few columns, the contents of column A disappear, then column B, and so on. A similar thing happens when you scroll down beyond row 20; row 1 disappears and then row 2, etc. Often the leftmost columns and/or topmost rows contain labels or values you would prefer to fix on the screen for constant reference. The Titles command does this.

A. Move the cursor to the row below or column to the right of that which you would like to fix on the screen.

B. Type /.

C. Select Worksheet from the menu and press [ENTER].

D. Select Titles from the submenu and press [ENTER].

E. If you want to set a horizontal title (a row), select Horizontal from the menu. For a vertical title (a column), choose Vertical. You may fix both a horizontal and vertical title by using the Both command.

Once you have fixed the titles, the cursor cannot be moved into the title area(s) except by using the F5 (Go To) key. To remove any Title command that is in effect, select the Clear command from the Title submenu.

6. Built-In Functions

Some of the mathematical relationships are used so frequently that they have been built into 1-2-3. To specify one of the functions, you should first type (@), then the function, followed by the required value or range for that function. When it is necessary to specify a value, you may either indicate a numeric value or a cell position in the worksheet. If a range of values is required, the standard procedure of indicating the first position followed by a period and the last position should be used.

Some of the available functions are:

@ABS(x)	Absolute value of x
@EXP(x)	Exponential value of x
@INT(x)	Integer part of the value of x

@LN(x)	Log on the base e for x
@LOG(x)	Log on the base 10 for x
@RAND	Random number between 0 and 1
@ROUND(x,n)	Round the number x to n decimal places
@SQRT(x)	Square root of x
@NPV(x,range)	Net present value of the range using the discount rate x
@TODAY	Today's date
@COUNT(range)	Counts the number of items in the range
@SUM(range)	Sums the values of all items in the range
@AVG(range)	Averages the values of all items in the range
@MIN(range)	Selects the minimum of all items in the range
@MAX(range)	Selects the maximum of all items in the range
@STD(range)	Standard deviation of all items in the range
@VAR(range)	Variance of all items in the range

V. USING GRAPHICS

The graphics facility of Lotus 1-2-3 allows you to present data so that it is attractive and easily understood. The Graphics section of the Lotus 1-2-3 package displays data that have been entered into or generated by the worksheet. You must specify which data is to be displayed and how it is to be displayed, then 1-2-3 does the rest. To illustrate how to use the graphics, you can create a graph using the data from the simple six-year income statements you created in the previous sections.

1. Selecting Graphics

To enter the Graphics subprogram, you should:

A. Type /.

B. Select Graphics from the menu. You will then see the following submenu.

EXHIBIT B-9 Graphics Command Submenu

Type	X	A	B	C	D	E	F	Reset	View	Save	Options	Name	Quit

C. Press T to select the type of graph. You may choose between a line chart, bar graph, X-Y graph, stacked bar graph, or a pie chart. Select the line chart.

D. Select A to set the first data range. You will see the prompt "Enter first data range:". You may specify any row or column of data to be graphed. For our example, you should enter "B11..G11".

E. Select View from the menu. If you have a graphics monitor, you should now see the following graph:

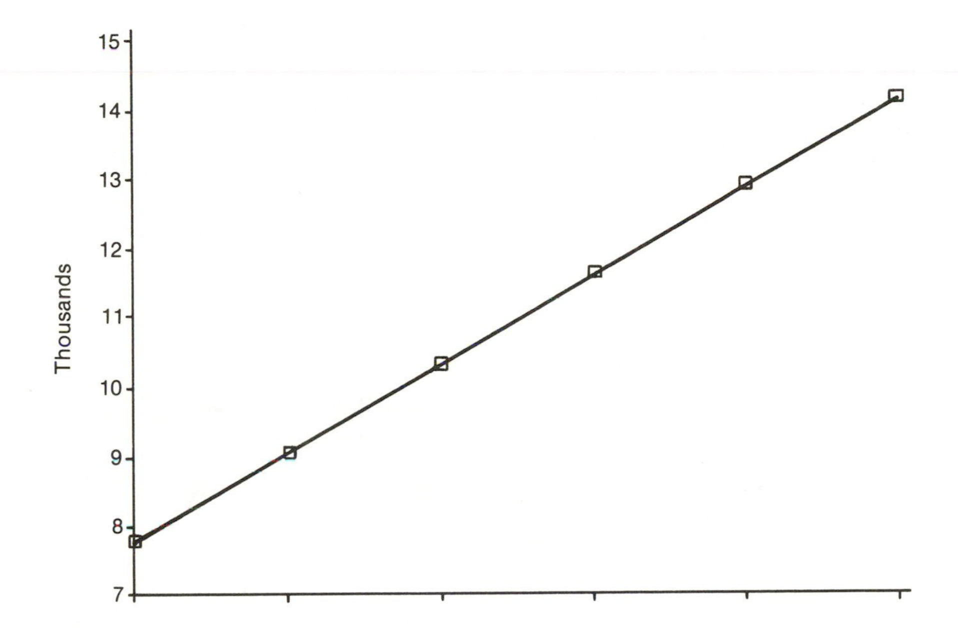

Press any key to return to the worksheet text.

The IBM PC monochrome monitor does not display graphs. You can still create graphs and then print them as will be explained later.

2. Adding Additional Data Ranges

The graph is not very impressive with just one line of data. You may include up to six different data ranges to be graphed. To add additional ranges, you do the following:

A. Select B from the graphics submenu. You will then be prompted for the second data range. Enter "B4..G4". You could of course specify data ranges for C through F.

B. Press V to view the graph. You will see the graph shown at the top of page 178. Notice that the left-hand axis (Y-axis) has been automatically rescaled.

3. Adding Labels

With two lines on the graph, it is confusing as to what each line represents. To eliminate confusion, which is of course the purpose of using graphs, you should label the lines. To do this:

A. Select Options. Then select L for Legends from the submenu.

B. Press A. The entry line now reads "Enter legend for A-range:". Since the A-range is the profit after tax, you should enter "PAT".

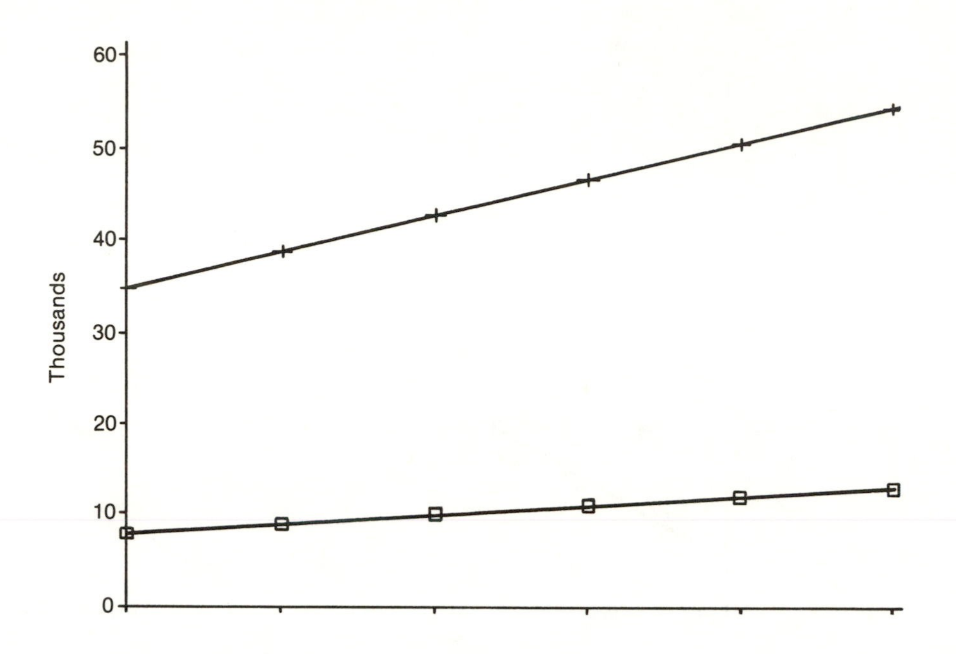

C. Press L and then B. You should now enter the legend for the B-range. This was the gross margin, so enter "MARGIN".

D. Select Quit and then press V. You will see the following graph.

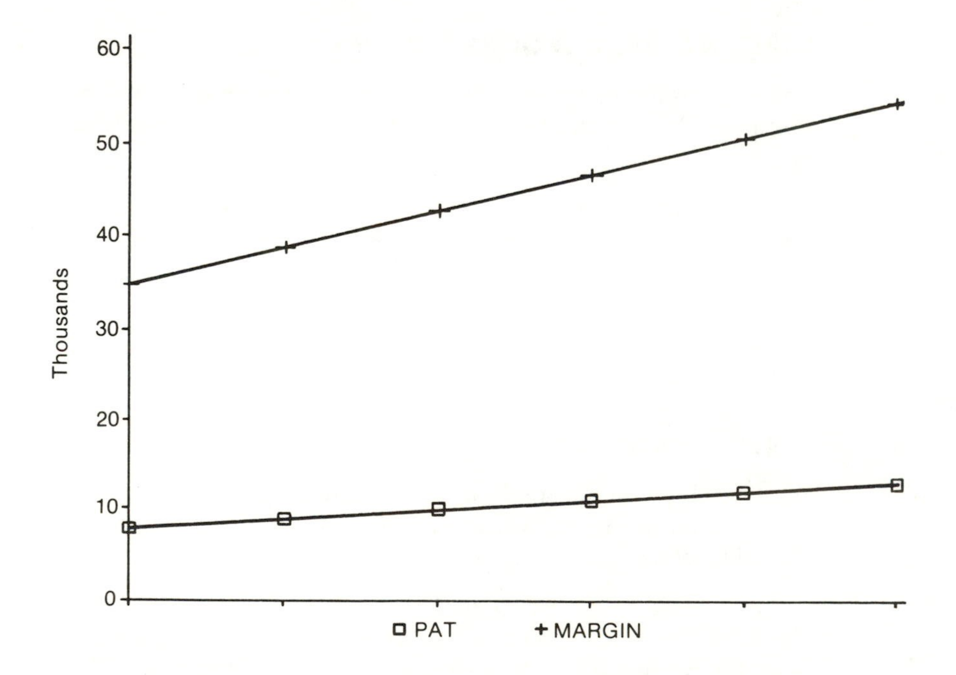

Once the graph has been created, you can return to the ready mode of the worksheet, change any data that you would like, and then view the results by pressing the F10 key. It is not necessary to access the graphics submenu to view the graph, only to change any of the graphics specifications.

4. Saving the Graph

In order to print the graph, you must first name and save it. This can be done through the following steps.

A. Select Name from the Graphics submenu.

B. Select Create from the submenu. You will see the prompt "Enter graph name". Type in the name you would like for the graph.

C. Select Save. Again you will be prompted "Enter graph name." The names of all previously saved graphics files will be displayed. Type in the name of the graphics files again, and the graph will be saved on the disk in the B drive.

5. Printing a Graph

The program to print a graph can only be accessed from the 1-2-3 Access menu.

A. Press the Esc key until you return to the ready mode of the worksheet with a clear prompt line.

B. Press / and then Q to exit from the worksheet. Press Y at the prompt to return to the Access menu.

C. Select PrintGraph from the Access menu. You will be prompted to remove the 1-2-3 Systems disk and to insert the PrintGraph disk. When you have done that, press [ENTER]. You will then see the PrintGraph menu.

EXHIBIT B-10 Printgraph Command Menu

Select	Options	Go	Configure	Align	Page	Quit

D. Press S to select the file that you would like printed. A directory of the graphics files (with the suffix .PIC) will be displayed. Scroll through the directory using the up and down arrow keys. Mark the file you would like printed by pressing the space bar when the highlighted cursor is on the file. Then press [ENTER].

E. Select Configure from the menu. Then select Device from the submenu. This allows you to select the type of printer you have. Scroll through the list of printers and select the appropriate one by marking it with the space bar. Then press [ENTER].

F. Press Q to exit from the Configure submenu.

G. Make sure that the printer is on and connected. Select Go for printing to commence. If the graphics are not printing, you should consult the 1-2-3 User's Manual for more detailed instructions.

VI. OTHER MODELING SYSTEMS

While Lotus 1-2-3 is a powerful and popular spreadsheet program, many other similar programs are also available. These include SuperCalc 3, Multiplan, and VisiCalc Advanced Version. In addition, several so-called integrated programs such as Enable, Symphony, and Framework also include spreadsheet programs.

Another approach to modeling is presented by programs such as IFPS/Personal, ENCORE! and PLAN80. These programs were originally designed to be used on mainframe computer systems. They allow the user to specify relationships between variables using English language-like statements. Rather than requiring specific cell references as with the spreadsheet programs, these programs generate the matrix of cells based on the model relationships.

A detailed review of all of these programs is beyond the scope of this book. However, a wide variety of different types of modeling programs are available. We believe that, wisely used, these programs are an effective managerial tool.

Solutions to Study Questions

This appendix consists of three parts. The first section has detailed solutions to the questions. The second section explains the entries that could be used in creating Lotus 1-2-3 models for solving the study questions. The third part lists IFPS models for the study questions.

I. MANUAL SOLUTIONS TO STUDY QUESTIONS

Chapter 1

1-1.

Sales	$340,000
Cost of goods	261,800
Other expenses	68,000
Profit after tax	$ 10,200

Balance Sheet

Cash	$9,898	Accounts payable	$21,518
Accounts receivable	32,603	Other short-term liabilities	21,549
Inventories	43,633		
Total current assets	86,134	Total current liabilities	43,067
		Long-term debt	81,600
		Common stock	40,000
		Retained earnings	62,000
Net property, plant, and equipment	140,533	Total long-term debt and equity	183,600
Total assets	$226,667	Total liabilities and equity	$226,667

These statements were determined using the following steps:

a. Long-term debt/Equity = .80.
LTD/($40,000 + $62,000) = .80.
LTD = $81,600.

b. Return on equity = 10%.
Profit after tax/($40,000 + $62,000) = .10.
PAT = $10,200.

c. PAT = 3% sales.
$10,200/Sales = .03.
Sales = $10,200/.03.
Sales = $340,000.

d. Cost of goods/Sales = .77.
CGS/$340,000 = .77.
CGS = $261,800.

e. PAT = Sales − CGS − Other expenses.
$10,200 = $340,000 − $261,800 − Other expenses.
Other expenses = $68,000.

f. Days' sales outstanding in AR = 35 days.
(AR/Sales) × 365 = 35.
AR/$340,000 = 35/365.
AR = $32,603.

g. Inventory turnover = 6 times.
CGS/Inventory = 6.
$261,800/Inventory = 6.
Inventory = $43,633.

h. Asset turnover = 1.5.
Sales/Assets = 1.5.
$340,000/Assets = 1.5.
Total assets = Total liabilities = $226,667.
Total liabilities = Total equity + Long-term debt + Current liabilities.
$226,667 = $81,600 + $102,000 + Current liabilities.
Current liabilities = $43,067.

i. Current ratio = 2.0.
Current assets/Current liabilities = 2.0.
Currents assets/$43,067 = 2.0.
Current assets = $86,134.

j. Current assets = Cash + AR + Inventories.
$86,134 = Cash + $32,603 + $43,633.
Cash = $9,898.

k. Total assets = PP&E + Current assets.
$226,667 = PP&E + $86,134.
PP&E = $140,533.

l. Days payables = 30 days.
(Accounts payable/CGS × 365 = 30.
AP/$261,800 = .082.
AP = $21,518.

m. Other ST liabilities = Current liabilities − AP.
Other ST liabilities = $43,067 − $21,518 = $21,549.
Other ST liabilities = $21,549.

1-2. Marvel Company

	1980	*1981*	*1982*	*1983*	*1984*
Percent of sales:					
Sales	100.0%	100.0%	100.0%	100.0%	100.0%
Cost of goods sold	87.0	85.0	83.0	80.0	80.0
Advertising	2.0	1.8	2.2	4.0	6.0
Interest expense	1.0	1.2	1.4	1.3	1.5
Other expenses	6.0	5.7	5.4	5.1	4.9
Profit before tax	4.0	6.3	8.0	9.6	7.6
Change from previous year:					
Sales	—	+5.0%	+4.6%	+5.7%	+8.0%
Cost of goods sold	—	+2.6	+2.1	+1.9	+8.0
Advertising	—	−5.6	+28.0	+92.0	+62.0
Interest expense	—	+26.0	+22.0	−1.7	+25.0
Other expenses	—	−0.2	−1.0	−0.1	+3.8
Profit before tax	—	65.4	32.9	26.8	−14.5

Marvel Company was apparently unhappy with its relatively steady 5%/year increase in sales and the low (4%) return on the sales (PBT/Sales). It did two things:

a. It undertook cost reduction programs in CGS (declining from 87% sales to a steady 80%) and other expenses (declining from 6% sales to a steady 4–5% sales).

b. It stepped up its advertising to increase the annual sales. (Advertising increased from 2% to 6% of sales.)

The program was successful—by the end of 1984, sales were up 8% on an annual basis. PBT/Sales were at a level of 7.6%.

However, Marvel Company apparently had to issue some extra debt to meet its financial needs as Interest/Sales increased throughout the period. In fact, increases in interest expense brought the company's return down in the last period, indicating that Marvel may have to forfeit profitability for growth.

1-3. The current ratios were higher than the industry, indicating high liquidity. A comparison of current ratios with acid-test ratios indicates that the bulk of the current assets were in inventory. The possibility that PBJ had overstocked its inventory is reflected in the lower-than-normal inventory turnover. Changes between PBJ's 1983 and 1984 data indicate that efforts were underway to cut inventories back and increase the turnover. The downward trend in the acid-test ratio is disturbing, but PBJ was still very close to the industry average.

PBJ was supplying far more credit to its customers than was the industry, as reflected in the number of days' sales outstanding. The fact that the trend in this figure was upwards is alarming. The fact that PBJ's days' payables outstanding were in line with the industry average indicates that little slippage was possible with suppliers—PBJ needed to continue to pay its bills on time. Since PBJ must provide the funds to support its credit sales from somewhere, it is likely that its short-term borrowings have increased. The fact is reflected in the decline in the current and the acid-test ratios.

While PBJ's debt/equity ratio was hovering around the industry average, the upward trend indicates that the company had issued new debt. The company may have undertaken capital investments in new production facilities.

PBJ had tight control over its CGS as reflected in its higher-than-average gross profit margin. However, due to its high interest expense, the company's PBT/sales ratio was lower than the industry's.

PBJ's return on equity was close to that of the industry's. Evidently, the company's lower returns had been offset by a smaller equity base (also reflected in the lower debt/equity ratio).

Chapter 2

2–1.

W&H MANUFACTURING COMPANY

	1983	*1984*
Income statement:		
Sales	$250,000	$510,000
Cost of goods sold	195,000	397,800
Gross margin	55,000	112,200
Administrative and other expenses	40,000	40,000
Profit before tax	15,000	72,200
Taxes @ 40%	6,000	28,880
Profit after tax	$ 9,000	$ 43,320
Balance sheet:		
Cash	$ 50,000	$102,000
Accounts receivable	20,548	41,918
Inventory	65,000	66,300
Current assets	135,548	210,218
Net property, plant, and equipment	80,000	76,000
Total assets	$215,548	$286,218
Acounts payable	$ 16,027	$ 32,696
Other short-term liabilities	30,521	41,202
Total current liabilities	46,548	73,898
Long-term debt	60,000	60,000
Common stock	100,000	100,000
Retained earnings	9,000	52,320
Total LTD and equity	169,000	212,320
Total liabilities and equity	$215,548	$286,218
Net working capital:		
Current assets	$135,548	$210,218
Current liabilities	46,548	73,898
Net working capital	$ 89,000	$136,320

These statements were determined using the following:

a. CGS = 78% × Sales = .78 × 510,000 = $397,800.

b. PAT = $34,320.

c. Retained earnings = 1984 RE + 1983 PAT.
Retained earnings = $43,320 + $9,000 = $52,320.

d. Total LTD + OE = LTD + CS + RE.
Total LTD + Equity = $60,000 + $100,000 + $52,320 = $212,320.
e. Cash = .20 × $510,000 = $102,000.
f. Accounts receivable = 30 days' sales.
Accounts receivable/$510,000 + 365 = 30.
Accounts receivable = $41,918.
g. Inventory turnover = 6.
$397,800/Inventory = 6.
Inventory = $66,300.
h. Accounts payable = 30 days of goods.
Accounts payable/397,800 × 365 = 30.
Accounts payable = $32,696.
i. Short-term liabilities = the plug figure.

W&H Manufacturing Company will need to borrow an additional $10,681 in short-term debt, raising the balance to $41,202. Working capital has increased from $89,000 to $136,320.

2–2.

	1984	*1985*
Income statement:		
Sales	$510,000	$663,000
Cost of goods sold	397,800	517,140
Gross margin	112,200	145,860
Other expenses	40,000	40,000
Profit before tax	72,200	105,860
Taxes @ 40%	28,880	42,344
Profit after tax	$ 43,320	$ 63,516
Balance sheet:		
Cash	$102,000	$132,600
Accounts receivable	41,918	81,740
Inventory	66,300	86,190
Total current assets	210,218	300,530
Net property, plant, and equipment	76,000	72,000
Total assets	$286,218	$372,530
Accounts payable	$ 32,696	$ 42,505
Other short-term liabilities	41,202	54,189
Total current liabilities	73,898	96,694
Long-term debt	60,000	60,000
Common stock	100,000	100,000
Retained earnings	52,320	115,836
Total LTD and equity	212,320	275,836
Total liabilities and equity	$286,218	$372,530
Net working capital:		
Current assets	$210,218	$300,530
Current liabilities	73,898	96,694
Net working capital	$136,320	$203,836

These statements were determined using the following:

a. Cost of goods = $663,000 × .78 = $517,140.
Completing the income statement gives PAT of $63,516.

b. Retained earnings = 1984 Retained earnings balance of \$52,320 plus 1985 Profit after tax of \$63,516 = \$115,836.

c. Total long-term debt + Equity = Long-term debt \$ 60,000

Long-term debt	\$ 60,000
Common stock	100,000
Retained earnings	115,836
	\$275,836

d. Cash = .20 × \$663,000 = \$132,600.

e. Accounts receivable = Sales of \$663,000 to be paid in 45 days.
Accounts receivable/\$663,000 × 365 = 45.
Accounts receivable = \$81,740.

f. Inventory turnover = 6.
\$517,140/Inventory = 6.
Inventory = \$86,190.

g. Total current assets = \$132,600 + \$81,740 + \$86,190 = \$300,530.

h. Total assets = \$300,530 + \$72,000 = \$372,530.

i. Total current liabilities = Total assets − (Total LTD + OE) = \$372,530 − \$275,836 = \$96,694.

j. Accounts payable = 30 days.
Accounts payable/\$517,140 × 365 = 30.
Accounts payable = \$42,505.

k. Other short-term liabilities = Total current liabilities − Accounts payable = \$96,694 − \$42,505 = \$42,505.

Net working capital increased from \$136,320 to \$203,836. The change was funded from W&H's 1985 anticipated profits and the \$4,000/year depreciation figure.

2–3.

	1985
Income statement:	
Sales	\$700,000
Bad debt losses	14,000
Net sales	686,000
Cost of goods sold	546,000
Gross margin	140,000
Other expenses	40,000
Profit before tax	100,000
Taxes @ 40%	40,000
Profit after tax	\$ 60,000
Balance sheet:	
Cash	\$140,000
Accounts receivable	86,301
Inventory	91,000
Total current assets	317,301
Net property, plant, and equipment	72,000
Total assets	\$389,301
Accounts payable	44,877
Other short-term liabilities	72,104
Total current liabilities	116,981

Long-term debt	60,000
Common stock	100,000
Retained earnings	112,320
Total LTD and equity	272,320
Total liabilities and equity	$389,301
Net working capital:	
Current assets	$317,301
Current liabilities	116,981
Net working capital	$200,320

These statements were prepared using the following data:

a. Bad debts = 2% Sales = \$700,000 × .02 = \$14,000.

b. Completing the 1985 income statement gives profit after tax of \$60,000.

c. 1985 Retained earnings = 1984 RE + 1985 profit-after-tax balance.
1985 Retained earnings = \$52,320 + \$60,000 = \$112,320.

d. Total long-term debt and equity = \$60,000 + \$100,000 + \$112,320 = \$272,320.

e. Cast = 20% of sales = \$700,000 × .20 = \$140,000.

f. Accounts receivable = 45 days.
Accounts receivable/\$700,000 × 365 = .45.
Accounts receivable = \$86,301.

g. Inventory turnover = 6.
(\$700,000 × .78)/Inventory = 6.
Inventory = \$91,000.

h. Total assets = \$389,301.

i. Current liabilities = \$389,301 − \$272,320 = \$116,981.

j. Accounts payable = 30 days.
Accounts payable/(\$700,000 × .78) × 365 = 30.
Acounts payable = \$44,877.

k. Short-term liabilities = Current liabilities − Accounts payable.
Short-term liabilities = \$116,981 − \$44,877 = \$72,104.
Net working capital increased from \$136,320 in 1984 to \$200,320. The net profit after tax was lower than the previous alternative because of the bad debt losses of uncollectable credit sales. The short-term liabilities would increase over the 1984 amount.

Chapter 3

3–1.

SUN COMPANY
1985 Cash Budget
(in thousands)

	Jan.	*Feb.*	*Mar.*	*Apr.*	*May*	*June*	*July*	*Aug.*	*Sept.*	*Oct.*	*Nov.*	*Dec.*
Sales	65	70	90	100	115	125	150	175	130	110	80	70
Receipts:												
Beginning accounts receivable	$70	$ 52	$ 56	$ 72	$ 80	$ 92	$ 100	$ 120	$140	$104	$ 88	$ 64
Credit sales	52	56	72	80	92	100	120	140	104	88	64	56
Less collections	70	52	56	72	80	92	100	120	140	104	88	64
Ending accounts receivable	$52	$ 56	$ 72	$ 80	$ 92	$100	$ 120	$ 140	$104	$ 88	$ 64	$ 56
Cash sales	$13	$ 14	$ 18	$ 20	$ 23	$ 25	$ 30	$ 35	$ 26	$ 22	$ 16	$ 14
Collections	70	52	56	72	80	92	100	120	140	104	88	64
Total receipts	$83	$ 66	$ 74	$ 92	$ 103	$117	$ 130	$ 155	$166	$126	$104	$ 78
Disbursements:												
Beginning accounts payable	$51	$ 54	$ 70	$ 78	$ 89	$ 97	$ 117	$ 136	$101	$ 85	$ 62	$ 54
Purchases	54	70	78	89	97	117	136	101	85	62	54	51
Less payments	51	54	70	78	89	97	117	136	101	85	62	54
Ending accounts payable	$54	$ 70	$ 78	$ 89	$ 97	$117	$ 136	$ 101	$ 85	$ 62	$ 54	$ 51
Payments	$51	$ 54	$ 70	$ 78	$ 89	$ 97	$ 117	$ 136	$101	$ 85	$ 62	$ 54
Selling and administrative costs	5	5	6	7	8	9	11	12	9	8	6	5
Fixed costs	6	6	6	6	6	6	6	6	6	6	6	6
Lease and interest	3	3	3	3	3	3	3	3	3	3	3	3
Total disbursements	$65	$ 68	$ 85	$ 94	$ 106	$115	$ 137	$ 157	$119	$102	$ 77	$ 68

Receipts less disbursements	$18	$ (2)	$(11)	$ (2)	$ (3)	$ 2	$ (7)	$ (2)	$ 47	$ 24	$ 27	$ 10
Cumulative cash flow	18	16	5	3	0	2	(5)	(7)	40	64	91	101
Monthly cash change:												
Beginning cash balance	$11	$ 29	$ 27	$ 16	$ 14	$ 11	$ 13	$ 6	$ 4	$ 51	$ 75	$102
Change in cash	18	(2)	(11)	(2)	(3)	2	(7)	(2)	47	24	27	10
Ending cash	$29	$ 27	$ 16	$ 14	$ 11	$ 13	$ 6	$ 4	$ 51	$ 75	$102	$112

SUN's net cumulative cash flow for the year is $101,000. Its cumulative cash outflow will be the highest in August, when it will reach $7,000; however, because of the cash balance accumulated in the previous months, the company will still have a positive cash balance. Since the balance is so low, the company may wish to borrow on a short-term basis to provide more of a liquidity margin.

3–2.

SUN Company Pro Forma Income Statement—1985

Sales	$1,280
Cost of goods sold	947
Gross margin	333
Selling and administrative	91
Fixed costs	72
Depreciation	36
Lease and interest payments	36
Net income	$ 98

3–3.

SUN Company Balance Sheets

	1984 Actual		*1985 Pro Forma*
Assets			
Cash	$ 11		$112
Accounts receivable	70		56
Inventories	60	(+ Purchases $994 − CGS $947)	107
Total current assets	141		275
Property, plant, and equipment	540	(less depreciation $36)	504
Total assets	$681		$779
Liabilities and Equity			
Accounts payable	51		$ 51
Notes payable	89		89
Total current liabilities	140		140
Equity	541	(+ Net income $98)	639
Total liabilities and equity	$681		$779
Net Working Capital			
Current assets	$141		$275
Current liabilities	140		140
Net working capital	$ 1		$135

Chapter 4

4–1. Payback = 3.87 years.
B/C Ratio = 5.17.

There is no clear-cut answer whether the new assembly line should be installed since the payback of 3.87 is very close to the cut-off. In light of the very high B/C ratio, Marvel might want to undertake the project, especially if it had no alternatives available or if the management thought their sales forecasts might be low.

Sales	$1,250,000	
Raw materials	462,500	
Gross margin	787,500	
Depreciation	40,000	
Gas, etc.	10,000	
Employees	450,000	
PBT	287,500	
Taxes @ 42%	120,750	
PAT	166,750	
Plus depreciation	40,000	
Net cash flow	$ 206,750	(same cash flow each year)

Payback = $800,000/$206,750 = 3.87 years.
Benefit/Cost ratio = ($206,750 × 20)/$800,000 = 5.17.

4–2. The project's NPV is $45,000. The major component of the project's cash flows are the high depreciation allowances. The analysis would be done as follows (in thousands).

	0	*1*	*2*	*3*	*4*	*5*
Investments	$(200)		$(60)			
Sales		$120	138	$159	$183	$210
Cost of goods sold		47	54	62	71	82
Gross margin		73	84	97	112	128
Depreciation Inv. 1		30	44	42	42	42
Depreciation Inv. 2				15	23	22
Profit before tax		43	40	40	47	64
Taxes @ 40%		17	16	16	19	26
		26	24	24	28	38
Depreciation		30	44	57	65	64
Cash flow	$(200)	$ 56	$ 68	$ 81	$ 93	$102

The net present value would be determined in the following way:
a. PV of total investment cash outflows

$$= \$200 + \text{PV of } \$60, \text{ in 2 yrs. @ } 10\%$$
$$= \$200 + (\$60/(1 + .10)^2)$$
$$= 200 + \$60/1.21$$
$$= \$250$$

b. PV of cash flows:

Year	*CF*	*PV Factor*	*Present Value*
1	56	$(1.10)^1$	\$51
2	68	$(1.10)^2$	56
3	81	$(1.10)^3$	61
4	93	$(1.10)^4$	64
5	102	$(1.10)^5$	63
Total			\$295

c. NPV = PV cash flows − PV investment
= \$295 − \$250
= \$45

4–3. *a.* Project 1: Plant expansion (in thousands).

	0	1	2	3	4	5	6	7	8	9	10
Investment	$(800)										
Sales		$500	$500	$500	$500	$500	$500	$500	$500	$500	$500
Cost of goods sold (49%)		245	245	245	245	245	245	245	245	245	245
Gross margin		255	255	255	255	255	255	255	255	255	255
Advertising		50	50	50	50	50	50	50	50	50	50
Depreciation		64	112	96	80	80	80	72	72	72	72
PBT		141	93	109	125	125	125	133	133	133	133
Taxes (45%)		63	42	49	56	56	56	60	60	60	60
PAT		78	51	60	69	69	69	73	73	73	73
Plus depreciation		64	112	96	80	80	80	72	72	72	72
Cash flow	$(800)	$142	$163	$156	$149	$149	$149	$145	$145	$145	$145

Year	CF	Factor	Present Value
1	$ 142	1.10	$129
2	163	1.21	135
3	156	1.33	117
4	149	1.46	102
5	149	1.61	92
6	149	1.77	84
7	145	1.94	74
8	145	2.14	68
9	145	2.35	62
10	145	2.59	56
	$1,487		$919

Benefit/Cost ratio = $1,488/$800 = 1.86.

Payback = $800 – ($142 + $163 + $156 + $149 + $149) = $41
$41/$149 = .28
5 + .28 = 5.28 years.

Net present value = $919 – $800 = $119.

b. Project 2: New product (in thousands).

	0	*1*	*2*	*3*	*4*	*5*	*6*	*7*	*8*	*9*	*10*
Investment	$(600)										
Training	(200)										
Total	(800)										
Sales		$350	$385	$424	$466	$536	$616	$709	$779	$857	$943
Cost of goods sold (50% for three years, 42% after)		175	192	212	196	225	259	298	327	360	396
Gross margin		175	193	211	270	311	357	411	452	497	547
Advertising		88	96	106	100	100	100	100	100	100	100
Depreciation		48	84	72	60	60	60	54	54	54	54
PBT		40	12	34	110	150	197	257	298	343	393
Taxes (45%)		18	6	15	50	68	89	116	134	154	177
PAT		22	7	19	61	83	109	141	164	189	216
Plus depreciation		48	84	72	60	60	60	54	54	54	54
Cash flow	$(800)	$ 70	$ 91	$ 91	$121	$143	$169	$195	$218	$243	$270

Year	*CF*	*Factor*	*Present Value*
1	$ 70	1.10	$ 63
2	91	1.21	75
3	91	1.33	68
4	121	1.46	82
5	143	1.61	89
6	169	1.77	95
7	195	1.94	100
8	218	2.14	102
9	243	2.35	103
10	270	2.59	104
	$1,609		$881

Benefit/Cost ratio = \$1,609/\$800 = 2.01

Payback = \$800 − (\$70 + \$91 + \$91 + \$121 + \$143 + \$169) = \$115

115/196 = .59

6 + .59 = 6.59 years.

Net present value = \$881 − \$800 = \$81.

	Project 1 Expansion	*Project 2 New Product*
Payback	5.28 years	6.59 years
B/C ratio	1.86	2.01
NPV	\$119	\$81

Kertin should expand its current production and not undertake the new product at this time. Despite a higher benefit/cost ratio, the new product project offers a lower NPV because the higher cash flows occur much later. Additionally, the new product project is riskier than the expansion, and the projected returns are not high enough to offset the risk.

Chapter 5

5-1. The marginal weighted average cost of capital for Kauph Company would be calculated as follows:

A. Capital structure: 35% debt; 65% equity.

B. Cost of debt:
Before tax 11¾%.
After tax .1175 × (1 − .42) = .068.

C. Cost of equity:

1. *Dividend discount model:* $R_e = \frac{D_1}{P_0} + g$

   a. To calculate the dividend yield: $\frac{D_1}{P_0}$
   Projected earnings = $554,400.
   Dividend payout = .24 × $554,400 = $133,056.
   Dividend/share = $133,056/300,000 shares = $0.44.
   Current market price/share = $18.50.
   D_1/P_0 = $0.44/$18.50 = .024.

   b. To calculate the growth (g):
   g = (1 − Payout)(ROE).
   g = (1 − .24) × .12 = .091.

   c. To calculate the weighted cost:
   Cost of equity = .024 + .091 = .115.
   Weighted cost of equity = .65 × .115 = .075.
   Weighted cost of debt = .1175 × .35(1 − t)
   = .04(1 − .42)
   = .024.

   Weighted average cost of capital = .024 + .075 = 9.9%.

2. *Stock-bond yield spread:* $R_e = R_d + (\dot{R}_e - \dot{R}_d)$
   Re = .175 + (.12 − .10) = .1375.
   Weighted cost of equity = .65 × .1375 = .089.
   Weighted cost of debt = .1175 × .35(1 − t)
   = .04(1 − .42)
   = .024.
   Weighted average cost of capital = .089 + .024 = 11.3%.

3. *CAPM:* $R_{ej} = R_f + \beta_j(R_m - R_f)$
   R_{ej} = .085 + 0.98(.16 − .085) = .159.
   Weighted cost of equity = .65 × .159 = .103.
   Weighted average cost of capital = .103 + .024 = 12.7%.

Chapter 6

6–1.

	Earnings per Share at Current Sales Level	
	Debt	*Common Stock*
Sales	$125,000	$125,000
EBIT @ 13% sales	16,250	16,250
Current interest	1,750	1,750
New interest	1,500	—
PBT	13,000	14,500
Taxes @ 50%	6,500	7,250
PAT	6,500	7,250
Current preferred dividends	1,200	1,200
New preferred dividends	—	—
Funds to common shareholders	$ 5,300	$ 6,050
Number of shares	2,000	3,000
EPS	$2.65	$2.02

	Earnings per Share at Projected Sales Level	
	Debt	*Common Stock*
Sales	$150,000	$150,000
EBIT @ 13% sales	19,500	19,500
Current interest	1,750	1,750
New interest	1,500	—
PBT	16,250	17,750
Taxes @ 50%	8,125	8,875
PAT	8,125	8,875
Current preferred dividends	1,200	1,200
New preferred dividends	—	—
Funds to common shareholders	$ 6,925	$ 7,675
Number of shares	2,000	3,000
EPS	$3.46	$2.56

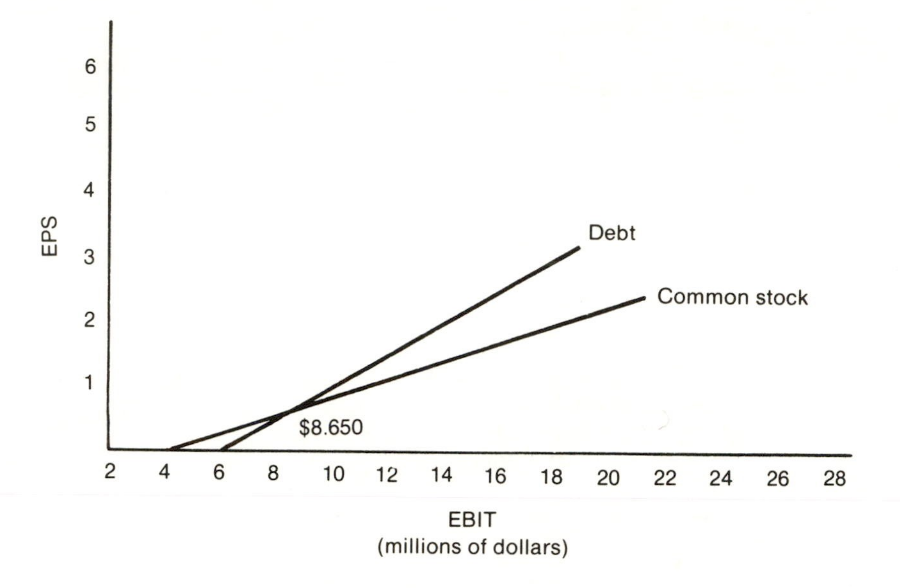

To determine the equivalency point between debt and common stock:

$$\frac{(X - 1750 - 1500)(1 - .5) - 1{,}200}{2{,}000} = \frac{(X - 1750)(1 - .5) - 1{,}200}{3{,}000}$$

$$\frac{.5X - 1{,}625 - 1{,}200}{2{,}000} = \frac{.5X - 875 - 1{,}200}{3{,}000}$$

$$\frac{.5X - 2{,}825}{2{,}000} = \frac{.5X - 2.075}{3{,}000}$$

$$1500X - 8{,}475{,}000 = 1000X - 4{,}150{,}000$$

$$500X = 4{,}325{,}000$$

$$X = \$8{,}650 \text{ (equivalency EBIT point)}$$

$$EPS = \$0.75$$

The equivalency EBIT point of $8,650 is almost 50% lower than the prevailing figure of $16,250, and current EPS of $3.03 is well above the $0.75 level implied by the analysis. Debt would appear to be significantly more attractive than equity.

6–2. *a.* Current dividends = $6,050 × .25 = $1512.5
$1,512.5/2,000 shares = $0.76/share.
b. Projected dividends:
Debt: $6,925 × .25 = $1,731.25
1,731.25/2,000 = $0.87/share.
Equity: $7.675 × .25 = $1,918.75
1,918.75/3,000 = $0.64/share.

Despite the increase in sales, dividends per share would decline under the equity alternative, although the absolute amount paid out by Traie would increase. This again would tend to favor the debt alternative.

6–3. Explicit Costs:
Debt = 10% × (1 − t) = 10% × .50 = 5%.
Equity = Initial EPS/Proceeds per share = $3.03/$15 = 20.2%.
Implicit Costs of Equity: (Assuming Constant PE)

	Equity	*Debt*
Projected EPS	$2.56	$3.46
Constant PE	6	6
Estimated stock price	$15.36	$20.76
or		
Estimated PE	6	4.4
Constant market price	$15.36	$15.36

The PE would have to fall 27% to 4.4 before the shareholders lost all advantages resulting from the increased leverage. Traie had a PE of 4 two years ago. Based on its continued earnings and dividend growth, it appears unlikely that the PE, viewed discretely, would fall by 30%. Again, the debt alternative appears more attractive.

6–4. A. *Compared to industry:*

Ratio	*Debt*	*Common Stock*	*Industry*
a. Total assets	134,000 + 15,000 = 149,000	149,000	
ROA	4.6%	5.2%	10%
b. Equity	54,000 + 6925 − 1731 = 59,194	54,000 + 15,000 + 7675 − 1919 = 74,756	
ROE	11.7%	10.3%	12%
c. Debt/Total capital (preferred stock considered long-term debt)	(25 + 15 + 15 − 2)/(94 + 15 + 7 − 2 − 2) = 47%	(25 + 15 − 2)/(94 + 15 + 8 − 2 − 2) = 34%	45%
d. Interest/Sales	2.2%	1.2%	1.5%

With regard to the industry statistics, Traie does not appear to be doing very well. The low ROA under either financial strategy implies that the company needs to improve its productivity or margins. The lower ROE figures also suggest low profits or low leverage. The debt alternative results in an ROE closer to the average which strengthens that alternative's attractiveness. Although the resulting Debt/Total capital figure is higher than average, the difference is not great and will decline over time.

The debt alternative appears attractive.

B. Other risk measures:

1. Interest coverage: (EBIT/Interest)
   Current: $16,250/$1,750 = 9.3.
   Proposed:
   Debt: $19,500/($1,750 + $1,500) = 6.
   Equity: $19,500/$1,750 = 11.1.
2. Current burden coverage:
   a. Cash flow = EBIT + Depreciation
   $16,250 + $4000 = $20,250.
   b. Burden:
   Interest: $1,750
   Sinking fund before tax: $2,500/(1 − .5) = $5,000.
   Preferred dividend before tax:
   $1,200/(1 − .5) − $2,400.
   c. Burden coverage:
   Total without common dividends = $20,250/$9,150 = 2.2.
   Total with common dividends = $20,250/$12,175 = 1.7.
3. Projected burden coverage:
   a. Cash flows: $19,500 + $4,750 = $24,250.
   b. Burden

Debt Alternative	*Equity Alternative*
Interest: $1,750 + $1,500 = $3,250	$1,750
Sinking fund: ($2,500 + $1,500)/(1 − .5) = $8,000	$2,500/(1 − .5) + $5,000
Preferred dividends: $1,200/(1 − .5) = $2,400	$1,200/(1 − .5) $2,400
Common dividends: $1,731/(1 − .5) = $3,462	$1,919/(1 − .5) = $3,838
Total without common dividends: $13,650	$9,150
Total with common dividends: $17,112	$12,988

   c. Burden coverage

Debt Alternative	*Equity Alternative*
Without common dividends: 1.7	2.7
With common dividends: 1.4	1.9

6–5. Traie's burden coverage including common dividends is already low at 1.7. Even under the least risky alternative, the equity issue, the projected increase in sales would increase the burden coverage to only 1.9 when common dividends are included. The major factor in computing the company's burden are the dividends adopted by management. If these were maintained at their current level rather than increased as earnings increase, the company would be far less risky. In the absence of any change, however, management would appear wiser to go with the equity issue at this point in time, despite all other considerations which seem to point toward the debt issue. In this case, risk would be the overriding consideration. Even if the common dividends are excluded from consideration, burden coverage under the equity alternative would increase to only 2.7. The company's estimated cash flow is apparently not sufficiently large to handle both an increase in interest sinking fund payments and common dividends without taking on a significant amount of risk.

Chapter 7

7-1.

	Net Cash Flow/Year (EPS/Number of Shares)	
	X Company	*Y Company*
1976	$700,000	$501,000
1977	756,000	561,200
1978	816,000	625,000
1979	880,000	701,950
1980	952,000	785,850
Increase in EPS	Average 8% per year	Average 12% per year

If the Ray Company is interested primarily in growth, they should pursue the Y Company.

7-2. *a.* Book value of Klick = $543,000 – ($137,000 + $111,000) = $295,000.

This is the lowest of any of the values identified and, based on the nature of the assets involved, should be the minimum price acceptable to Klick's management. If the assets have appreciated in value since their purchase (e.g., land), this price might be unacceptable. In such a case, the minimum acceptable price might be based on a market appraisal of the assets' value.

b. Current market price = 50,000 shares × $6.00 = $300,000.

c. PV of Klick's net cash flow = $40,000/.1125 = $355,556.

d. Implied PE and market value = PV/share/EPS
($355,556/50,000)/($30,000/50,000) = $11.85
$11.85 × 50,000 shares = $592,500.

e. Price of indifference to Kupp:
[PV combined – (PV Kupp + PV Klick)] = [(Price) – PV Klick]
[$1,000,000 – ($480,000 + $355,556)] = (X – $355,556)
Breakeven price X = $520,000.

This is the price at which Kupp should be indifferent about acquiring Klick. Unless Kupp felt they had underestimated Klick's future potential or value, they should not pay more than $520,000 for the company.

The fact that the PE and market value of the company implied by its cash flow exceeds this amount ($592,500) indicates that the company may have potential in areas not reflected on the balance sheet.

7–3. Valuation of Smyth, Robinson, and the combined company can be done with the dividend discount formulation.

$$P = D/(k - g)$$

Using this approach, the calculations are as follows:

A. Value of Smyth:
$6.45/(.122 − .04) = $78.66 million.

B. Value of Robinson:
$2.2/(.105 − .04) = $33.85 million.

C. Value of combined company:
$9.45/(.11 − .04) = $135 million.

Since there are no debtholder claims on Robinson, Smyth could offer up to $56.34 million ($135 − $78.66), and Robinson should accept an offer above $33.85 million.

II. LOTUS 1-2-3 MODELS FOR STUDY QUESTIONS

The following section shows examples of solutions to the chapter problems using Lotus 1-2-3 and is provided to allow the user of this financial planning tool to practice.

For each of the models, the entries for the rows and columns are stated. The results of these models may differ slightly from the manual solutions to the study questions because of differences in rounding.

Chapter 1

1–1.

	A	B
1	INCOME STATEMENT	
2	------------------------------------	
3	SALES	+ B7/.03
4	CGS	.77*B3
5	OTHER EXP	(B3 – B4) – B7
6	--------	--------
7	PAT	.1*(B31 + B32)
8		
9	************************************	
10	BALANCE SHEET	
11	------------------------------------	
12	ASSETS	
13	CASH	+ B17 – B14 – B15
14	A/R	(B3/365)*35
15	INV	+ B4/6
16	--------	--------
17	TOT C/A	2*B28
18		
19	NET P&E	+ B21 – B17
20	--------	--------
21	TOT ASSET	+ B3/1.5
22		========
23		
24	LIAB & EQ	
25	A/P	(B4/365)*30
26	OTHER STL	+ B28 – B25
27	--------	--------
28	TOT C LIA	+ B21 – B34
29		
30	LTD	.8*(B31 – B32)
31	C/S	40000
32	RET EARN	62000
33	--------	--------
34	TOT CAP	@SUM(B30..B32)
35	--------	--------
36	TOT L&OE	+ B28 + B34
37		========

1–2.

	A	B	C	D	E	F
1	YEAR	1980	+B1+1	+C1+1	+D1+1	+E1+1
2	------------------------------	------------------------------	------------------------------	------------------------------	------------------------------	------------------------------
3	SALES	27000	28350	29654	31344	33852
4	COGS	23490	24098	24613	25075	27082
5	ADVERT	540	510	652	1254	2031
6	INTEREST	270	340	415	408	508
7	OTHER EXP	1620	1616	1601	1599	1659
8	---------	---------	---------	---------	---------	---------
9	PBT	+B3−(@SUM(B4..B7))	+C3−(@SUM(C4..C7))	+D3−(@SUM(D4..D7))	+E3−(@SUM(E4..E7))	+F3−(@SUM(F4..F7))
10						
11	COMP %					
12	---------------------					
13	SALES	+B3/B3	+C3/C3	+D3/D3	+E3/E3	+F3/F3
14	COGS	+B4/B3	+C4/C3	+D4/D3	+E4/E3	+F4/F3
15	ADVERT	+B5/B3	+C5/C3	+D5/D3	+E5/E3	+F5/F3
16	INTEREST	+B6/B3	+C6/C3	+D6/D3	+E6/E3	+F6/F3
17	OTHER EXP	+B7/B3	+C7/C3	+D7/D3	+E7/E3	+F7/F3
18	---------	---------	---------	---------	---------	---------
19	PBT	+B9/B3	+C9/C3	+D9/D3	+E9/E3	+F9/F3
20						
21	TREND %					
22	---------------------					
23	SALES		(+C3/B3)−1	(+D3/C3)−1	(+E3/D3)−1	(+F3/E3)−1
24	CGS		(+C4/B4)−1	(+D4/C4)−1	(+E4/D4)−1	(+F4/E4)−1
25	ADVERT		(+C5/B5)−1	(+D5/C5)−1	(+E5/D5)−1	(+F5/E5)−1
26	INTEREST		(+C6/B6)−1	(+D6/C6)−1	(+E6/D6)−1	(+F6/E6)−1
27	OTHER EXP		(+C7/B7)−1	(+D7/C7)−1	(+E7/D7)−1	(+F7/E7)−1
28	---------		---------	---------	---------	---------
29	PBT		(+C9/B9)−1	(+D9/C9)−1	(+E9/D9)−1	(+F9/E9)−1

1–3. The nature of this problem does not lend itself to modeling.

Chapter 2

2–1.

	A	B	C
1	YEAR	1983	1984
2	------------------------------	------------------------------	------------------------------
3	INCOME STATEMENT		
4			
5	SALES	250000	510000
6	COGS	195000	.78*C5
7	--------	--------	--------
8	GR MARGIN	+B5 – B6	+C5 – C6
9	OTHER EXP	40000	40000
10	--------	--------	--------
11	PBT	+B8 – B9	+C8 – C9
12	TAXES	.4*B11	.4*C11
13	--------	--------	--------
14	PAT	+B11 – B12	+C11 – C12
15			
16	------------------------------	------------------------------	------------------------------
17	BALANCE SHEET		
18			
19	ASSETS		
20	CASH	50000	.2*C5
21	A/R	20548	(C5/365)*30
22	INVEN	65000	+C6/6
23	--------	--------	--------
24	CURR ASST	@SUM(B20..B22)	@SUM(C20..C22)
25	NET P&E	80000	76000
26	--------	--------	--------
27	TOT ASST	+B24 + B25	+C24 + C25
28			
29	L&E		
30	A/P	16027	(C6/365)*30
31	OTHER STL	30521	+C27 – C30 – C38
32	--------	--------	--------
33	CURR LIAB	+B30 + B31	+C30 + C31
34	LTD	60000	60000
35	C/S	100000	100000
36	RET EARN	9000	+B36 + C14
37	--------	--------	--------
38	TOT LTD&E	@SUM(B34..B36)	@SUM(C34..C36)
39	--------	--------	--------
40	TOT L&E	+B33 + B38	+C33 + C38
41			
42	NET W CAP		
43	CURR ASST	+B24	+C24
44	CURR LIAB	+B33	+C33
45	--------	--------	--------
46	NET W CAP	+B43 – B44	+C43 – C44

2–2.

	A	B	C	D
1	YEAR	1983	1984	1985
2	--			
3	INCOME STATEMENT			
4				
5	SALES	250000	510000	663000
6	COGS	195000	.78*C5	.78*D5
7	--------	--------	--------	--------
8	GR MARGIN	+ B5 – B6	+ C5 – C6	+ D5 – D6
9	OTHER EXP	40000	40000	40000
10	--------	--------	--------	--------
11	PBT	+ B8 – B9	+ C8 – C9	+ D8 – D9
12	TAXES	.4*B11	.4*C11	.4*D11
13	--------	--------	--------	--------
14	PAT	+ B11 – B12	+ C11 – C12	+ D11 – D12
15				
16	--			
17	BALANCE SHEET			
18				
19	ASSETS			
20	CASH	50000	.2*C5	.2*D5
21	A/R	20548	(C5/365)*30	(D5/365)*45
22	INVEN	65000	+ C6/6	+ D6/6
23	--------	--------	--------	--------
24	CURR ASST	@SUM(B20..B22)	@SUM(C20..C22)	@SUM(D20..D22)
25	NET P&E	80000	76000	72000
26	--------	--------	--------	--------
27	TOT ASST	+ B24 + B25	+ C24 + C25	+ D24 + D25
28				
29	L&E			
30	A/P	16027	(C6/365)*30	(D6/365)*30
31	OTHER STL	30521	+ C27 – C30 – C38	+ D27 – D30 – D38
32	--------	--------	--------	--------
33	CURR LIAB	+ B30 + B31	+ C30 + C31	+ D30 + D31
34	LTD	60000	60000	60000
35	C/S	100000	100000	100000
36	RET EARN	9000	+ B36 + C14	+ C36 + D14
37	--------	--------	--------	--------
38	TOT LTD&E	@SUM(B34..B36)	@SUM(C34..C36)	@SUM(D34..D36)
39	--------	--------	--------	--------
40	TOT L&E	+ B33 + B38	+ C33 + C38	+ D33 + D38
41				
42	NET W CAP			
43	CURR ASST	+ B24	+ C24	+ D24
44	CURR LIAB	+ B33	+ C33	+ D33
45	--------	--------	--------	--------
46	NET W CAP	+ B43 – B44	+ C43 – C44	+ D43 – D44

2–3.

	A	B	C	D
1	YEAR	1983	1984	1985
2	--			
3	INCOME STATEMENT			
4				
5	SALES	250000	510000	700000
6	BAD DEBTS	0	0	.02*D5
7	COGS	195000	.78*C5	.78*D5
8	--------	--------	--------	--------
9	GR MARGIN	+B5-B7	+C5-C7	+D5-D7-D6
10	OTHER EXP	40000	40000	40000
11	--------	--------	--------	--------
12	PBT	+B9-B10	+C9-C10	+D9-D10
13	TAXES	.4*B12	.4*C12	.4*D12
14	--------	--------	--------	--------
15	PAT	+B12-B13	+C12-C13	+D12-D13
16				
17	--			
18	BALANCE SHEET			
19				
20	ASSETS			
21	CASH	50000	.2*C5	.2*D5
22	A/R	20548	(C5/365)*30	(+D5/365)*45
23	INVEN	65000	+C7/6	+D7/6
24	--------	--------	--------	--------
25	CURR ASST	@SUM(B21..B23)	@SUM(C21..C23)	@SUM(D21..D23)
26	NET P&E	80000	76000	72000
27	--------	--------	--------	--------
28	TOT ASST	+B25+B26	+C25+C26	+D25+D26
29				
30	L&E			
31	A/P	16027	(C7/365)*30	(D7/365)*30
32	OTHER STL	30521	+C28-C31-C39	+D28-D31-D39
33	--------	--------	--------	--------
34	CURR LIAB	+B31+B32	+C31+C32	+D31+D32
35	LTD	60000	60000	60000
36	C/S	100000	100000	100000
37	RET EARN	9000	+B37+C15	+C37+D15
38	--------	--------	--------	--------
39	TOT LTD&E	@SUM(B35..B37)	@SUM(C35..C37)	@SUM(D35..D37)
40	--------	--------	--------	--------
41	TOT L&E	+B34+B39	+C34+C39	+D34+D39
42				
43	NET W CAP			
44	CURR ASST	+B25	+C25	+D25
45	CURR LIAB	+B34	+C34	+D34
46	--------	--------	--------	--------
47	NET W CAP	+B44-B45	+C44-C45	+D44-D45

Chapter 3

3–1.

	A	B	C	D	E	F	G	H	I	J	K	L	M
1		JAN	FEB	MAR	APR	MAY	JUN	JUL	AUG	SEP	OCT	NOV	DEC
2		--------	--------	--------	--------	--------	--------	--------	--------	--------	--------	--------	--------
3	SALES	65	70	90	100	115	125	150	175	130	110	80	70
4													
5	RECEIPTS												
6	BEG A/R	70	+B10	+C10	+D10	+E10	+F10	+G10	+H10	+I10	+J10	+K10	+L10
7	+CRED SLS	.8*B3	.8*C3	.8*D3	.8*E3	.8*F3	.8*G3	.8*H3	.8*I3	.8*J3	.8*K3	.8*L3	.8*M3
8	−COLLECT	+B6	+C6	+D6	+E6	+F6	+G6	+H6	+I6	+J6	+K6	+L6	+M6
9	--------	--------	--------	--------	--------	--------	--------	--------	--------	--------	--------	--------	--------
10	END A/R	+B6+B7−B8	+C6+C7−C8	+D6+D7−D8	+E6+E7−E8	+F6+F7−F8	+G6+G7−G8	+H6+H7−H8	+I6+I7−I8	+J6+J7−J8	+K6+K7−K8	+L6+L7−L8	+M6+M7−M8
11	======	======	======	======	======	======	======	======	======	======	======	======	======
12	COLLECT	+B8	+C8	+D8	+E8	+F8	+G8	+H8	+I8	+J8	+K8	+L8	+M8
13	+CASH PAY	.2*B3	.2*C3	.2*D3	.2*E3	.2*F3	.2*G3	.2*H3	.2*I3	.2*J3	.2*K3	.2*L3	.2*M3
14	--------	--------	--------	--------	--------	--------	--------	--------	--------	--------	--------	--------	--------
15	TOT RCPTS	+B12+B13	+C12+C13	+D12+D13	+E12+E13	+F12+F13	+G12+G13	+H12+H13	+I12+I13	+J12+J13	+K12+K13	+L12+L13	+M12+M13
16	======	======	======	======	======	======	======	======	======	======	======	======	======
17													
18	DISBURSMT												
19	BEG A/P	51	+B23	+C23	+D23	+E23	+F23	+G23	+H23	+I23	+J23	+K23	+L23
20	+PURCH	1.05*(.7 4*C3)	1.05*(.7 4*D3)	1.05*(.7 4*E3)	1.05*(.7 4*F3)	1.05*(.7 4*G3)	1.05*(.7 4*H3)	1.05*(.7 4*I3)	1.05*(.7 4*J3)	1.05*(.7 4*K3)	1.05*(.7 4*L3)	1.05*(.7 4*M3)	51
21	−PAYMENTS	+B19	+C19	+D19	+E19	+F19	+G19	+H19	+I19	+J19	+K19	+L19	+M19
22	--------	--------	--------	--------	--------	--------	--------	--------	--------	--------	--------	--------	--------
23	END A/P	+B19+B20 −B21	+C19+C20 −C21	+D19+D20 −D21	+E19+E20 −E21	+F19+F20 −F21	+G19+G20 −G21	+H19+H20 −H21	+I19+I20 −I21	+J19+J20 −J21	+K19+K20 −K21	+L19+L20 −L21	+M19+M20 −M21
24	======	======	======	======	======	======	======	======	======	======	======	======	======
25	A/P PYMNT	+B21	+C21	+D21	+E21	+F21	+G21	+H21	+I21	+J21	+K21	+L21	+M21
26	S&A	.07*B3	.07*C3	.07*D3	.07*E3	.07*F3	.07*G3	.07*H3	.07*I3	.07*J3	.07*K3	.07*L3	.07*M3
27	FIXED	6	6	6	6	6	6	6	6	6	6	6	6
28	LSE+INT	3	3	3	3	3	3	3	3	3	3	3	3
29	--------	--------	--------	--------	--------	--------	--------	--------	--------	--------	--------	--------	--------
30	TOT DSBMT	@SUM(B25 ..B28)	@SUM(C25 ..C28)	@SUM(D25 ..D28)	@SUM(E25 ..E28)	@SUM(F25 ..F28)	@SUM(G25 ..G28)	@SUM(H25 ..H28)	@SUM(I25 ..I28)	@SUM(J25 ..J28)	@SUM(K25 ..K28)	@SUM(L25 ..L28)	@SUM(M25 ..M28)
31	======	======	======	======	======	======	======	======	======	======	======	======	======
32													
33	NET CF	+B15−B30	+C15−C30	+D15−D30	+E15−E30	+F15−F30	+G15−G30	+H15−H30	+I15−I30	+J15−J30	+K15−K30	+L15−L30	+M15−M30
34													
35	CUM CF	+B33	+B35+C33	+C35+D33	+D35+E33	+E35+F33	+F35+G33	+G35+H33	+H35+I33	+I35+J33	+J35+K33	+K35+L33	+L35+M33
36													
37	BEG CASH	11	+B40	+C40	+D40	+E40	+F40	+G40	+H40	+I40	+J40	+K40	+L40
38	+CHANGE	+B33	+C33	+D33	+E33	+F33	+G33	+H33	+I33	+J33	+K33	+L33	+M33
39	--------	--------	--------	--------	--------	--------	--------	--------	--------	--------	--------	--------	--------
40	END CASH	+B37+B38	+C37+C38	+D37+D38	+E37+E38	+F37+F38	+G37+G38	+H37+H38	+I37+I38	+J37+J38	+K37+K38	+L37+L38	+M37+M38

3–2. Add to the model developed for 3–1 the following:

	A	B	C
34			
35	CUM CF	+ B33	+ B35 + C33
36			
37	BEG CASH	11	+ B40
38	+ CHANGE	+ B33	+ C33
39	--------	--------	--------
40	END CASH	+ B37 + B38	+ C37 + C38
41			
42	--		
43			
44		1984	1985 PF
45		--	
46	SALES		@SUM(B3..M3)
47	CGS		.74*C46
48	--------		--------
49	GR MARGIN		+ C46 – C47
50	S&A		@SUM(B26..M26)
51	FIX COSTS		(36 + @SUM(B27..M27))
52	LSE & INT		@SUM(B28..M28)
53	--------		--------
54	NET INC		+ C49 – C50 – C51 – C52
55	= = = =		= = = = =

3–3. Add to the model developed for 3–2 the following:

	A	B	C
57	--		
58	BALANCE SHEET		
59	ASSETS		
60	CASH	+ B37	+ M40
61	A/R	+ B6	+ M10
62	INVEN	60	+ B62 + (@SUM(B20..M20)) – C47
63	--------	--------	--------
64	TOT CA	@SUM(B60..B62)	@SUM(C60..C62)
65	NET P&E	540	+ B65 – (12*3)
66	--------	--------	--------
67	TOT ASSTS	+ B64 + B65	+ C64 + C65
68	= = = = = = =	= = = = = = = =	= = = = = = = =
69			
70	L&E		
71	A/P	+ B19	+ M23
72	N/P	89	+ B72
73	--------	--------	--------
74	TOT CL	+ B71 + B72	+ C71 + C72
75	EQUITY	541	+ B75 + C54
76	--------	--------	--------
77	TOTAL L&E	+ B74 + B75	+ C74 + C75
78	= = = = = = =	= = = = = = = =	= = = = = = = =
79			
80	NET WC		
81	CA	+ B64	+ C64
82	CL	+ B74	+ C74
83	--------	--------	--------
84	NET WC	+ B81 – B82	+ C81 – C82
85	= = = = = = =	= = = = = = = =	= = = = = = = =
86			

Chapter 4

4–1.

	A	B	C
1		0	(B1+1)
2		--	--
3	SALES		1250
4	COGS		.37*C3
5	--------		--------
6	GR MARGIN		+C3−C4
7	OP COSTS		200/20
8	WAGES		30*15
9	DEPREC		800/20
10	--------		--------
11	PBT		+C6−C7−C8−C9
12	TAXES		.42*C11
13	--------		--------
14	PAT		+C11−C12
15	DEPREC		+C9
16	--------		--------
17	NET CF		+C14+C15
18			
19	--	--	--
20			
21	INVEST	800	
22			
23	PAYBACK	+B21/C17	
24			
25	B/C RATIO	(@SUM(C17..V17))/B21	
26			

Copy the range C1..C19 to the column range D1..V1.

4–2.

	A	B	C	D	E	F	G
1		0	1	2	3	4	5
2		--------	--------	--------	--------	--------	--------
3	INVEST1	200					
4	INVEST2			60			
5							
6							
7	SALES		120	1.15*C7	1.15*D7	1.15*E7	1.15*F7
8	COSTS		.39*C7	.39*D7	.39*E7	.39*F7	.39*G7
9	DEPREC1		.15*B3	.22*B3	.21*B3	.21*B3	.21*B3
10	DEPREC2				.24*D4	.38*D4	.37*D4
11	--------		--------	--------	--------	--------	--------
12	PBT		+C7 – @SUM(C8..C10)	+D7 – @SUM(D8..D10)	+E7 – @SUM(E8..E10)	+F7 – @SUM(F8..F10)	+G7 – @SUM(G8..G10)
13	TAXES		.4*C12	.4*D12	.4*E12	.4*F12	.4*G12
14	--------		--------	--------	--------	--------	--------
15	PAT		+C12 – C13	+D12 – D13	+E12 – E13	+F12 – F13	+G12 – G13
16	DEPREC		+C9 + C10	+D9 + D10	+E9 + E10	+F9 + F10	+G9 + G10
17	--------		--------	--------	--------	--------	--------
18	NET CF		+C15 + C16	+D15 + D16	+E15 + E16	+F15 + F16	+G15 + G16
19							
20	--------	--------	--------	--------	--------	--------	--------
21							
22	DISC RATE	.1					
23							
24	NPV	(@NPV(B22,C18..G18) – B3) – (D4/((1 + B22)*D1))					
25							

4–3.

	A	B	C	D	E	F	G	H	I	J	K	L
1		0	1	2	3	4	5	6	7	8	9	10
2		----------	----------	----------	----------	----------	----------	----------	----------	----------	----------	----------
3	PROJ #1											
4												
5	INVEST	800000										
6	SALES		500000	500000	500000	500000	500000	500000	500000	500000	500000	500000
7	COGS		.49*C6	.49*D6	.49*E6	.49*F6	.49*G6	.49*H6	.49*I6	.49*J6	.49*K6	.49*L6
8	--------		--------	--------	--------	--------	--------	--------	--------	--------	--------	--------
9	GR MARGIN		+C6 – C7	+D6 – D7	+E6 – E7	+F6 – F7	+G6 – G7	+H6 – H7	+I6 – I7	+J6 – J7	+I6 – I7	+L6 – L7
10	ADV		50000	50000	50000	50000	50000	50000	50000	50000	50000	50000
11	DEPR		.08*B5	.14*B5	.12*B5	.1*B5	.1*B5	.1*B5	.09*B5	.09*B5	.09*B5	.09*B5
12	--------		--------	--------	--------	--------	--------	--------	--------	--------	--------	--------
13	PBT		+C9 – C10 – C 11	+D9 – D10 – D 11	+E9 – E10 – E 11	+F9 – F10 – F 11	+G9 – G10 – G 11	+H9 – H10 – H 11	+I9 – I10 – I 11	+J9 – J10 – J 11	+K9 – K10 – K 11	+L9 – L10 – L 11
14	TAXES		.45*C13	.45*D13	.45*E13	.45*F13	.45*G13	.45*H13	.45*I13	.45*J13	.45*K13	.45*L13
15	--------		--------	--------	--------	--------	--------	--------	--------	--------	--------	--------
16	PAT		+C13 – C14	+D13 – D14	+E13 – E14	+F13 – F14	+G13 – G14	+H13 – H14	+I13 – I14	+J13 – J14	+K13 – K14	+L13 – L14
17	DEPR		+C11	+D11	+E11	+F11	+G11	+H11	+I11	+J11	+K11	+L11
18	--------		--------	--------	--------	--------	--------	--------	--------	--------	--------	--------
19	CASH FLOW		+C16 + C17	+D16 + D17	+E16 + E17	+F16 + F17	+G16 + G17	+H16 + H17	+I16 + I17	+J16 + J17	+K16 + K17	+L16 + L17
20	----------	----------	----------	----------	----------	----------	----------	----------	----------	----------	----------	----------

4–3. *(concluded)*

	A	B	C	D	E	F	G	H	I	J	K	L
1		0	1	2	3	4	5	6	7	8	9	10
2		--------	--------	--------	--------	--------	--------	--------	--------	--------	--------	--------
21												
22	PROJ #2											
23												
24	INVEST-FL	60000										
25	INVEST-TN	20000										
26	--------	--------										
27	TOT INVES	(B24 + B25)										
28	SALES		350000	1.1*C28	1.1*D28	1.1*E28	1.15*F28	1.15*G28	1.15*H28	1.1*I28	1.1*J28	1.1*K28
29	COGS		.5*C28	.5*D28	.5*E28	.42*F28	.42*G28	.42*H28	.42*I28	.42*J28	.42*K28	.42*L28
30	--------		--------	--------	--------	--------	--------	--------	--------	--------	--------	--------
31	GR MARGIN		+ C28 – C29	+ D28 – D29	+ E28 – E29	+ F28 – F29	+ G28 – G29	+ H28 – H29	+ I28 – I29	+ J28 – J29	+ K28 – K29	+ L28 – L29
32	ADV		.25*C28	.25*D28	.25*E28	100000	100000	100000	100000	100000	100000	100000
33	DEPR		.08*B24	.14*B24	.12*B24	.1*B24	.1*B24	.1*B24	.09*B24	.09*B24	.09*B24	.09*B24
34	--------		--------	--------	--------	--------	--------	--------	--------	--------	--------	--------
35	PBT		+ C31 – C32 – C33	+ D31 – D32 – D33	+ E31 – E32 – E33	+ F31 – F32 – F33	+ G31 – G32 – G33	+ H31 – H32 – H33	+ I31 – I32 – I33	+ J31 – J32 – J33	+ K31 – K32 – K33	+ L31 – L32 – L33
36	TAXES		.45*C35	.45*D35	.45*E35	.45*F35	.45*G35	.45*H35	.45*I35	.45*J35	.45*K35	.45*L35
37	--------		--------	--------	--------	--------	--------	--------	--------	--------	--------	--------
38	PAT		+ C35 – C36	+ D35 – D36	+ E35 – E36	+ F35 – F36	+ G35 – G36	+ H35 – H36	+ I35 – I36	+ J35 – J36	+ K35 – K36	+ L35 – L36
39	DEPR		+ C33	+ D33	+ E33	+ F33	+ F33	+ H33	+ I33	+ J33	+ K33	+ L33
40	--------		--------	--------	--------	--------	--------	--------	--------	--------	--------	--------
41	CASH FLOW		+ C38 + C39	+ D38 + D39	+ E38 + E39	+ F38 + F39	+ G38 + G39	+ H38 + H39	+ I38 + I39	+ J38 + J39	+ K38 + K39	+ L38 + L39
42												
43	--------	--------	--------	--------	--------	--------	--------	--------	--------	--------	--------	--------
44												
45			PROJ #1		PROJ #2							
46												
47	B/C RATIO		(@SUM(C19 ..L19)/B5)		(@SUM(C41 ..L41)/B2 7)							
48	NPV		(@NPV(.1, C19..L19) – B5)		(@NPV(.1, C41..L41) – B27)							
49												

Chapter 5

5–1.

	A	B
1	LTD	2261538
2	C/S	1500000
3	R/E	2700000
4	--------	--------
5	TOT CAP	+B1+B2+B3
6		
7	DEBT	+B1/B5
8	EQUITY	1−B7
9		
10	COST-DEBT	
11	MRGN INT	.1175
12	TAX RATE	.42
13		
14	WGTD COD	(1−B12)*B11*B7
15	================	================
16		
17	COST-EQ	
18		
19	DIVD DISC	
20	# SHARES	300000
21	PROJ PAT	554400
22	DIV P/O	.24
23	PROJ DPS	(B21/B20)*B22
24	MKT PRICE	18.5
25	ROE	.12
26	PROJ G	(1−B22)*B25
27	COE	(B23/B24)+B26
28	WGTD COE	+B27*B8
29		
30	WACC	+B28+B14
31	================	================
32		
33	YLD SPRD	
34		
35	MRGN INT	+B11
36	AVG INT	.1
37	ROE	+B25
38	COE	+B35+B37−B36
39	WGTD COE	+B38*B8
40		
41	WACC	(B39+B14)
42	================	================
43		
44	CAPM	
45		
46	T-BILL	.085
47	EXP MKT	.16
48	BETA	.98
49	COE	+B46+(B48*(B47−B46))
50	WGTD COE	+B49*B8
51		
52	WACC	+B50+B14
53	================	================

Chapter 6

6–1.

	A	B	C	D	E	F
1		CURRENT	SALES		PROJECTE	D SALES
2		---------	---------	---------	---------	--------
3		DEBT	C/S		DEBT	C/S
4		--------	--------		--------	--------
5	SALES	125000	125000		+ B5*1.2	+ E5
6	EBIT	.13*B5	.13*C5		.13*E5	.13*F5
7	CURR INT	1750	1750		1750	1750
8	NEW INT	(15000*.1)	0		+ B8	0
9	-------	--------	--------		--------	--------
10	PBT	+ B6 – B7 – B8	+ C6 – C7 – C8		+ E6 – E7 – E8	+ F6 – F7 – F8
11	TAXES	+ B10*.5	+ C10*.5		+ E10*.5	+ F10*.5
12	-------	--------	--------		--------	--------
13	PAT	+ B10 – B11	+ C10 – C11		+ E10 – E11	+ F10 – F11
14	PREF DIV	(15000*.08)	+ B14		+ B14	+ B14
15	-------	--------	--------		--------	--------
16	AVAIL C/S	+ B13 – B14	+ C13 – C14		+ E13 – E14	+ F13 – F14
17	# SHARES	2000	(1000 + B17)		2000	+ C17
18	EPS	+ B16/B17	+ C16/C17		+ E16/E17	+ F16/F17
19						
20		= = = = = =	= = = = = =	= = = = = =	= = = = = =	= = = = = =
21						
22	B/E EBIT	(((+ B17*B7) – (C17*B7) – (C17*B8))/(B 17 – C17)) + (B 14/.5)				
23						
24		DEBT	C/S			
25		--------	--------			
26	B/E EPS	(((B22 – B7 – B8)*.5) – B1 4)/B17	(((B22 – C7 – C8)*.5) – C1 4)/C17			
27						
28	**********	**********	**********	**********	**********	**********

6–2.

	A	B	C	D	E	F
1		CURRENT	SALES		PROJECTE	D SALES
2		---------	---------	---------	---------	---------
3		DEBT	C/S		DEBT	C/S
4		--------	--------		--------	--------
5	SALES	125000	125000		+ B5*1.2	+ E5
6	EBIT	.13*B5	.13*C5		.13*E5	.13*F5
7	CURR INT	1750	1750		1750	1750
8	NEW INT	(15000*.1)	0		+ B8	0
9	-------	--------	--------		--------	--------
10	PBT	+ B6 – B7 – B8	+ C6 – C7 – C8		+ E6 – E7 – E8	+ F6 – F7 – F8
11	TAXES	+ B10*.5	+ C10*.5		+ E10*.5	+ F10*.5
12	-------	--------	--------		--------	--------
13	PAT	+ B10 – B11	+ C10 – C11		+ E10 – E11	+ F10 – F11
14	PREF DIV	(15000*.08)	+ B14		+ B14	+ B14
15	-------	--------	--------		--------	--------
16	AVAIL C/S	+ B13 – B14	+ C13 – C14		+ E13 – E14	+ F13 – F14
17	# SHARES	2000	+ B17		2000	3000
18	EPS		+ C16/C17		+ E16/E17	+ F16/F17
19						
20	DPS		+ C18*.25		+ E18*.25	+ F18*.25

6–3. This problem does not lend itself to modeling.

6–4. Add to the model developed for 6–2 the following:

	E	F	G	H
26	TOT ASSET	(134000 + 15000)	(134000 + 15000)	
27	ROA	(+ F13 – F14)/F26	(+ G13 – G14)/G26	.1
28				
29	TOT EQ	4000 + 50000 + F17	15000 + 4000 + 50000 + G17	
30	ROE	(+ F13 – F14)/F29	(+ G13 – G14)/G29	.12
31				
32	LTD	25000 + 15000 + 15000 – 2500	25000 + 15000 – 2500	
33	LTD/CAP	+ F32/(F32 + F29)	+ G32/(G32 + G29)	.45
34				
35	INT/SALES	(F7 + F8)/F5	(G7 + G8)/G5	.015

Note on 6–4: It might be useful to have the titles remain on the screen while scrolling. This can be done by placing the cursor at A3 and typing /WTH.

Chapter 7

The data for these problems do not allow the development of useful models. Models in general are useful in evaluating acquisitions because they facilitate sensitivity analysis on earnings and cash flow projections.

III. IFPS MODELS FOR STUDY QUESTIONS

This section provides models for solving the study questions using the Interactive Financial Planning System (IFPS). As explained in Appendix A, this modeling system allows for structuring the model with a series of statements.

For each of the models, a full listing is given. The listings are models for the microcomputer version, IFPS/Personal. To use these models on the mainframe version of IFPS, you will need to change the backslash "\" to an asterisk "*" to indicate a comment line. The results of these models may differ slightly from the manual solutions to the study questions because of differences in rounding.

Chapter 1

1-1.

```
COLUMNS 1
\ INCOME STATEMENT
\-----------------------------------
SALES = PAT / .03
COGS = .77 * SALES
OTHER EXP = SALES - COGS - PAT
\-----------------------------------
PAT = .1 * (CS + RET EARN)
\
\***********************************
\ BALANCE SHEET
\-----------------------------------
\ ASSETS
CASH = TOT CA - AR - INV
AR = (SALES/365) * 35
INV = COGS / 6
\-----------------------------------
TOT CA = 2 * TOT C LIA
\
NET PE = TOT ASSET - TOT CA
\-----------------------------------
TOT ASSET = SALES / 1.5
\
\ LIAB & EQ
AP = (COGS/365) * 30
OTHER STL = TOT C LIA - AP
\-----------------------------------
TOT C LIA = TOT ASSET - TOT CAP
\
LTD = .8 * (CS + RET EARN)
CS = 40000
RET EARN = 62000
\-----------------------------------
TOT CAP = LTD + CS + RET EARN
\-----------------------------------
TOT LOE = TOT C LIA + TOT CAP
\
```

1–2.

```
COLUMNS 1980 THRU 1984
\-------------------------------------------------------------------------
SALES = 27,000, 28350, 29654, 31344, 33852
COGS = 23490, 24098, 24613, 25075, 27082
ADVERT = 540, 510, 652, 1254, 2031
INTEREST = 270, 340, 415, 408, 508
OTHER EXP = 1620, 1616, 1601, 1599, 1659
\-------------------------------------------------------------------------
PBT = SALES - COGS - ADVERT - INTEREST - OTHER EXP
\
\COMP %
\-------------------------------------------------------------------------
SALES1 = (SALES / SALES) * 100
COGS1 = (COGS / SALES) * 100
ADVERT1 = (ADVERT / SALES) * 100
INTEREST1 = (INTEREST / SALES) * 100
OTHER EXP1 = (OTHER EXP / SALES) * 100
\-------------------------------------------------------------------------
PBT1 = (PBT / SALES) * 100
\
\TREND %
\-------------------------------------------------------------------------
SALES2 = 0, ((SALES / PREVIOUS SALES) - 1) * 100
COGS2 = 0, ((COGS / PREVIOUS COGS) - 1) * 100
ADVERT2 = 0, ((ADVERT / PREVIOUS ADVERT) - 1) * 100
INTEREST2 = 0, ((INTEREST / PREVIOUS INTEREST) - 1) * 100
OTHER2 = 0, ((OTHER EXP / PREVIOUS OTHER EXP) - 1) * 100
\-------------------------------------------------------------------------
PBT2 = 0, ((PBT / PREVIOUS PBT) - 1) * 100
```

1–3. The nature of this problem does not lend itself to modeling.

Chapter 2

2–1.

```
COLUMNS 1983, 1984
\------------------------------------------
\ INCOME STATEMENT
\
SALES = 250000, 510000
COGS = 195000, .78 * SALES
\------------------------------------------
GR MARGIN = SALES - COGS
OTHER EXP = 40000
\------------------------------------------
PBT = GR MARGIN - OTHER EXP
TAXES = .4 * PBT
\------------------------------------------
PAT = PBT - TAXES
\
\------------------------------------------
\ BALANCE SHEET
\
\ ASSETS
CASH = 50000, .2 * SALES
AR = 20548, (SALES / 365) * 30
INVEN = 65000, (COGS / 6)
\------------------------------------------
CURR ASST = CASH + AR + INVEN
NET PE = 80000, 76000
\------------------------------------------
TOT ASST = CURR ASST + NET PE
\
\ L & E
AP = 16027, (COGS / 365) * 30
OTHER STL = 30521, (TOT ASST - AP - TOT LTDE)
\------------------------------------------
CURR LIAB = AP + OTHER STL
LTD = 60000
CS = 100000
RET EARN = 9000, PREVIOUS RET EARN + PAT
\------------------------------------------
TOT LTDE = LTD + CS + RET EARN
\------------------------------------------
TOT LE = CURR LIAB + TOT LTDE
\
\ NET W CAP
CURR ASSET = CURR ASST
CURR LIA = CURR LIAB
\------------------------------------------
NET W CAP = CURR ASSET - CURR LIA
\
```

2–2.

```
COLUMNS 1983, 1984, 1985
\--------------------------------------------------
\ INCOME STATEMENT
\
SALES = 250000, 510000, 663000
COGS = 195000, .78 * SALES
\--------------------------------------------------
GR MARGIN = SALES - COGS
OTHER EXP = 40000
\--------------------------------------------------
PBT = GR MARGIN - OTHER EXP
TAXES = .4 * PBT
\--------------------------------------------------
PAT = PBT - TAXES
\
\--------------------------------------------------
\ BALANCE SHEET
\
\ ASSETS
CASH = 50000, .2 * SALES
AR = 20548, (SALES/365)*30, (SALES / 365)*45
INVEN = 65000, (COGS / 6)
\--------------------------------------------------
CURR ASST = CASH + AR + INVEN
NET PE = 80000, 76000, 72000
\--------------------------------------------------
TOT ASST = CURR ASST + NET PE
\
\ L & E
AP = 16027, (COGS / 365) * 30
OTHER STL = 30521, (TOT ASST - AP - TOT LTDE)
\--------------------------------------------------
CURR LIAB = AP + OTHER STL
LTD = 60000
CS = 100000
RET EARN = 9000, PREVIOUS RET EARN + PAT
\--------------------------------------------------
TOT LTDE = LTD + CS + RET EARN
\--------------------------------------------------
TOT LE = CURR LIAB + TOT LTDE
\
\ NET W CAP
CURR ASSET = CURR ASST
CURR LIA = CURR LIAB
\--------------------------------------------------
NET W CAP = CURR ASSET - CURR LIA
```

2–3.

```
COLUMNS 1983, 1984, 1985
\--------------------------------------------------
\ INCOME STATEMENT
\
SALES = 250000, 510000, 700000
COGS = 195000, .78 * SALES
BAD DEBTS = 0, 0, .02 * SALES
\--------------------------------------------------
GR MARGIN = SALES - COGS - BAD DEBTS
OTHER EXP = 40000
\--------------------------------------------------
PBT = GR MARGIN - OTHER EXP
TAXES = .4 * PBT
\--------------------------------------------------
PAT = PBT - TAXES
\
\--------------------------------------------------
\ BALANCE SHEET
\
\ ASSETS
CASH = 50000, .2 * SALES
AR = 20548, (SALES/365)*30, (SALES / 365) *45
INVEN = 65000, (COGS / 6)
\--------------------------------------------------
CURR ASST = CASH + AR + INVEN
NET PE = 80000, 76000, 72000
\--------------------------------------------------
TOT ASST = CURR ASST + NET PE
\
\ L & E
AP = 16027, (COGS / 365) * 30
OTHER STL = 30521, (TOT ASST - AP - TOT LTDE)
\--------------------------------------------------
CURR LIAB = AP + OTHER STL
LTD = 60000
CS = 100000
RET EARN = 9000, PREVIOUS RET EARN + PAT
\--------------------------------------------------
TOT LTDE = LTD + CS + RET EARN
\--------------------------------------------------
TOT LE = CURR LIAB + TOT LTDE
\
\ NET W CAP
CURR ASSET = CURR ASST
CURR LIA = CURR LIAB
\--------------------------------------------------
NET W CAP = CURR ASSET - CURR LIA
```

Chapter 3

3–1.

```
COLUMNS JAN THRU DEC
\--------------------------------------------------------------------------------
SALES = 65, 70, 90, 100, 115, 125, 150, 175, 130, 110, 80, 70
\
\ RECEIPTS
BEG AR = 70, PREVIOUS ENDING
CRED SALES = .8 * SALES
COLLECT = BEG AR
\--------------------------------------------------------------------------------
ENDING = BEG AR + CRED SALES - COLLECT
\================================================================================
CASH PAY = .2 * SALES
\--------------------------------------------------------------------------------
TOT RCPTS = COLLECT + CASH PAY
\================================================================================
\
\ DISBURSEMENTS
BEG AP = 51, PREVIOUS ENDING AP
PURCH = 1.05 * (.74 * FUTURE SALES) for 11, 51
PAYMENTS = BEG AP
\--------------------------------------------------------------------------------
ENDING AP = BEG AP + PURCH - PAYMENTS
\================================================================================
SA = .07 * SALES
FIXED = 6
LSEwINT = 3
\--------------------------------------------------------------------------------
TOT DSBMT = PAYMENTS + SA + FIXED + LSEwINT
\================================================================================
NET CF = TOT RCPTS - TOT DSBMT
\
CUM CF = NET CF, PREVIOUS CUM CF + NET CF
\
BEG CASH = 11, PREVIOUS ENDING CASH
CHANGE = NET CF
\--------------------------------------------------------------------------------
ENDING CASH = BEG CASH + CHANGE
```

3–2.

```
COLUMNS JAN THRU DEC
\-------------------------------------------------------------------------------
SALES = 65, 70, 90, 100, 115, 125, 150, 175, 130, 110, 80, 70
\
\ RECEIPTS
BEG AR = 70, PREVIOUS ENDING
CRED SALES = .8 * SALES
COLLECT = BEG AR
\-------------------------------------------------------------------------------
ENDING = BEG AR + CRED SALES - COLLECT
\===============================================================================
CASH PAY = .2 * SALES
\-------------------------------------------------------------------------------
TOT RCPTS = COLLECT + CASH PAY
\===============================================================================
\
\ DISBURSEMENTS
BEG AP = 51, PREVIOUS ENDING AP
PURCH = 1.05 * (.74 * FUTURE SALES) for 11, 51
PAYMENTS = BEG AP
\-------------------------------------------------------------------------------
ENDING AP = BEG AP + PURCH - PAYMENTS
\===============================================================================
SA = .07 * SALES
FIXED = 6
LSEwINT = 3
\-------------------------------------------------------------------------------
TOT DSBMT = PAYMENTS + SA + FIXED + LSEwINT
\===============================================================================
```

```
NET CF = TOT RCPTS - TOT DSBMT
\
CUM CF = NET CF, PREVIOUS CUM CF + NET CF
\
BEG CASH = 11, PREVIOUS ENDING CASH
CHANGE = NET CF
\-----------------------------------------------------------------------------------
ENDING CASH = BEG CASH + CHANGE
\
\-----------------------------------------------------------------------------------
\
\                              1984        1985 PF
\---------------------------------------------------------
SALE = 0, COLSUM (1..12, SALES), 0
CGS = 0, .74 * SALE, 0
\---------------------------------------------------------
GR MARGIN = 0, SALE - CGS, 0
S ADM = 0, COLSUM (1..12, SA), 0
FIX COSTS = 0, 36 + COLSUM (1..12, FIXED), 0
LSEwINTER = 0, COLSUM (1..12, LSEwINT), 0
\---------------------------------------------------------
NET INC = 0, GR MARGIN - S ADM - FIX COSTS - LSEwINTER, 0
\=========================================================
```

3–3.

```
COLUMNS JAN THRU DEC
\-------------------------------------------------------------------------------
SALES = 65, 70, 90, 100, 115, 125, 150, 175, 130, 110, 80, 70
\
\ RECEIPTS
BEG AR = 70, PREVIOUS ENDING
CRED SALES = .8 * SALES
COLLECT = BEG AR
\-------------------------------------------------------------------------------
ENDING = BEG AR + CRED SALES - COLLECT
\===============================================================================
CASH PAY = .2 * SALES
\-------------------------------------------------------------------------------
TOT RCPTS = COLLECT + CASH PAY
\===============================================================================
\
\ DISBURSEMENTS
BEG AP = 51, PREVIOUS ENDING AP
PURCH = 1.05 * (.74 * FUTURE SALES) for 11, 51
PAYMENTS = BEG AP
\-------------------------------------------------------------------------------
ENDING AP = BEG AP + PURCH - PAYMENTS
\===============================================================================
SA = .07 * SALES
FIXED = 6
LSEwINT = 3
\-------------------------------------------------------------------------------
TOT DSBMT = PAYMENTS + SA + FIXED + LSEwINT
\===============================================================================
NET CF = TOT RCPTS - TOT DSBMT
\
CUM CF = NET CF, PREVIOUS CUM CF + NET CF
\
BEG CASH = 11, PREVIOUS ENDING CASH
CHANGE = NET CF
\-------------------------------------------------------------------------------
ENDING CASH = BEG CASH + CHANGE
\
\-------------------------------------------------------------------------------
```

```
\
\                              1984        1985 PF
\--------------------------------------------------------------------------------
SALE = 0, COLSUM (1..12, SALES), 0
CGS = 0, .74 * SALE, 0
\--------------------------------------------------------------------------------
GR MARGIN = 0, SALE - CGS, 0
S ADM = 0, COLSUM (1..12, SA), 0
FIX COSTS = 0, 36 + COLSUM (1..12, FIXED), 0
LSEwINTER = 0, COLSUM (1..12, LSEwINT), 0
\--------------------------------------------------------------------------------
NET INC = 0, GR MARGIN - S ADM - FIX COSTS - LSEwINTER, 0
\================================================================================
\
\ BALANCE SHEET
\ASSETS
CASH = BEG CASH, FUTURE 10 ENDING CASH, 0
AR = BEG AR, FUTURE 10 ENDING, 0
INVEN = 60, PREVIOUS INVEN + COLSUM (1..12, PURCH) - CGS, 0
\--------------------------------------------------------------------------------
TOT CA = CASH + AR + INVEN FOR 2, 0
NET PE = 540, PREVIOUS NET PE - (12 * 3), 0
\--------------------------------------------------------------------------------
TOT ASSTS - TOT CA + NET PE FOR 2, 0
\================================================================================
\
\L & E
AP = BEG AP, FUTURE 10 ENDING AP, 0
NP = 89 FOR 2, 0
\--------------------------------------------------------------------------------
TOT CL = AP + NP FOR 2, 0
EQUITY = 541, PREVIOUS EQUITY + NET INC, 0
\--------------------------------------------------------------------------------
TOTAL LE = TOT CL + EQUITY FOR 2, 0
\================================================================================
\
\ NET WC
CA = TOT CA FOR 2, 0
CL = TOT CL FOR 2, 0
\--------------------------------------------------------------------------------
NET WC = CA - CL FOR 2, 0
```

Chapter 4

4–1.

```
COLUMNS 1 THRU 20
\--------------------------------------------------------------------------
SALES = 1250
COGS = .37 * SALES
\--------------------------------------------------------------------------
GR MARGIN = SALES - COGS
OP COSTS = 200/20
WAGES = 30 * 15
DEPREC = 800/ 20
\--------------------------------------------------------------------------
PBT = GR MARGIN - OP COSTS - WAGES - DEPREC
TAXES = .42 * PBT
\--------------------------------------------------------------------------
PAT = PBT - TAXES
DEPRE = DEPREC
\--------------------------------------------------------------------------
NET CF = PAT + DEPRE
\
\--------------------------------------------------------------------------
\
INVEST = 800,0
\
PAYBACK = INVEST/ NET CF
BC RATIO = COLSUM (1..20, NET CF)/ INVEST
```

4–2.

```
COLUMNS 1 THRU 5
\--------------------------------------------------------------------------
INVEST1 = 200, 0
INVEST2 = 0, 0, 60, 0
\--------------------------------------------------------------------------
TOTAL INVESTMENT = INVEST1 + INVEST2
\
SALES = 120, PREVIOUS SALES * 1.15
COSTS = .39 * SALES
DEPREC1 = INVEST1 * .15, INVEST1[1] * .22, '
          INVEST1[1] * .21, INVEST1[1] * .21, '
          INVEST1[1] * .21
DEPREC2 = 0,0, INVEST2 * .25, INVEST2[3] * .38, '
          INVEST2[3] * .37
\--------------------------------------------------------------------------
PBT = SALES - COSTS - DEPREC1 - DEPREC2
TAXES = .4 * PBT
\--------------------------------------------------------------------------
PAT = PBT - TAXES
DEPREC = DEPREC1 + DEPREC2
\--------------------------------------------------------------------------
NET CF = PAT + DEPREC
\
\--------------------------------------------------------------------------
\
DISCOUNT RATE = 10%
\
NET PRESENT VALUE = NPVC (NET CF, DISCOUNT RATE, TOTAL INVESTMENT)
```

4–3.

```
COLUMNS 1 THRU 10
\-------------------------------------------------------------------
PROJECT #1
\
INVEST = 800000, 0
SALES = 500000
COGS = .49 * SALES
\-------------------------------------------------------------------
GR MARGIN = SALES - COGS
ADV = 50000
DEPR = .08 * INVEST, .14 * PREVIOUS 1 INVEST, .12 * PREVIOUS '
          2 INVEST, .10 * PREVIOUS 3 INVEST, .10 * PREVIOUS 4 INVEST, .10 '
          * PREVIOUS 5 INVEST, .09 * PREVIOUS 6 INVEST, .09 * PREVIOUS 7 '
          INVEST, .09 * PREVIOUS 8 INVEST, .09 * PREVIOUS 9 INVEST
\-------------------------------------------------------------------
PBT = GR MARGIN - ADV - DEPR
TAXES = .45 * PBT
\-------------------------------------------------------------------
PAT = PBT - TAXES
DEPREC = DEPR
\-------------------------------------------------------------------
CASH FLOW = PAT + DEPREC
\
\-------------------------------------------------------------------
\
\PROJECT #2
\
INVEST FL = 600000, 0
INVEST TN = 200000, 0
\-------------------------------------------------------------------
TOT INVEST = INVEST FL + INVEST TN, 0
SALES2 = 350000, 1.1*PREVIOUS SALES2 FOR 3, 1.15 * PREVIOUS SALES2 '
            FOR 3, 1.1 * PREVIOUS SALES2 FOR 3
COGS2 = .5 * SALES2 FOR 3, .42 * SALES2
\-------------------------------------------------------------------
GR MARGIN2 = SALES2 - COGS2
ADV2 = .25 * SALES2 FOR 3, 100000
DEPRE2 = .08 * INVEST FL, .14 * PREVIOUS 1 INVEST FL, '
            .12 * PREVIOUS 2 INVEST FL, .10 * PREVIOUS 3 INVEST FL, '
            .10 * PREVIOUS 4 INVEST FL, .10 * PREVIOUS 5 INVEST FL, '
            .09 * PREVIOUS 6 INVEST FL, .09 * PREVIOUS 7 INVEST FL, '
            .09 * PREVIOUS 8 INVEST FL, .09 * PREVIOUS 9 INVEST FL
\-------------------------------------------------------------------
PBT2 = GT MARGIN2 - ADV2 - DEPR2
TAXES2 = .45 * PBT2
\-------------------------------------------------------------------
PAT2 = PBT2 - TAXES2
DEPREC2 = DEPR2
\-------------------------------------------------------------------
CASH FLOW2 = PAT2 + DEPREC2
\
\-------------------------------------------------------------------
DISCOUNT RATE = .10
\
\-------------------------------------------------------------------
\                                       PROJECT #1        PROJECT #2
\
BC RATIO = COLSUM (1..10, CASH FLOW) / INVEST, COLSUM (1..10, '
              CASH FLOW2) / PREVIOUS TOT INVEST
\
PROJECT 1 NET PV = NPVC (CASH FLOW, DISCOUNT RATE, INVEST)
PROJECT 2 NET PV = NPVC (CASH FLOW2, DISCOUNT RATE, TOT INVEST)
\
```

Chapter 5

5-1.

```
COLUMNS 1
LTD = 2261538
CS = 1500000
RE = 2700000
\ ----------------------------------
TOT CAP = LTD + CS + RE
\
DEBT = LTD / TOT CAP
EQUITY = 1 - DEBT
\
\ COST - DEBT
MRGN INT = .1175 * 100
TAX RATE = .42
\
WGTD COD = ((1 - TAX RATE) * MRGN INT) * DEBT
\ = = = = = = = = = = = = = = = = = = = = = =
\
\ COST - EQUITY
\
\ DIVD DISC
SHARES = 300000
PAT PROJ = 554400
DIV PO = .24
DPS PROJ = (PAT PROJ / SHARES) * DIV PO
MKT PRICE = 18.5
ROE = .12*100
PROJ G = (1 - DIV PO) * ROE
COE = ((DPS PROJ / MKT PRICE) * 100) + PROJ G
WGTD COE = EQUITY * COE
\
WACC = WGTD COE + WGTD COD
\ = = = = = = = = = = = = = = = = = = = = = =
\
\ YLD SPRD
MRGN INT1 = MRGN INT
AVG INT = .10 * 100
ROE1 = ROE
COE1 = MRGN INT1 + ROE1 - AVG INT
WGTD COE1 = COE1 * EQUITY
\
WACC1 = WGTD COE1 + WGTD COD
\ = = = = = = = = = = = = = = = = = = = = = =
\
\ CAPM
T BILL = .085 * 100
EXP MKT = .16 * 100
BETA = .98
COE2 = T BILL + (BETA * (EXP MKT - T BILL))
WGTD COE2 = COE2 * EQUITY
\
WACC2 = WGTD COE2 + WGTD COD
\ = = = = = = = = = = = = = = = = = = = = = =
```

Chapter 6

6–1.

```
COLUMNS DEBT1, CS1, DEBT2, CS2
\                                    CURRENT SALES        PROJECTED SALES
\------------------------------------------------------------------------
SALES = 125000, PREVIOUS SALES, PREVIOUS SALES * 1.2, PREVIOUS SALES
EBIT = .13 * SALES
CURR INT = 1750
NEW INT = 15000 * .1, 0, PREVIOUS 2 , 0
\------------------------------------------------------------------------
PBT = EBIT - CURR INT - NEW INT
TAXES = PBT * .5
\------------------------------------------------------------------------
PAT = PBT - TAXES
PRE DIV = 15000 * .08
\------------------------------------------------------------------------
AVAIL CS = PAT - PREF DIV
SHARES = 2000, 1000 + PREVIOUS SHARES, PREVIOUS 2 SHARES, PREVIOUS 2 SHARES
EPS = AVAIL CS / SHARES
\
\========================================================================
\
BE EBIT = ((2000*CURR INT - 3000*CURR INT - 3000*NEW INT)/(2000 - 3000)) + '
            (PREF DIV/.5), 0
\
\ DEBT CS
\------------------------------------------------------------------------
D EQUIV = (((BE EBIT - CURR INT - NEW INT) * .5) - PREF DIV)/ SHARES, 0
E EQUIV = 0, (((PREVIOUS BE EBIT - CURR INT - NEW INT) * .5) - PREF DIV)/'
            SHARES, 0
```

6–2.

```
COLUMNS CS1, DEBT2, CS2
\                         CURRENT SALES        PROJECTED SALES
\-------------------------------------------------------------
SALES = 125000, PREVIOUS SALES * 1.2, PREVIOUS SALES
EBIT = .13 * SALES
CURR INT = 1750
NEW INT = 0, 15000 * .1, 0
\-------------------------------------------------------------
PBT = EBIT - CURR INT - NEW INT
TAXES = PBT * .5
\-------------------------------------------------------------
PAT = PBT - TAXES
PREF DIV = 15000 * .08
\-------------------------------------------------------------
AVAIL CS = PAT - PREF DIV
SHARES = 2000 FOR 2, 3000
EPS = AVAIL CS / SHARES
\
DPS = EPS * .25
```

6–3. This problem does not lend itself to modeling.

6–4.

```
COLUMNS DEBT1, CS1, DEBT2, CS2
\                                          CURRENT SALES          PROJECTED SALES
\-----------------------------------------------------------------------------------
SALES = 125000, PREVIOUS SALES, PREVIOUS SALES * 1.2, PREVIOUS SALES
EBIT = .13 * SALES
CURR INT = 1750
NEW INT = 15000 * .1, 0, PREVIOUS 2, 0
\-----------------------------------------------------------------------------------
PBT = EBIT - CURR INT - NEW INT
TAXES = PBT * .5
\-----------------------------------------------------------------------------------
PAT = PBT - TAXES
PREF DIV = 15000 * .08
COMM DIV = 0, 0, .25 * (PAT - PREF DIV)
\------------------------------------------------------------------------------
AVAIL CS = PAT - PREF DIV - COMM DIV
\
\ = = = = = = = = = = = = = = = = = = = = = = = = = = = = = = = = = = = = = = = = = = =
\
\
\                                       INDUSTRY
\                                       ----------
TOTASSET = 0, 0, 134000 + 15000, PREVIOUS
ROA = .10 * 100, 0, ((PAT - PREF DIV)/ TOTASSET ) * 100
\
TOT EQ = 0, 0, (4000 + 50000) + AVAIL CS, (54000 + 15000) + AVAIL CS
ROE = .12 * 100, 0, ((PAT - PREF DIV)/ TOT EQ) * 100
\
LTD = 0, 0, 55000 - 2500, 40000 - 2500
LTDwCAP = .45 * 100, 0, (LTD/(LTD + TOT EQ)) * 100
\
INTwSALES = .015 * 100, 0, ((CURR INT + NEW INT)/ SALES) * 100
```

Chapter 7

The data for these problems do not allow the development of useful models. Models in general are useful in evaluating acquisitions because they facilitate sensitivity analysis on earnings and cash flow projections.

INDEX

This book has been set Compugraphic in 10 point Times Roman, leaded 2 points. Chapter numbers are 10 point and chapter titles are 18 point Avant Garde Demi. The size of the type page is 27 by 47 picas.

06-1611-02 ISBN 0-256-03413-3